Hardouin de Péréfixe de Beaumont

The History of Henry IV.

Hardouin de Péréfixe de Beaumont

The History of Henry IV.

ISBN/EAN: 9783337328146

Printed in Europe, USA, Canada, Australia, Japan

Cover: Foto ©ninafisch / pixelio.de

More available books at **www.hansebooks.com**

Uniform with the present volume:

"Historical and Secret Memoirs of the Empress Josephine." 2 vols.
"Memoirs of Marmontel." 2 vols.
"Memoirs of C. M. Talleyrand de Perigord." 2 vols.
"Memoirs of Cardinal de Retz." 1 vol.
"Memoirs of Madame du Barri." 4 vols.
"Memoirs of Joseph Fouché." 2 vols.

HISTORY
OF
HENRY THE GREAT

Edition strictly limited to 500 copies.

Five extra copies have been printed on Japanese vellum, but are not offered for sale.

HENRY IV OF FRANCE

SURNAMED THE GREAT

THE

HISTORY OF HENRY IV

(SURNAMED "THE GREAT")

KING OF FRANCE AND NAVARRE

TRANSLATED FROM THE FRENCH

LONDON

H. S. NICHOLS

3 SOHO SQUARE AND 62A PICCADILLY W.

MDCCCXCVI

Printed and Published by
H. S. NICHOLS
AT 3 SOHO SQUARE, LONDON W.

PUBLISHER'S NOTE

This History of Henry IV. of France forms the seventh issue of my Historic Memoir Series. The character of this King is one that recommends itself to the sympathy of the English people, inasmuch as he was so closely allied with, and received considerable assistance from, Queen Elizabeth of England.

Henry IV. bore arms from the age of fifteen to forty-five, taking part in more than a hundred combats.

This history was written by Hardouin de Beaumont de Péréfixe, successively Bishop of Rhodez and Archbishop of Paris. It was written for the edification of Louis XIV., grandson of Henry IV., and was translated for another grandson, Charles II. of England, by James Dauncey. The first French edition was published at Amsterdam in 1661. The English edition, published at London, appeared in 1663. Numerous French editions have been published, the latest and best being that issued at Paris in 1876. There is no trace of any other English issue than one published at Paris in 1785, and that is not absolutely correct.

For the purpose of this present issue the first

English version has been made use of. It was soon perceived, however, that reliance could not be placed upon the translation, and the French edition of 1662, revised by the author, has been carefully consulted from beginning to end. A few notes have been added, and also, at the end, short biographical sketches of notable personages mentioned in the work.

The next issue of this series will be the "Letters of Madame d'Épinay," in three volumes.

LONDON, *August, 1896.*

TRANSLATOR'S ADDRESS

To His Sacred Majesty Charles II., King of Great Britain, France and Ireland.

Dread Sir,—With all that humble reverence that becomes a lowly but loyal subject and servant to his sovereign lord and master, cast I at your feet this present Address. Those stars that move in the lowest orb receive their light and lustre from the sun, as well as those that wander in a more exalted heaven, and therefore may possibly be capable of returning some grateful influences, though not in so great a quantity, yet in a quality as pure and candid.

However, all my courage could not have inspired me with a presumption to present anything of mine to so glorious a majesty, had it not borne in its frontispiece the name of Henry the Great, your royal and renowned grandfather: a prince of so sublime a virtue, of so heroic a courage, of such activity in war and such prudence in peace, that he justly became both the love and terror of the age he lived in.

And, great Sir, give me leave to tell you, that never did the life of any prince since the Creation bear so equal a parallel with your Majesty's as that of this renowned king. If your miseries and misfortunes have exceeded his, God hath made it by evident demonstrations appear that He intends to make your glories and happiness as far surpass those of your royal grandfather. You both had Leaguers armed with rebellion, obstinacy and ambition, under a cloak of zeal to religion, to oppose you; and you both, assisted by a miraculous providence of Heaven, overcame them. You both by arms long struggled for your rights; but, as if God had intended you both for true fathers of your countries and the foundations whereon He would settle an absolute happiness in your kingdoms, so long afflicted with civil wars and those terrors which attend them, He brought you both to spotless thrones, unbesmeared with blood.

How soon was France redeemed from those plagues it so long had endured, at the entrance into the chair of royalty of the great Henry, who as a rising sun, darted forth those salutiferous rays which shone upon and enriched the remotest parts of his territories! How soon were all factions dissipated! and how soon did he by his prudent conduct reconcile the most obstinate spirits! In fine, in how short time was France, from a den of atheists, thieves, and robbers, become the nursery of piety, arts, and industry!

England, dread Sovereign, suffered under the same fate her neighbouring sister had long since been subject to, when Heaven was graciously pleased to restore you to your crown; and you have already made us not only hope, but see, that you have designed to restore to us such happiness, that we cannot justly envy those which France enjoyed under her beloved Henry. How well have you settled both our Church and State! How well have you reconciled our dissensions! With how much too great a mercy (give me, Sir, leave to fear so) have you pardoned the most obstinate of your enemies! And how may we hope (if the malice of those obstinate spirits yet disturb not our tranquillity) to enjoy under your government the most happy and flourishing days that ever Great Britain beheld!

But, Sir, that I may conclude, and not seem tedious to your Majesty, may the God of Heaven inspire into the hearts of your people a true sense of your goodness and paternal love to them; may He correct the unjust malice of those who yet dare to be your enemies; may He incline you still to prosecute such maxims of good government, both in Church and State, as may make both equally flourish; may He augment your glories, and raise them above those of your grandfather Henry the Fourth; may He bless us all, by giving you a long and happy reign; and when that affliction (though late) comes to us of losing you, may we yet be made blessed in that succession from your loins that may endure for ever.

Thus prays, Sir, the humblest and most faithful, though the meanest of your Majesty's subjects and servants,

J. D.

THE
AUTHOR TO THE READER

READER,—This History of Henry the Great is only a small part of the summary or epitome of the general history of France which I have composed by the command of the King and for the instruction of his Majesty. It having been my intention only to gather together all that might serve to instruct a great prince and render him capable of reigning well, I have not thought it convenient to enter into a particular recital of things, or to recount at length all wars and affairs as historians do who are to write for all sorts of persons. I have only taken the sum, and recounted those circumstances I have judged the fairest and the most instructive, leaving apart all the rest, to shorten matter, and to give in epitome an account of all that passed, which might inform the mind of the King without surcharging his memory. This hath been my design : if it hath not succeeded so well as could be wished, I hope, Reader, that my endeavour may appear praiseworthy. I doubt not but there are in this work some mistakes which I may not have perceived, but which cannot escape eyes more clear-sighted. The History is accompanied with so many circumstances, that it is almost impossible not to have been deceived in some; yet I believe I have written nothing for which I have not my warrant. And if you find in any author the contrary of what I have said, I entreat you to consider that our historians do in many things so differ among themselves, that he who takes the judgment of one must necessarily contradict the other. In this diversity I have followed those whom I believed the best and most assured. I acknowledge likewise that I could not refrain borrowing from them whole paragraphs where they have pleased me, and where I have thought I could better explain myself by their expressions than my own. However, if this be a fault, it is but a light one, and ought to be pardoned, since ingenuously confessed. For other more remarkable ones I may have committed, I presume on your goodness that, Reader, you will not treat me with the utmost rigour, but that you will have as much indulgence for me as I have in this work had zeal for the service of my King and affection for the good of France.

THE
TRANSLATOR TO THE READER

Behold here a History compiled by one of the most able, and (let me testify thus much) one of the most moderate and impartial pens of Europe. It was fitted for the hand of a king; and is the life of one whom his own actions will declare to have better deserved the name of Great than that proud Macedonian who wept that he had no more worlds to conquer. For though he gained not such signal victories, nor overran so many countries, yet he was possessed of more virtues than the other of cities; and virtue is the fairest mother of true greatness. But, Reader, I forestall thy delight in its reading: go on, therefore, but with deliberation.

J. D.

TO THE KING.

SIRE,—That respect and love which all good Frenchmen have still preserved for the happy memory of King Henry the Great, your grandfather, represents itself as vivid to their remembrance as if he still reigned, and renown preserves the splendour of his fair actions in the hearts and mouths of men as fresh and entirely as in the time of his triumphs. But we may say, moreover, when we consider your Majesty, that he has regained a new life in your person, and that he makes himself daily be seen under a visage yet more august, and by virtues which appear as redoubtable to the enemies of France as they are sweet and charming to its people.

In truth, Sire, that praiseworthy impatience which your Majesty has testified (when I presented our history to your reading) to come to this glorious reign, and for it to leave behind seven or eight others of kings that preceded him, is a most certain proof that you desire him for your model, and that you have resolved to study his conduct and conserve it in the government of your estates. Your happy birth,[1]

---

[1] Referring, doubtless, to the fact that Louis XIV. was the first-born after twenty-three years of his parents' wedded life, and was therefore called *Dieudonné*.

and your inclinations wholly royal, lead you to it; the hopes and votes of your subjects agree to it; the necessities of your kingdom, afflicted with the miseries of the longest war it ever sustained, oblige you to it; and Heaven has disposed you to it by so many graces and eminent qualities that it would be difficult for you not to follow the fair examples of this great monarch. I dare likewise say (and I may speak it with truth) that it will not be impossible for you to surpass him, if you school yourself to improve well all those advantages wherewith Heaven has endowed you above other princes of your age.

Yes, Sire, Heaven has likewise given you a generous soul, good and beneficent; a spirit elevated and capable of the greatest things; a memory happy and facile; a courage heroic and martial; a judgment neat and solid; a strong and vigorous health; but you have, moreover, been vouchsafed one advantage the King, your grandfather, never had, that is, a majestic presence; an air and port almost divine; a person and beauty worthy the empire of the universe, which attracts the eye and respect of all the world, and which, without the force of arms, without the authority of commands, will attach to your person all those whom your Majesty shall admit to your presence.

I will not speak of the prosperity of this kingdom since your happy advancement to the crown: how you have been proclaimed conqueror as soon as king; how, by the helpful counsels of your great ministers, your frontiers have been extended on all sides, and your enemies everywhere defeated; but I ought not to forget that singular grace which Heaven has conferred on you, by instructing you in the Catholic religion and in true piety, through the continual diligence and example of the Queen your mother; this was without doubt wanting to the youth of our Henry.

You cannot, Sire, with so fair a disposition, with so many superabundant favours of Heaven, be content to rest on the glory and reputation of this great prince. Remember, if you please, that you have done me the honour to tell me more than once that you ardently aspire to a like perfection, and that you have no greater ambition. All France, who at present have their eyes upon you, rejoice to see the effects already second your desires, and that you strive as earnestly to imitate as you have passionately desired to hear the recital of so fair a life.

Your Majesty knows that wills pass but for weaknesses when they render not themselves efficacious, and are so far from being worthy of praise that they condemn those who have them so much the more, because they see well what they ought to do, and have not the heart to attempt or undertake it. The way of virtue at first glance seems rough, but it conducts to the temple of glory, where it is certain we arrive not by simple thoughts and idle discourses, but by labour, application, and perseverance.

I have often taken the liberty to represent to your Majesty that royalty is no *métier de fainéant;* that it consists almost altogether in action; that a king ought to make his duty his delight; and that he ought to know how to reign; that is, how to hold in his own grasp the helm of his states, the better to conduct them with vigour, wisdom, and justice.

Who knows not that there is no honour in bearing a title without executing the functions of it? That it is in vain to have acquired the best knowledge, without labouring to reduce it to practice. That it is ridiculous to propose to ourselves a great model unless it be effectually imitated. And, in fine, that it is nothing to understand by heart all the maxims of policy, if we apply them not to their right use? Without doubt, he that hath eyes and will not open them, who hath arms and will not take the pains to move them, is in a worse state than the blind or the cripple.

I cannot dissemble, Sire, that unspeakable joy I have sometimes conceived when I have understood from the mouth of your Majesty *that you would choose rather never to have worn a crown than not yourself to govern it*, but resemble those lazy kings of the first race, who, as all our historians say, served only as idols to the mayors of their palace, and who had had no name other than to mark the year in the chronology.

But it will be enough to make France know how much your Majesty condemns that sleepy lethargy, to tell them that you are at present resolved to imitate your grandfather, Henry the Great, who was the most active and most laborious of all our kings, who dedicated himself with great diligence to the management of his affairs, and who cherished his states and people with the utmost affection and tenderness. This is to declare that your Majesty has taken a firm resolution to put your hand to the work, to know both the inside and outside of your realm, to preside in your councils, to give weight and motion to all resolutions, to have a continual eye over your revenues, to cause a true, faithful and exact account to be given, to distribute graces and recompenses to those of your creatures who shall prove worthy; in fine, fully and amply to enjoy your authority. It is thus the incomparable Henry acted, whom we have seen to reign, not only in France by right of blood, but over all Europe by the esteem of his virtue.

In effect, since the first foundation of the French monarchy, history furnishes us not with any reign more memorable by reason of the great events, more replete with the wonders of Divine assistance, more glorious for the prince, and more happy for the people than his; and it is without flattery or envy that all the universe has given him the surname of Great, not so much for the greatness of his victories, however comparable to those of Alexander or Pompey, as for the greatness of his soul and of his courage, for he never bowed either under the insults of fortune or under the stratagems of his enemies, or under the resentments of revenge, or under the artifices of favourites or ministers—he remained always in the same temper, always master of himself. In a word, he remained always King and sovereign, without acknowledging other superior than God, justice, and reason.

Let us then proceed to write the history of his life, which we shall divide into three principal parts.

The first shall contain what happened from his birth till his coming to the crown of France. The second shall speak of what he did after he came to it until the peace of Vervins; and the third shall recount his actions after the peace of Vervins until the unhappy day of his death.

But before all, it is necessary to say something briefly of his genealogy. He was the son of Anthony de Bourbon, Duke of Vendôme and King of Navarre, and Jane d'Albret, heiress of that kingdom.

Anthony was a descendant in a direct male line of Robert, Count of Clermont, fifth son of King St. Louis. This Robert espoused Beatrix, daughter and heiress of John of Burgundy, Baron of Bourbon, by his wife Agnes; for which cause, Robert took the name of Bourbon, but not the arms, still keeping those of France.

This wise precaution served well to his descendants, to maintain themselves in the degree of princes of the blood, which those of Courtnay[1] lost for not having

[1] Peter, son of Louis le Gros, espoused Isabella, heiress of Courtnay, and took both name and arms—a fault very prejudicial to his descendants, for they tried in 1603 and later to be recognised as princes of the Royal line, but were always unsuccessful.

acted in the same manner. And besides the virtue which gave a splendour to their actions, the good management and economy which they exercised to conserve and augment their revenues, the great alliances in which they were diligent to match themselves, ever refusing to mingle their noble with vulgar blood, and above all, their rare piety towards God and that singular goodness wherewith they acted towards their inferiors, conserved them and elevated them above princes of elder branches; so that the people, seeing them always rich, puissant, wise, and in a word worthy to command, had imprinted in their spirits, as it were, a prophetic persuasion that this house would one day come to the crown; and they on their side seemed to have conceived this hope, though it were at great distance, having taken for their word or device, Hope.

Among the younger branches which issued from this branch of Bourbon, the most considerable and the most illustrious was that of Vendôme. It carried this name because they possessed that great country, which came to them in the year 1364 by the marriage of Catherine of Vendôme (sister and heiress to Bouchard, last Count of Vendôme) with John of Bourbon, Count of the Marches. At this time it was but a county, but was afterwards made a duchy by King Francis I. in the year 1515, in favour of Charles, who was great-grandchild to John and father of Anthony. This Charles had seven male children: Louis, Anthony, Francis, another Louis, Charles, John, and a third Louis. The first Louis and the second died in their infancy, and Anthony remained the eldest. Francis, who was Count of Enghien and gained the battle of Cerisoles, died without being married. Charles was a Cardinal of the title of Chrysogone, and Archbishop of Rouen; he it was who was named the old Cardinal de Bourbon. John lost his life at the battle of St. Quentin. The third Louis was called the Prince of Condé, and by two marriages had several male children. From the first descended Henry Prince of Condé, Francis Prince of Conti, and Charles, who was Cardinal and Archbishop of Rouen after the death of the old Cardinal de Bourbon. From the second came Charles Count of Soissons.

There were eight generations from male in male from St. Louis to Anthony, who was Duke of Vendôme, King of Navarre, and father to our Henry.

As for Jane d'Albret his wife, she was daughter and heiress of Henry d'Albret, King of Navarre, and of Margaret de Valois, sister of King Francis I., and widow of the Duke of Alençon. Henry d'Albret was son of John d'Albret, who became King of Navarre, by his wife Catherine du Foix, sister of King Phœbus, who died without children; for that realm had entered into the house of Foix by marriage, as it entered afterwards into that of Albret, and since into that of Bourbon.

Ferdinand, King of Arragon, had invaded and taken Upper Navarre, that is, that part which is beyond the Pyrenean Hills, and the most considerable of that realm, from King John d'Albret; so that by consequence there remained to the latter only the Lower, that is, that beneath the mountains towards France; but with it he had the countries of Bearn, of Albret, of Foix, of Armagnac, of Bigorre, and many other great seignories which came to him by the houses of Foix and Albret.

Henry his son had only one daughter, Jane, who was called the "favourite of kings," for King Henry her father and the great King Francis her uncle, with envy of each other, strove most to cherish her.

The Emperor Charles V. had cast his eyes on her, and caused her to be demanded of her father for his son Philip II., proposing this as a means to pacify their differences touching the kingdom of Navarre. But King Francis I., not thinking it fit to introduce so powerful an enemy into France, causing her to come to Chastellerault, affianced her to the Duke of Cleves, and after releasing her of that contract, married her to Anthony of Bourbon, Duke of Vendôme; and the marriage was solemnised at Moulins in the year 1547, the same year that Francis I. died.

The two young spouses had in their first three or four years two sons, both of whom died in infancy by accidents very extraordinary: the first, because its governess, being herself cold of nature, kept it so hot that she stifled it with heat; and the second by the carelessness of the nurse, who, playing with a gentleman, as they danced the child from one to another, let it fall to the ground, so that it died in agony. Thus

Heaven deprived them of these two little princes, to make way for our Henry, who merited well both the birthright and to be an only son.

Let us now come to the history of his life.

THE HISTORY
OF
HENRY THE GREAT
KING OF FRANCE AND NAVARRE

PART I

CONTAINING THE HISTORY OF HENRY THE GREAT, FROM HIS BIRTH UNTIL HE CAME TO THE CROWN OF FRANCE.

HENRY THE GREAT, son of Anthony of Bourbon, Duke of Vendôme, and the Princess of Navarre, was born at Pau, in Bearn, on the 13th of December, 1553.

His grandfather, Henry d'Albret, who yet lived, having understood that his daughter was with child, recalled her home to him from the camp in Picardy, where she was with her husband, who was governor of that province, and who was gone from La Flèche to command an army against Charles V. He was desirous to take every care for the preservation of this new fruit, which, by a secret presentiment, he was wont to say ought to revenge him of those injuries the Spaniards had done him.

This courageous princess, then taking leave of her husband, left Compiègne on the 15th of November, traversed all France to the Pyrenees, and arrived at Pau, where the King her father was, on the 4th of December, and on the 13th of the same month she was happily brought to bed of a son.

Before this, King Henry d'Albret had made his will, which the princess, his daughter, had a great desire to see, because it was reported that it was made to her disadvantage, in favour of a lady that the good man had loved. She durst not speak to him of it; but he, being advised of her desire, promised to show it to her and put it in her hands when her child was born; but on condition that at her delivery she should sing a song, "to the end," said he, "that thou bringest not into the world a weak and weeping infant." The princess promised him, and had so much courage that, despite the great pains she suffered, she kept her word, and sang one in the Bearnais language so soon as she understood he had entered the chamber. It was observed that the infant, contrary to the common order of nature, came into the world without weeping or crying. Nor was it fit that a prince who ought to be the joy of all France should be born amidst tears and groans.

So soon as he was born his grandfather carried him in the skirt of his robe into his own chamber, giving his will, which was in a box of gold, to his daughter, and telling her, " My daughter, see there what is for you ; but this is for me." Whilst he held the infant he rubbed his little lips with a clove of garlic, and made him suck a draught of wine out of a golden cup, that he might render his temperament more masculine and vigorous.

The Spaniards had formerly said, in raillery, concerning the birth of the mother of our Henry, "O wonder, the cow has brought forth an ewe," meaning by the word "cow" Queen Margaret, her mother, whom they called so, and her husband cowkeeper, alluding to the arms of Bearn, which are two cows. And King Henry, resting assured of the future greatness of his little grandchild, taking him often in his arms, kissing him, and remembering the foolish raillery of the Spaniards, spoke with joy to all those who came to visit him and congratulate this happy birth. "See," said he, "how my ewe has now brought forth a lion!"

He was baptised the year following, on Twelfthday, being the 6th of January, 1554. For this baptism were expressly made fonts of silver richly gilded, in which he was baptised, in the chapel of the castle of Pau. His godfathers were Henry II., King of France, and Henry d'Albret, King of Navarre, who gave him their name; and the godmother was Madame Claudia of France, afterwards Duchess of Lorraine. Jacques de Foix, then Bishop of Lescar, and afterwards Cardinal, held him over the font in the name of the most Christian King; and Madame d'Andovins in the name of Madame Claudia of France. He was baptised by the Cardinal of Armagnac, Bishop of Rodez and Vicelegate of Avignon.

He was, however, difficult to bring up, having seven or eight nurses, of which the last had all the honour. On his being weaned, the King gave him for governess Susan de Bourbon, wife of John d'Albret, Baron of Miossens, who educated him in the castle of Coarasse in Bearn, situated amongst the rocks and mountains.

His grandfather would not permit him to be nourished with that delicacy ordinarily used to persons of his quality, knowing well that there seldom lodged other than a mean and feeble soul within a soft and tender body. He likewise denied him rich habiliments and children's usual baubles; or that he should be flattered or treated like a prince, "because all those things were only the causes of vanity, and rather raised pride in the hearts of infants than any sentiments of generosity"; but he commanded that he should be habited and nourished[1] like the other infants of the country, and likewise that they should accustom him to run and mount up the rocks, that by such means he might use himself to labour, and, if we may speak so, give a temperament to that young body to render it the more strong and vigorous, which was without doubt most necessary for a prince who was to suffer so much to reconquer his estate.

King Henry d'Albret died at Hagetmau in Bearn, on the 25th of May, 1555, being fifty-three years old or thereabouts. He ordained by his will that his body should be carried to Pampeluna to be interred with his predecessors, and that in the meantime it should be laid in state in the cathedral of Lescar in Bearn. This prince was courageous, of a great spirit,

[1] It has been said that he was ordinarily nourished with coarse bread, beef, cheese, and garlic, and that often he was made to march bareheaded and with naked feet.

sweet and courteous to all the world, and so nobly liberal that Charles V. once passing through Navarre, was in such manner received that he protested he had never seen a more magnificent prince.

After his death, Jane his daughter, and Anthony, Duke of Vendôme, his son-in-law, succeeded him. They were at that time at the court of France, and had much difficulty in obtaining leave to retire to Bearn; for King Henry II., pressed to it by bad counsel, would have deprived them of the Lower Navarre, which yet remained to them, pretending that all below the Pyrenees belonged to the realm of France. They knew how justly to oppose against him the states of the country, and the King durst not too much pursue this subject, lest despair should force them to call the Spaniards to their assistance; but he still remained troublesome to them, and, giving to Anthony the government of Guienne, which had been likewise held by Henry d'Albret, his father-in-law, he deprived him of Languedoc, which he had a long time enjoyed.

About two years after they returned to the court of France, whither they brought their son, aged about four or five years, who was the jolliest and best-composed lad in the world; but they stayed only a few months, and returned again to Bearn.

A little time after, King Henry II. was slain with a blow of a lance by Montgomery. Francis II., his eldest son, succeeded him; and the Guises, uncles to Mary Stuart, his Queen, seized the government. The princes of the blood would not suffer this, and Louis, Prince of Condé, younger brother to Anthony, called that King to the court to oppose it.

During these divisions the Huguenots hatched the Amboise conspiracy against the government; and the two brothers, Anthony and Louis, being accused as chiefs of it, were arrested in Orleans, and evidence was so strong against Louis that it was believed he would have been beheaded if the death of King Francis II. had not happened.

Charles IX., who succeeded him, being under age, Queen Catherine, his mother, caused herself to be declared regent of the states, and the King of Navarre, first prince of the blood, was declared lieutenant-general of the realm, to govern the state with her; so that by this means he was kept in France, whither he caused his Queen, Jane, and his young son, Prince Henry, to come. But he did not long enjoy this new dignity, for, the troubles daily continuing, by reason of the surprises which the new reformers made of the chief cities of the kingdom, after having retaken Bruges from them, he came to besiege Rouen, where, visiting one day the trenches, he received a musket shot in the left shoulder, of which he in a few days died at Andely, on the Seine. Had he lived longer the Huguenots had without doubt been but ill-treated in France, for he mortally hated them, though his brother, the Prince of Condé, was the principal chief of their party.

The Queen his wife and the little prince his son were at that time at the court of France. The mother returned to Bearn, where she publicly embraced Calvinism; but she left her son with the King, under the conduct of a wise tutor named La Gaucherie, who endeavoured to give him some degree of learning, not by the rules of grammar, but by discourses and entertainments. To this effect he taught him by heart many fair sentences such as:

> Ou vaincre avec justice,
> Ou mourir avec gloire.[1]

And this:

> Les princes sur leur peuple ont autorité grande,
> Mais Dieu plus fortement dessus les rois commande.[2]

In the year 1566 his mother took him from the court of France, and led him to Pau; and in the place of La Gaucherie, who had died, she gave him Florentius Christian, an ancient servant of the house of Vendôme, a man of a very agreeable conversation and well versed in learning, but, however, a Huguenot, who, according to the orders of the Queen, instructed the prince in that false doctrine.

In the first troubles of the religion, Francis Duke of Guise had been assassinated by Poltrot at the siege of Orleans, leaving his children in minority. This was in the year 1563. In the second, the Constable of Montmorency received a wound at the battle of St. Denis, of which he died at Paris three days after, the Eve of St. Martin in the year 1567. In the third, in the year 1569, Queen Jane rendered herself protectress of the Huguenot party, being for this purpose come to Rochelle with her son, whom she now devoted to the defence of that new religion.

In this quality he was declared chief, with his uncle the Prince of Condé his lieutenant, in colleague with

---

[1] Either justly gain the victory,
Or learn with glory how to die.

[2] Kings rule their subjects with a mighty hand;
But God with greater power doth kings command.

Admiral Coligny. These were two great chieftains, but they committed notable errors; and this young prince, though not exceeding thirteen years of age, had the spirit to observe them. For he judged well at the great skirmish of Loudun that if the Duke of Anjou[1] had had troops ready to assault them, he had done it; and that, not doing it, he was without doubt in a sorry plight, and therefore should the rather have been assaulted by them; but they, by not doing it, gave time to all his troops to arrive.

At the battle of Jarnac he represented to them yet more judiciously that there was no means to fight, because the forces of the princes were dispersed, and those of the Duke of Anjou firmly embodied: but they were engaged too far to be able to retreat. The Prince of Condé was killed in this battle, or rather assassinated in cold blood after the combat, in which he had had his leg broken.

After that all the authority and hope of the party remained in Admiral Coligny who, to speak truth, was the greatest man of that time of the religion he sided with, but the most unfortunate.

This admiral having gathered together new forces, hazarded a second battle at Montcontour, in Poitou. He had caused to come to the army our little Prince of Navarre, and the young Prince of Condé, who was likewise named Henry, and placed them in charge of Prince Lodovic of Nassau, who guarded them on a distant hill with four thousand horse.

The young prince burned with desire to engage in person, but they permitted him not to run so great

[1] This Duke of Anjou was afterwards Henry III.

a hazard. Nevertheless, when the advance guard of the Duke of Alençon was disordered by that of the admiral, there had been no danger to let him fall upon the enemy who were taken with surprise. However, they hindered him, and he now cried out, "We shall lose our advantage, and in consequence the battle." It happened as he had foreseen; and it was at that hour judged by some that a young man of sixteen years of age had more understanding than the old soldiers. Thus he applied himself thoroughly to what he did: nor had he only a body, but spirit and sound judgment.

Being saved with the remnants of his army, he made a tour almost round the kingdom, fighting in retreat, and rallying together the Huguenot troops here and there for five or six months, during which he suffered so many hardships that had he not been brought up in the manner he was he would not have been able to support them.

This young prince, always accompanied with the admiral, led his troops into Guienne, and from thence through Languedoc, where he took Nimes by stratagem, forced several small places, and burned the suburbs of Toulouse in such manner that the sparks of that fire flew into that great city. The war being thus kindled in the heart of France, he showed himself on the other bank of the Rhone with his troops, gained by storm the towns of St. Julien and St. Just, and obliged St. Etienne-en-Forêt to capitulate. From thence he descended to the banks of the Saône, and afterwards into the middle of Burgundy. Paris trembled a second time at the approach of an army so much the more formidable, because it seemed to be reinforced by the loss of two battles, and to have now gained some advantage over the army of the Catholics which the Marshal de Cossé commanded.

The council of the King, fearing to hazard all by a fourth encounter, judged it more to the purpose to patch up a peace with that party. It was therefore entered upon, the two armies being near each other, and concluded in the little town of Arnay-le-Duc, on the 11th of August, 1570.

This peace made, everyone returned home. The Prince of Navarre went to Bearn, King Charles IX. married Elizabeth, daughter of the Emperor Maximilian II.; and nothing else seemed thought of but feasts and rejoicings. In the meantime the King, having found that he could never compass his desires on the Huguenots by force, resolved to make use of means more easy, but much more wicked. He began to caress them, to feign that he would treat them favourably, to accord them the greater part of those things they desired, and to lull them asleep with hopes of his making war against the King of Spain in the Low Countries, a thing they passionately desired; and the better to allure them he promised, as a gage of his faith, to marry his sister Margaret to our Henry; and by these means drew the principal chiefs of their party to Paris.

His mother Jane, who was come in advance to make preparations for the marriage, died a few days after her arrival—a princess of a spirit and courage above her sex, and whose soul, wholly virile, was not subject to the weaknesses and defects of other women; but, in truth, a passionate enemy of the Catholic religion.

Some historians say that she was poisoned with a pair of perfumed gloves, because they feared that she, having a great spirit, would discover the design they had to massacre all the Huguenots; but if I be not deceived, this is a falsity; it being more likely, which others say, that she died of a phthisical affection, since those that were about her and served her have so testified.

Henry her son, who came after her, being in Poitou, received news of her death, and presently took the quality of King; for hitherto he had only borne that of Prince of Navarre. As soon as he came to Paris, the unhappy nuptials were celebrated, the two parties being married by the Cardinal de Bourbon, on a daïs erected for that purpose before the church of Notre-Dame.

Six days after, which was the day of St. Bartholomew, all the Huguenots who were come to the solemnity had their throats cut; amongst others, the admiral and twenty other lords of note, twelve hundred gentlemen, three or four thousand soldiers and burgesses, and through all the cities of the kingdom, after the example of Paris near a hundred thousand men. Execrable action! which never had, nor ever shall again have, if it please God, its parallel.

What grief must it needs be to our young King to see instead of wines and perfumes so much blood shed at his nuptials, and his best friends murdered, and to hear their pitiful cries, which pierced his ears into the Louvre, where he was lodged! And, moreover, what visions and fears must needs surprise his very person! For in effect it was considered whether they should murder him and the Prince of Condé with the rest, and all the murderers concluded their death. Nevertheless, by a miracle, they afterwards resolved to spare them.

Charles IX. caused them to be brought to his presence, and, having showed them a mountain of dead bodies, with horrible threats, not hearkening to their reasons, told them "Either death or the mass!" They elected rather the last then the first, and abjured Calvinism; but because it was known they did it not heartily, they were so straitly observed that they could not escape the court during those two years that Charles IX. lived, nor until a long time after his death.

During this time our Henry exquisitely dissembled his discontent, though it was very great, and notwithstanding those vexations which might trouble his spirit, he clothed his visage with a perpetual serenity, and humour wholly jolly. This was without doubt the most difficult passage of his life. He had to do with a furious King, and with his two brothers—to wit, the Duke of Anjou, a dissembling prince, who had been educated in massacres, and with the Duke of Alençon, who was deceitful and malicious; with Queen Catherine, who mortally hated him, because her divines had foretold his reign; and lastly, with the house of Guise, whose power and credit were at present almost boundless.

He was doubtless necessitated to act with a marvellous prudence in the conduct of himself with all these people that he might not create in them the least jealousy, but rather beget a great esteem of himself, make submission and gravity accord, and preserve his dignity and life. In the meantime he disengaged himself from all these difficulties and from all these dangers with an unparalleled address.

He contracted a great familiarity with the Duke of Guise, who was about his own age, and they often made secret parties of pleasure together; but he agreed not so well with the Duke of Alençon, who had a capricious spirit; nor was he overmuch troubled at his ill accord with him, because neither the King nor Queen-mother had any affection for this duke. However, he gave no credit to the bad counsel of that Queen's emissary, who endeavoured to engage his contending in a duel against him; so much the rather because, considering him as the brother of his King, to whom he owed respect, he knew well it would have proved his loss, and that she would not have been wanting to take so fair a pretext to ruin him.

He shunned, likewise, other snares laid for him; but yet not all, for he suffered himself to be overtaken with the allurements of some ladies of the court, whom it is said that the Queen engaged expressly to amuse the princes and nobles and to discover all their thoughts.

From that time (for vices contracted in the blossom of youth generally accompany men to their tomb) a passion for women proved to be the greatest weakness of our Henry, and possibly was the cause of his last misfortune; for God punishes sooner or later those who wickedly abandon themselves to this criminal passion.

Besides this, he contracted no other crimes in this court; and it ought to be attributed to a particular grace of Heaven that he was not infected with all, for there never was a court more vicious or more corrupted. Impiety, atheism, witchcraft, black ingratitude and perfidy, poisoning and assassination, reigned there in a sovereign degree; yet all these abominations, instead of affecting him, fortified him in the natural horror he had against them, and though amongst wicked persons, he had never any thoughts to become their companion, but many to be their enemy.

On the succeeding St. Bartholomew's Day they looked to finish exterminating the Huguenots; and to this purpose the Duke of Anjou went to besiege Rochelle, carrying Henry with him, but caused him to be so well observed that he could neither turn to the right hand nor to the left. It may be judged what heart-grief it was to him to be made an instrument in the destruction of those who yet remained his friends and servants, and had sought refuge in this city. After a long siege it was relieved by the arrival of the ambassadors of Poland, who came to seek the Duke of Anjou, whom the estates of that country had elected their King. The siege raised, Henry returned to Paris or, rather, was led there, and the Duke of Anjou left France with great regret in order to take possession of his new kingdom.

Some months afterwards Charles IX. fell mortally sick, vomiting forth blood through all the conduits of his body, so that by many it was believed he was poisoned.

His extreme malady gave birth to a league made by the Duke of Alençon, the Marshals of Montmorency and Cossé, and some Catholics with the Huguenot party, to deprive the Queen-mother of the government, and drive the Guises from the court, where they were very powerful. Our Henry entered into it, not out of any design to stand well with those people, but only that he might have the means to retire with security into his own country.

The Queen-mother having heard of these doings, caused him and the Duke of Alençon to be arrested and committed to prison. The Prince of Condé saved himself happily in Germany. She caused likewise the two Marshals of Montmorency and Cossé to be secured; and to let the world see she treated not princes of their degree in this manner without sufficient cause, she caused them to be strictly examined on many treasonable interrogatories, which were all false. There were only put to death La Mole, Coconas, and Tourtray, three gentlemen of note, who had engaged themselves in their intrigues; and possibly this execution was necessary to calm the spirit of the nobility and people, who began to murmur that a son of France, and the first prince of the blood, should be treated in this manner.

In this affair the chancellor would have examined the King of Navarre; but though captive and threatened, he would not so much wrong his dignity as to reply to him. However, to content the Queen-mother, he made a long discourse, addressing his speech to her, by which he declared many things touching the present state of affairs, but charged no person, as the Duke of Alençon had weakly and unworthily done.

King Charles IX. being near his death, and hating, possibly not without reason, both his two brothers and his mother, sent to seek our Henry, in whom alone he acknowledged to have found faith and honour, and most affectionately recommended to him his wife and daughter.

Catherine de Medicis, knowing that he had sent for him, was fearful lest he should leave to him the regency, and to this purpose wished to cast some fear into his soul, to the end he should not dare to accept it. As he went to attend the King, who was at Bois de Vincennes, she gave orders that he should be made to pass under the arches, between the guards, who lay in ambush and posture to massacre him. He startled at first with fear, and recoiled two or three paces backwards. However, Nanzay le Châtre, captain of the lifeguards, reassured him, swearing to him that he should receive no harm: he was therefore constrained, though he trusted but little to his words, to pass through the carbines and halberds.

After the death of Charles IX., Catherine de Medicis, partly by force and partly by cunning, seized on the regency, *en attendant* the return of her dear son, the Duke of Anjou, who was named Henry III.

When he was returned from Poland she brought the two princes before him to do with them what he pleased, whom, after some chidings and threatenings, he set at liberty.

These two princes making reflection on the continual dangers they had for two years past been in, resolved with the first occasion to deliver themselves from these fears. The Prince of Condé, who was in Germany, had raised levies for the Huguenot party, who about the end of the reign of Charles IX. had retaken arms; and Damville, second son of the late Constable and brother of the Marshal of Montmorency, who was a prisoner in the Bastille, had joined himself to their party, not taking religion for his pretext (because he was a Catholic), but the public liberty and reformation of the state. Those Catholics who joined themselves in league with the Huguenots were named the Politicians.

Our Henry could not escape from the court so soon as he desired. He was diligently watched, and his very domestics were as so many spies over him. He knew that if he were surprised whilst trying to leave he would certainly be murdered; and now, whilst he sought occasions to do so with security, he became enamoured of Madame de Sauves, wife of the secretary of state, then the fairest woman in the whole court.

In the meantime the Queen-mother, who with so much diligence kept him at court, would have been well contented had he been gone, for the King, her dear son, began to take some knowledge of his own affairs—a thing much displeasing to her, because she would have governed all. She therefore, apprehending that as he took the authority into his own hands, hers would be diminished, believed that she ought to embroil all by factions and civil wars, of which she alone, as it may be said, had the key, so that nothing could pass without her. This explains the reason why so long as she lived she did nothing but craftily generate troubles and animate different parties, both at court and abroad.

Amongst these transactions, as the King went to Rheims to be installed, a conspiracy was discovered against his person, fostered by the Duke of Alençon, at the instigation of the friends of the defunct admiral and of La Mole, who had been his favourite. Many believed this to be a thing devised by the Queen-mother, on purpose to astound and weaken the spirit of her son; the more so because it was she who obliged the King to pardon this crime so lightly, neither of the accomplices or instigators being punished for it. However it was, Henry III. testified on this occasion a particular confidence in our King of Navarre, who, assisted by his friends, served him as captain of his guards the whole way, never stirring from the boot of his coach; and in this he appeared so much the more generous, having no reason to love him beside the obligation of his duty, being his kinsman and his vassal.

Henry III. having arrived at Rheims, was on the 15th of February installed by the Cardinal of Guise, and on the morrow espoused to Louise de Lorraine, daughter of the Count of Vaudemont, which added yet a greater lustre to the house of Guise, of which Duke Henry was chief, who was then in favour, but afterwards killed at Blois. This prince, one of the bravest in every way that age produced, had ever promised himself to govern the King by Queen Louise, his kinswoman. He had contracted a very close familiarity with the King of Navarre, whom he called his master, as that King called him his gossip.

Queen Margaret, who, to speak the truth, could not live without intrigues and gallantries, contributed with all her power to the maintenance of this good understanding, and essayed to make Monsieur (the Duke of Alençon) whom she most passionately loved, enter into it.

But the union of princes being the overthrow of

favourites and governors, the Queen-mother straightway
spoilt this design, by begetting in the King a jealousy
of his wife, incensing Monsieur against the Duke of
Guise by the remembrance of the massacre of the
admiral, continually confounding the King of Navarre
by the intrigue of some ladies, but particularly of De
Sauves, who, enjoying such person as Catherine commanded her, received the love and services of Monsieur
to create a difference between them.

The Queen-mother maintained likewise an irrecon-
cilable hatred between the King and Monsieur, by
which means there happened an affair which as much
proclaimed the greatness of courage and generosity of
our Henry as any action he had done in his life.

The King, having fallen sick, and being in great
danger of death with a pain in his ear, believed himself to be poisoned, as Francis II.[1] had been, and
accused Monsieur. In this belief he sent to seek the
King of Navarre, and commanded him to dispatch
Monsieur as soon as he (the King) was dead, endeavouring by all reasons possible to persuade him that that
wicked man would make him perish and all his if he
prevented it not. The favourites of the King, having
the same opinion as their master, seeing Monsieur
pass, sacrificed him already to their revenge by murdering regards.

Our Henry endeavoured to sweeten the fury of the
King, and demonstrated to him the horrible consequences of the command; but the King, not content
with reasons, contrary to them, comported himself in

[1] Francis II. died of an aposteme in his ear, which was
believed to be the effects of poison.

such manner that he wished him to presently execute it, for fear he should fail of it when he was dead.

If the two brothers—to wit, the King and Monsieur—had been out of the world, the crown appertained to him. Now one in all appearances was about to die, and he might easily find a death for the other, having the favourites, the officers of the King, the Guises, all their friends, and almost all the nobility at his devotion; for Monsieur was a prince of an ill presence and of low inclinations, yet malign and cruel; and for all these fine qualities hated by almost all the world, and sustained only by the brave Bussy d'Amboise. How few princes are there who would have let slip so fair an occasion! I dare boldly speak it, how few are there who would not seek it! and yet our hero (for in such an action I must perforce call him so) was so far from availing himself of it that he conceived a horror at the furious vengeance of Henry III. "There is no nobler ambition than to know how to moderate ambition when it is not just, and to endeavour to preserve our conscience and honour rather than acquire a crown by wicked ways. Diadems gained by ill means are not marks of glory to those brows that carry them, but rather frontlets of infamy, such as are placed on thieves and villains."

Heaven without doubt approved the generous sentiments of our Henry, and destined to him the sceptre of the *fleur de lis,* because guiltless of an impatience to reach it before his term. On the contrary, these brothers of the house of Valois who endeavoured to ravish it one from the other died all unhappily, and had for their successor him who by a crime refused to be so.

Henry III. having recovered, knew well that he had wrongfully accused his brother of having poisoned him, yet he loved him never a whit the more. He daily suffered his favourites to give him a thousand affronts, and to domineer over him in the public assemblies. He likewise wished Bussy d'Amboise, who was his favourite and only support, to be murdered by night at the gates of the Louvre; and it was believed he had given orders, if the Duke of Alençon had gone to his assistance (for there were people appointed to come and tell him that Bussy was assassinated) to slay him likewise. Then Monsieur, getting the bridle out of his mouth, escaped from court, put himself in the field, gathered together some malcontents, composed an army and joined with that of the Huguenots, commanded by the Prince of Condé and by Casimir, youngest son of the Count Palatine, who, in these civil wars of religion, twice or thrice led great levies of German horse into France.

Our Henry was earnestly solicited to follow him, and Monsieur said he had promised him to do it, but they had taken from about him all those who might favour his escape, and placed in their stead people of their own hire. He was moreover promised the lieutenant-generalship of the King's army, which was a strong lure to retain him; nor was the love of the fair De Sauves less powerful. However, the natural spurs of his courage and the fear he had lest Monsieur and the Prince of Condé should seize on the chief command amongst the Huguenot party, which had been his cradle and was to be his castle, as well as the remonstrances of some of his servants and the inventions of Queen Catherine, who expressly incensed the King against him, in the end obliged him to escape, and made him take his resolution.

He saved himself therefore by feigning to go hunting towards Senlis, and retired to Alençon, where, however, he did nothing, peace being soon after concluded with them all. There was granted to Monsieur a great portion in money and places; to the Huguenots many very advantageous conditions; to the Prince of Condé the government of Picardy, and the city of Peronne for his retreat; but to our Henry nothing else but hopes, of which being in the end disabused, he renounced the peace, and re-entered into the Huguenot party; and quitting the Catholic Church, returned anew to his first religion. It is to be believed that he did it because he was persuaded it was the better. Thus his fault will be worthy of excuse; nor can he be accused but for not having the true light. In the meantime it must not be forgotten to observe on this, that the greatest reproach his enemies ever made him—I mean those of the League—was his having thus relapsed; and this was likewise the greatest obstacle he found at Rome, when, being converted, he demanded the absolution of the Pope.

The Rochellers received him into their city, but not without great precautions, and not until he had driven from him some people who were neither Catholics nor Huguenots, but atheists, and horribly wicked persons. It has been held that they followed him against his will; that truly he had served himself of them in some intrigues; but that it was himself who by secret advice obliged the Rochellers to demand their expulsion.

After he had sojourned some months at Rochelle, he went to take possession of his government of Guienne, where he had the displeasure to see shut against him the gates of the city of Bordeaux, under the pretext that the inhabitants feared that if he became master of it he would banish the Catholic religion—a very sensible injury to a young prince full of courage; but he knew most wisely how to dissemble it at present, because he had not power to revenge it, and generously forgot it when he had the means to do it.

About this time the League took birth, that powerful faction which for twenty years together tormented France, which thought to introduce the Spanish domination, and which would have reversed the order of the succession of the royal family, under the fairest pretext in the world, to wit, the maintenance of the religion of our ancestors.

At other times, under the reign of Charles IX., there were divers leagues and associations made in Guienne and Languedoc to defend the Church against the Huguenots (our heirs will judge whether those who rendered themselves chief of them had most zeal or most ambition), but they were not pressed so forward nor so diligently formed, and therefore became extinct. The grandees of the realm, however, might by them observe that if at any time such associations were made, it would be a fair means to elevate to a great height him who could render himself their chief.

Henry Duke of Guise, who had a kinglike heart, had in all likelihood this thought; or if he at first had it not, the favourites of Henry III., by persecuting him, forced him to entertain it, and to apply himself to this party, to defend himself against them. There were of his house seven or eight princes, all brave to the utmost extent. The principal of them were his brothers, the Duke of Mayenne and the Cardinal de Guise, and the Duke d'Aumale and the Marquis d'Elbeuf, his cousins.

Now the secession of Monsieur, of which we have spoken, to the Huguenots, and the advantageous peace afterwards granted them, made the League show itself, which was but little in its commencement. Those who, to render themselves powerful, desired a new faction in the state, took up this subject in order to represent by their emissaries the great danger in which the Catholic religion was, and to demonstrate the excessive strength of its enemies, who had on their side the two first princes of the blood and Monsieur, who was their friend. "What would it be," said they, "if he should come to the crown with such ill intentions? that therefore they ought to advise in good time, and fortify themselves against that danger which threatened the holy Church." They then whispered these considerations, and others like them, into men's ears, and when they had thus disposed their minds published them aloud.

Upon this, the burgesses of Peronne, a free city, and which was accustomed to have so powerful a governor, refused to receive the Prince of Condé, because a Huguenot. He made his complaints to the King, and demanded the execution of the treaty of peace. The Picards opposed him, and were the first that made a league or union for the defence, as they said, of the Catholic Apostolic and Roman faith. The Prince of Condé could never come to terms, and was constrained to retire into Guienne.

James Lord d'Humières was made chief of this league in Picardy, and Aplincourt, a young gentleman, took the oath of the inhabitants of Peronne, by whose example the cities of Amiens, Corbie, St. Quentin, and many others, did the like. Louis de Trémoille began one likewise in Poitou. The Queen-mother secretly favoured this design, to the end that she might retain her authority among these discords and disturbances. The first model and the articles of this league were brought to Paris; and there were some so zealous as to carry them from house to house, endeavouring to engage the most backward; but Christopher de Thou, chief president, hindered for the present the progress of this conspiracy.

Those who were the first inventors of it had deliberated among themselves, that to the end to give it means to aggrandise itself and to keep the spirits of the people still warm, it was necessary to continue the war with the Huguenots. For this purpose they stirred up divers persons, who surprised their places and committed a thousand affronts against our Henry and the Prince of Condé. And much more, they raised so many factions and complaints on all sides of people who demanded the summoning of the estates, that the King was obliged to agree to it. They assembled at Blois, and began in the month of December, in the year 1576. The Huguenots themselves were not at all troubled at this convocation, because they imagined that the third estate, which ordinarily is the strongest, and which has most reason to apprehend war, would cause the peace to be confirmed; but the union of those who were for war was so strong that it was resolved to prosecute it with vigour.

They judged it, notwithstanding, convenient to depute beforehand some persons of the assembly to our Henry and to the Prince of Condé, to exhort them to return into the bosom of the Catholic Church. And this taking no effect, the King was obliged to declare himself chief of the League; and so from sovereign, become chief of a faction and enemy to a part of his subjects.

But to be revenged on the Duke of Guise, who was the cause of all these troubles, he issued an edict whereby the princes of the blood were to have precedency of all other princes and peers, as well at the King's coronation as in parliament and elsewhere. This considerably lessened the dignity of the Duke of Guise, who by ancient usage had had the precedency of the princes of the blood who were not peers or whose peerage was of a later date than was his.

He raised three or four armies who made war against the Huguenots in the Dauphinate, in Guienne, in Languedoc, and in Poitou; and reduced, and might have quite crushed them, if their ruin had been resolutely prosecuted before they could recover their surprise. But the Queen-mother, who only desired the war that she might have affairs in agitation, and not that they might have their issue, persuaded the King her son, for certain studied reasons, to grant them peace.

The treaty being concluded, the Queen-mother made a voyage into Guienne. She feigned that it was to cause it to be punctually executed, and to carry her daughter Margaret to the King of Navarre her husband; but it was in effect to sow seeds of discord among the Huguenots, to the end she might be mistress of that party as she had been of that of the Catholics. Henry now kept his little court at Nerac; he had before kept it at Agen, where he was beloved of the people by reason of his justice and goodness. But it happened that at a ball or dance some young people of his own train blew out the candles to commit insolencies, which so scandalised the inhabitants that they delivered up their city to the Marshal de Biron, whom the King had sent as governor into the province of Guienne.

A little time after Henry likewise lost La Reole by another folly of his young people. He had given the government of it to an old Huguenot captain named D'Ussac, who had his visage horribly deformed. His deformity, however, hindered him not from becoming enamoured of one of the ladies attending the Queen-mother, for she had brought many of the most bewitching with her, to kindle a fire everywhere. The Viscount of Turenne, afterwards Duke of Bouillon, then about twenty-one or twenty-two years of age, with some others of his age, would make raillery of this business. Our Henry, instead of commanding them to silence, made himself of their party, and having a fluent spirit, assisted them in launching some mockeries and jeers against this doting lover. No passion renders a heart so sensitive as this. D'Ussac could not suffer this raillery, though proceeding from his master; but, in spite of his honour and religion, he yielded and delivered up La Reole to Duras, a lord who, having been in favour with our Henry, had quitted him out of envy, because he testified less affection to him than to Roquelaire, who was without doubt one of the most honest and most pleasant men of his time.

The Queen-mother had taken with her, as we have said, Queen Margaret to her husband. Neither of the two spouses was over-well pleased. Margaret, who loved the splendour of the French court, where she swam, if we may so speak, in full intrigues, believed that to be in Guienne was a kind of banishment; and Henry, knowing her humour and carriage, would rather have chosen her room than her company.[1] However, seeing it an irremediable ill, he resolved to suffer it, leaving her an entire liberty. He considered her rather as a sister of his King than as his own wife. He likewise pretended some nullities in the marriage, but waited time and place to make them known. In the meantime, accommodating himself to the season and to the necessity of his affairs, he endeavoured to draw advantages from her intrigues and from her credit. He received no small one in the conference which he and the deputies of the Huguenots had at Nerac with the Queen-mother; for whilst she thought to enchant them by the charms of those fair ladies she had expressly brought with her, and by the eloquence of Pibrac, Margaret opposed the same articles, gained the gentlemen who were near her mother by the attractions of her ladies; and employed so well her own that she enchanted the spirit and will of

---

[1] The King of Navarre did not show any pleasure in receiving a woman whose gallantries had thrown ridicule upon his name. —Martin's *History of France*, vol. ix.

poor Pibrac in such manner that he acted only by her will, and quite contrary to the intentions of the Queen-mother, who, distrusting that a man so wise could be capable of such great folly, was deceived in many articles, and insensibly carried to grant much more to the Huguenots than she had resolved.

Scarce were eight months spent since the peace, when the Queen-mother, Monsieur, and the Guises began to be weary of it. The Queen-mother, because she would not have the King rest any long time without having need of her negotiations and intermission; Monsieur, because by rekindling the war he thought to render himself redoubtable to the King, and to make him give him forces to carry into the Low Countries, which, being revolted from Spain, demanded him for their sovereign; and, finally, the Guises, because they feared lest the ardour of the League should by too protracted a calm grow cold.

In these wishes they pressed the King to redemand the places of security granted to the Huguenots; and Monsieur and the Queen-mother cunningly caused it to be told to our Henry that he should not surrender them, but hold it out that his cause was just, and that his safety consisted in his arms. Margaret, who knew his weakness, and who likewise wished for the war, excited him by the persuasion of ladies whom she retained for this service; and by the same means animated alike all those braves who approached her; nor spared she herself with the Viscount of Turenne for this purpose; so that this prince, possibly with very little justice, and certainly to very ill purpose, was carried to a rupture, and engaged the Huguenots in a new civil war, which was named, for the reasons just spoken of, the "War of the Lovers."

This was the most disadvantageous they ever yet made. By it they lost a great number of strong places; and were in such manner weakened that had the pursuit of them been finished they could never have regained strength. But Monsieur, who desired to transport all the forces both of the one and the other party into the Low Countries, made himself mediator of the peace, and obtained it by an edict, which was concluded after the conference of Fleix.

This peace was the cause of almost as many evils to the state as all the former wars had been. The two courts of the two Kings, and the two Kings themselves, plunged headlong into their pleasures; with this difference, however, that our Henry was not so absolutely lulled asleep with his delights but he thought sometimes of his affairs, being awakened and vividly reminded by the remonstrances of the ministers of his religion, and by the reproaches of the old captains of the Huguenots, who spoke to him with great liberty. But Henry III. was wholly overwhelmed with softness and feebleness. He seemed to have neither heart nor motion; and his subjects could scarcely have known that he was in the world, but that he daily charged them with new imposts, all the money of which was disposed to the benefit of his favourites.

He had always three or four at a time, and at present he began to cast his graces on Joyeuse and the two Nogarets—to wit, Bernard and Jean-Louis, of whom the elder died five or six years after, and the younger was Duke d'Epernon, one of the most memorable and most wonderful subjects that the court had ever seen elevated in its favour, and who certainly had qualities as eminent as his fortune. In the meantime the excessive gifts which the King gave to all his favourites excited the cries of the people because they were trampled on; and their monstrous greatness displeased the princes because they believed themselves despised. In such manner they rendered themselves odious to all the world; and the hate carried to them fell likewise upon the King, whilst that violence which they obliged him to use towards his parliaments to confirm his edicts of creation and imposts augmented it yet more; for if his authority made his wishes pass as absolute, he drew upon him the people's curses; and if the vigour of the sovereign companies, as often happened, stopped them, he attracted their disdain.

The people, who easily lend themselves to rebellion against their prince when they have lost for him all sentiments of esteem and veneration, spoke strange things of him and his favourites. The Guises, whom the minions—for so the favourites were called—opposed on all occasions, endeavouring to deprive them of their charges and governments, to re-invest themselves, were not wanting to blow the fire and to increase the animosities of the people, particularly of the great cities, whom favourites have always feared, and who have always hated favourites. These were the principal dispositions to the aggrandisement of the League and to the loss of Henry III.

It is not to our purpose to recount here all the

intrigues of the court during five or six years, nor the war of the Low Countries, from which Monsieur[1] brought nothing but disgrace. It is only necessary to tell that in the year 1584 Monsieur died at the castle of Thierry, without having been married; that Henry III. had likewise no children; and that it was but too well known he was incapable of ever having any, by reason of an incurable disease which he contracted at Venice, on his return from Poland.[2] See here the reason why, as soon as Monsieur was adjudged dead by the physicians, the Guises and Queen-mother began to labour each on their side to assure themselves of the crown, as if the succession had been open to them; for neither the one nor the other accounted for anything our Henry, so much the rather because he was beyond the seventh degree, beyond which in ordinary successions is accounted no kindred, and because he was not of that religion of which all the kings of France have been since Clovis, and by consequence incapable to wear the crown or bear the title of "Thrice-Christian." Add to this that he was two hundred leagues distant from Paris, and, as it were, shut up in a corner of Guienne, where it seemed to them easy to ensnare or to oppress him.

The Queen-mother had a design to give the crown to the children of her daughter married to the Duke of Lorraine, whom she would have treated as princes of the blood, as if the crown of France could fall under

[1] Monsieur, intending to surprise Antwerp, and treating ill the people of the Low Countries, who had called him, was driven thence.
[2] From 1575 the rumour was spread that the King and his brother were as mentioned in the text.—Martin's *History of France*.

the command of the spindle. Nor was this merely out of the love she had for them, but out of a secret hatred she had conceived against our Henry, because she saw that, contrary to all her wishes, Heaven had opened him a way to come to the throne.

Besides, she was too much deceived, for so able a woman, to believe that the Duke of Guise would favour her in her design. There was much appearance, and after affairs sufficiently testified it, that, feeling himself persecuted by the favourites and ill-treated by the King himself, for their sakes he had thoughts to assure the crown for his own head, for ill-treatments work at least no other effect than to cast into extreme despair souls so noble and elevated as that of this prince. But he, knowing well that of himself he could not arrive at so high a pitch, and that especially because it would be difficult to divert the affection which the people of France naturally have for the princes of the blood, essayed to gain to his side the old Cardinal de Bourbon, who was uncle of our Henry. He promised him therefore that on the death of Henry III. he would employ all his power and that of his friends to make him king; and that good man, doting with age, permitting himself to be flattered with these vain hopes, made himself the bauble of the duke's ambition, who by this means drew to his party a great number of Catholics who leaned to the house of Bourbon.

The question was, if the uncle ought to precede the son of the elder brother in the succession; and to speak truth, the business was not without some difficulty, because, according to the custom of Paris, the capital of the kingdom, and many other customs, collateral representation has no place. This point of right was diversely held by the reverend judges, and many debates were held, some in favour of the uncle, and others of the nephew. These were but combats of words— the sword was to decide the difference. It seemed to many great politicians that the Duke of Guise acted contrary to his own interests and design by acknowledging that the Cardinal de Bourbon ought to succeed to the crown; this being to avow that after his death, which could suffer no long delay, it would appertain to our Henry, his nephew.

Henry III. knew well his design, or rather it was notified by his favourites, who saw in it their certain ruin, and therefore so much desired to bring back the King of Navarre to the Catholic Church, to the end he might deprive the Leaguers of that specious pretext they had to entertain the League. He sent therefore to him the Duke d'Epernon, who essayed to convert him by reasons of interest and policy. Our Henry hearkened to him; but he testified that those were not motives sufficiently strong to make him change, and sent him back with many civilities.

The Huguenots were so vain as to publish and cause to be printed the conference of this prince with the Duke d'Epernon, to show that he was unshaken in his religion, and possibly likewise to engage him more strongly in it. The Duke of Guise was not wanting to profit by it, and demonstrated to the Catholic people the stubbornness of this prince, and what they might hope if he came to the throne with such sentiments.

To stop, therefore, his way to it, he made the zealous openly renew the League; and boldly bringing it into

Paris, where some new religious persons inspired this ardour into people's souls by confessions, held the first public assembly at the college of Fortet, which was called the cradle of the League. Many burgesses, many tradesmen, and likewise some clerks of Paris, entered into it. They carried it to Rome, and presented it to Pope Gregory III. for his approbation; but he never would give it, and continually, so long as he lived, disavowed it.

As soon as it grew a little great and strong, those who had engendered it made it appear that it was not only to provide for the security of religion for the future, but that at present they might approach themselves near to the crown; and that they not only would have it against the King of Navarre, who was to succeed, but against Henry III., who now reigned. They kept in salary certain new divines, who durst openly sustain that a prince ought to be deposed who acquits himself not well of his duty: "That no power but that which is well ordered is of God; otherwise, when it passes due bounds it is not authority, but usurpation; and that it is as absurd to say that he ought to be king who knows not how to govern, or who is deprived of understanding, as to believe a blind man a fit guide or an immovable statue able to make living men move."

In the meantime the Duke of Guise had retired to his government of Champagne, feigning himself discontented; but it was to make the Duke of Lorraine sign the League, out of hopes he would cause his son to succeed to the crown, to which he pretended to have right by his mother, daughter to Henry II. He held to this purpose a treaty at Joinville, where he likewise found agents from the King of Spain, who signed the treaty, and, as it was reported, did by letters of exchange supply the Duke of Guise with great sums of money.

At his departure thence, the duke assembled troops on all sides. His friends seized on as many places as they could, not only amongst the Huguenots, but likewise amongst the Catholics. The King might easily have dissipated these levies had he taken the field; but the Queen-mother, like self-interested physicians, who would for their profit augment the disease, withheld and amused him in his closet, persuading him that if he would leave to her the management of this affair she would easily reduce the duke to his obedience. To this purpose she held a conference with him at Vitry, and so gave him time to augment his party; and when he saw himself in a state to fear nothing, he broke up the conference, and made show of some resolution to come directly to Paris.

The King, astonished, prayed his mother to conclude an accommodation upon any terms; which she did by the treaty of Nemours, by which she granted to the duke and other princes of his house the government of several provinces, many great sums of money, together with a most bloody edict against the Huguenots, which forbade the profession of any other religion than the Catholic, under penalty of confiscation of goods and estate; with command to all preachers and ministers to depart from the realm within one month, and all Huguenots of what degree or quality soever within six months, or otherwise abjure their false religion. This edict was called the Edict of Juillet, which the League further constrained the King to carry himself into the parliament, and cause it to be ratified.[1]

A little after news arrived from Rome that Sixtus V., who succeeded Gregory XVIII., had approved the League, and had besides fulminated terrible bulls against the King of Navarre and Prince of Condé, declaring them heretics, apostates, chiefs, favourers and protectors of heretics, and as such falling under the censures and pains concluded on the laws and canons, depriving them and their descendants of all lands and dignities, incapable to succeed to any principality whatsoever, especially to the kingdom of France; and not only absolving their subjects from all oaths of fidelity, but absolutely forbidding them to obey them.

It was now that our Henry had need of all the forces both of his courage and virtue to sustain such rude assaults. He seemed in a manner lulled asleep by his pleasures. When the noise of these great assaults awakened him, he recalled all his virtue, and began to make it appear more vigorously than ever before. And he certainly afterwards avowed that his enemies had highly obliged him by persecuting him in this manner; for had they left him in repose, he would not have been constrained to think of his affairs, and, at the death of Henry III., would not have been in a state to attempt or entertain the crown.

---

[1] It is said that when Henry of Navarre heard of the King's agreement with the League, his apprehension for his party was such that his moustache became white.—Mathieu: *History of France*, vol. i.

He now did two renowned actions. The first was his commanding Philippe de Mornay (du Plessis Mornay), a gentleman of excellent education, and who could be reproached with nothing but being a Huguenot, to answer the manifesto of the League by an apology, and by a declaration which he caused to be drawn (June 10th, 1585). In this last piece (the chiefs of the League having spread abroad divers calumnies against his honour) he with all submission besought the King his sovereign that he would not be offended if he did pronounce, having still the respect due to his Majesty, that they did falsely and maliciously lie; and moreover, that to spare the blood of his nobles and avoid the desolation of the poor people, those infinite disorders, and above all those blasphemies, burnings and violations which the license of war must cause, he offered to the Duke of Guise, chief of the League, to decide this quarrel by his person against his, one to one, two to two, ten to ten, or such number as he should please, with arms generally in use by cavaliers of honour, either in the realm of France, or in such place as his Majesty should command, or else in such place as the Duke of Guise himself should choose.

This declaration had a great effect on people's spirits. They said that force could not be justly employed against him who so far submitted himself to reason; and the greater part of the nobility approved this generous procedure, and proclaimed aloud that the Duke of Guise ought not to refuse so great an honour.

That duke wanted no courage to accept the defiance; but he considered that drawing his sword against a prince of the blood was in France accounted a kind of parricide; that otherwise he would willingly have reduced the cause of religion and of the public to a private quarrel. He therefore prudently answered that he esteemed the person of the King of Navarre, and would have no controversy with him; but that he only interested himself in the Catholic religion, which was threatened, and for the tranquillity of the kingdom, which only and absolutely depended on the unity of religion.

His other action was as follows. Having heard the noise of those paper thunderbolts which the Pope had thrown out against him, he dispatched a representative to the King to make his complaints to him, and to demonstrate to him that this procedure concerned his Majesty nearer than himself: that he ought to judge that if the Pope took upon himself to decide concerning his succession, and should seize to himself a right to declare a prince of the blood unable to succeed to the crown, he might afterwards well pass further, and dethrone the King himself, as Zachary is reported to have formerly degraded Childeric III.

Upon these remonstrances, the King hindered the publication of those bulls in his dominions. But our Henry, not contenting himself therewith, and knowing himself to have friends at Rome, waxed so bold as to fix his and the Prince of Condé's opposition at the corners of the chief streets of that city, by which those princes appealed from the sentence of Sixtus V. to the Court of Peerage of France, giving the lie to whoever accused them of the crime of heresy, offering to prove the contrary in a general council, and in the end professing that they would revenge upon him and upon all his successors the injury done their King, the royal family, and all the courts of parliament.[1]

It could not but be supposed that this opposition would incense to the utmost the spirit of Sixtus V.; and indeed at first he testified a very furious emotion. However, when his choler was a little assuaged, he admired the great courage of that King who at such a distance had known how to revenge himself and fix the marks of his resentment even at the gates of his palace; in such manner he conceived so great an esteem for him (so true is it that virtue makes itself reverenced by its very enemies) that he was often afterwards heard say that of all those who reigned in Christendom there was none but this prince and Elizabeth, Queen of England, to whom he would have communicated those great things which agitated his spirit, if they had not been heretics. Nor could all the prayers of the League ever oblige him to furnish anything towards the charges of this war, which possibly overwhelmed the greater part of their enterprises, because their hopes in part depended on a million which he had promised them.

Now, as on their side the chiefs of the League endeavoured to attract to their party all the lords and cities they could, our Henry on his part reunited with him all his friends both of the one and the other religion: the Marshal of Damville-Montmorency, governor of Languedoc; the Duke of Montpensier, prince of the blood, who was governor of Poitou,

[1] This piece of audacity was drawn up at Paris by Pierre de L'Estoile, King's counsellor.

with his son the Prince of Dombes; the Prince of
Condé, who held a part of Poitou, of Saintange, and
of Angoumois; the Count of Soissons, and the Prince
of Conti his brother. Of these five princes of the
blood, the three last were his cousins-german, the two
first were removed one degree further; and all professed the Catholic religion, save only the Prince of
Condé. He had likewise on his part Lesdiguières, who
from a plain gentleman had by his valour elevated himself to so high a point that he was master of the
Dauphinate, and made the Duke of Savoy tremble;
Claudius de la Trémoille, who possessed great lands
in Poitou and Brittany, and had some time before
turned Huguenot that he might have the honour to
marry his daughter to the Prince of Condé; Henry
de la Tour, Viscount of Turenne, who, either out of
complacency or true persuasion, had espoused the new
religion; Chastillon, son to the Admiral Coligny; La
Boulaye, Lord Poitevin; René, chief of the house of
Rohan; George de Clermont d'Amboise; Francis, Count
of Rochefoucauld; the Lord d'Aubeterre; James de
Caumont La Force; the Lords de Pons, Saint Gelais-
Lansac; with many other lords and gentlemen of renown, all or most of the new religion. At the same
time he dispatched to Elizabeth Queen of England and
to the Protestant princes of Germany such able agents,
that they all joined together in a strong union, the
one to maintain the other; so that all these being
united, all things happened contrary to what the League
expected; and our Henry found himself fortified in such
manner that he had no longer any apprehension of being
oppressed without having the means to defend himself.

King Henry III. was extremely perplexed at this war,[1] which was maintained at his expense and to his great prejudice, since they disputed the succession, he yet living and well, and already considered him as one dead. He loved neither the one nor the other party, but did so much cherish his favourites (strange blindness!) that he fain would have parted his estate amongst them had it been in his power. The League on their side pretended to have power enough to carry it; and our Henry hoped to frustrate the designs of both. The Queen-mother, having other wishes for the children of her daughter married to the Duke of Lorraine, promised the King to find means to calm all these tempests. To this purpose she procured a truce with our Henry, during which an interview was agreed upon between him and her at the castle of St. Brix, near Coignac, where both met in the month of December.

There was some difficulty to find security for both; but especially for the Queen-mother, who was wonderfully distrustful. Our Henry hereupon did an action of great generosity, which he managed in this manner. There had been a truce agreed upon for the security of this conference, in such sort that if either party broke it, they were in fault, and might justly be arrested. Now some of our Henry's followers, feigning to be traitors, had enticed some of the Catholic captains, too greedy of the booty, to Fontenay, which they would have let them take. By this means the Catholics would have remained convicted of perfidy, and he would have had good pretence to arrest the

[1] This war has been called the "War of the Three Henries," viz., Henry III., Henry Duke of Guise, and Henry of Navarre.

Queen-mother; but this generous prince, having heard of this foul conspiracy, was extremely vexed against those who contrived it, and forbade them to continue it. Was not this proof to all men that he had the true sentiments of honour founded in his soul, and not the mere semblance?

And as he testified his generosity in that *rencontre*, so he made known his constancy and the power of his spirit in all the discourse. The Queen demanding of him what it was he desired, he answered, regarding those ladies she had brought with her, "Madam, there is nothing that I would have;" as if he would have said that he would not allow himself to be drawn away by such allurements. She endeavoured above all things to disunite him from the other chiefs of his party, or to render him suspected, offering all that he demanded for himself; but he, knowing well her stratagem, held firmly to his point that he could not treat about anything without communicating it to his friends.

After a long conversation, she once demanding of him if the pains she had taken would produce no more fruit, especially to her, who only wished for repose, he answered her: "Madam, I am not the cause of it, nor is it I who hinder you from resting in your bed; it is you that hinder me from resting in mine. The pains you take please and nourish you, for repose is the greatest enemy of your life." (Dec. 14th, 1586.)

He made many other replies very lively and full of spirit; but above all, that was notable which he made to the Duke of Nevers, of the house of Gonzaga, who accompanied the Queen-mother. This nobleman presuming once to tell him that he might live much more honourably near the King than among those people who had no authority; and that if he should have occasion for money at Rochelle, he would scarce have the credit to raise one impost, he fiercely replied: "Sir, I do at Rochelle all that I please, because I shall please to do nothing but what I ought."

This conference at St. Brix having produced nothing but new exasperations, and the Queen-mother having returned, the Guises, who endeavoured by all means possible to revenge themselves on the favourites, made offer of their service to our Henry; and the Duke of Mayenne sent to tell him that there might be found means for an accommodation, if he would meet them; that he would come to find him with four horse at whatever place he pleased, and that he would give him his wife and children for hostage. This negotiation had no success, nor can I find the cause why it was interrupted.

The rest of the winter passed in the two courts in feasts and dances; for, notwithstanding the miseries and troubles of the kingdom, Queen Catherine had introduced the custom of dancing in all places and at all feasts. This she did, it was said, to amuse the great ones of the court in those vain diversions, there being nothing which more dissipates the powers of the spirit, nor which is more capable—if we may say so—to dissolve the forces of the soul, than the ravishing sound of violins, the continual agitation of the body, and the charms of ladies. After the examples of the court, dances and masks reigned in all the realm; nor could the remonstrances of the ministers hinder these dances among the greater part of the Huguenot lords, though there were still some who could not suffer it.

In the spring some enterprises began on both sides; but they were nothing in comparison to what was done towards the end of the summer. The Protestant princes of Germany sent an army to the assistance of the Huguenots, consisting of five thousand lansquenets or German foot, sixteen thousand Swiss, and six thousand German horse. They traversed Lorraine and Champagne, afterwards passed the Seine, and marched towards the Loire, as if they would have passed it, or coasted along it in their re-advancing. At the same time the King of Navarre had gathered his forces towards Rochelle, and endeavoured to come to meet them on the banks of the Loire; but he was hindered by an army of the King, commanded by the Duke of Joyeuse, who had orders to diligently pursue him. The Duke of Guise had likewise gathered the forces of his party; and though they were very small, followed sometimes the German horse, sometimes skirted them, and oftentimes mixed himself amongst them without any great danger; so much the rather because this too weighty body of strangers could not easily move, being troubled with a great baggage, not having a chief either of any great credit, or sufficiently intelligent to conduct, and all its captains being at variance one with the other.

By reason of all these acts this army could never take any good resolution. The Loire was fordable in many places, for it was about the end of September; but nevertheless they would not pass it, but spread themselves in the country of Beausse, expecting news from the King of Navarre, instead of advancing against the Nivernois, and gaining Burgundy. The intention of the King of Navarre was to advance along the Dordogne, and from thence enter into Guienne, and, after having gathered together all his forces, to meet the Protestant army in Burgundy, by the favour of those provinces which were his friends. But the Duke of Joyeuse obstinately pursued him, imagining he fled, because in effect he avoided fighting, having no other end than a conjunction with the Germans.

This duke had much declined in favour with the King, who had received advice that he inclined much to the League; not that he loved the Guises, but because he had permitted it to be put into his head by his flatterers that he deserved to be chief of that great party; and he held the destruction of the Huguenots so certain that he had obtained from the Pope the confiscation of all the sovereign territories of our Henry. Desiring, therefore, to sustain his reputation and favour, which were then tottering, he pursued him so closely that he overtook him near to Coutras.

The army of Joyeuse was, as one may say, all of gold, shining with silver and gold laces, with damasked arms, with feathers in great plumes, with embroidered scarfs and velvet coats, with which every lord, according to the mode of the times, had furnished his companies; but the army of the King of Navarre was all of iron, having no other than grizzled arms, without any ornament, with great belts of buff, and labourers' clothes. The first had the advantage in number, having six hundred horse and a thousand foot more than the other; the half of its infantry were dragoons and its cavalry almost all lancers, and mostly mounted on managed horses. It had besides for it the name and authority of the King and assurance of rewards; but the better half of it was composed of new troops, which wanted order and discipline. It had a general without authority; a hundred chiefs instead of one; and all young people, brought up in the delights of the court, having sufficient heart and courage, but without any experience.

The other, on the contrary, was composed of all the choice men of its party—the old remnant of the battles of Jarnac and Montcontour, people bred up in the mystery of war, and hardened by the continual endurance of fights and adversities. It had at its head three princes of the blood, the chief of them well obeyed and reverenced as the presumptive heir to the crown, the love of the soldiery, and hope of all good Frenchmen; besides, it was armed with a necessity either to overcome or die—armour of more proof than either steel or brass.

Orders being given, the King of Navarre called all his chiefs, and from a little rising ground exhorted them in a few words, but such as were agreeable both to his quality and the time; taking Heaven to witness that he fought not against his King, but for the defence of his religion and right. Afterwards addressing himself to the two princes of the blood, Condé and Soissons, "I shall say nothing else to you," said he, "but that you are of the house of Bourbon; and if

God live, I will now show you that I am worthy to be the first-born of the family."[1]

His valour that day appeared above that of all others. He had placed on his head-piece a plume of white feathers, both to make himself known and because he loved that colour; so that some putting themselves before him, out of design to shelter and defend his person, he cried out to them, "To your quarter, I pray you! Do not shadow me, for I would appear." (A bravery without doubt absolutely necessary for a conqueror, but which would be temerity and an unpardonable fault in a prince well established.) He broke the first ranks of the enemy, and took prisoners with his own hand, and came even to handigrips with one named Château-Reynard, cornet of a company of men-at-arms, saying to him, "Deliver thy colours!"

The battle being gained, some having seen the fugitives, who made a halt, came to tell him that the army of the Marshal of Matignon appeared. He received this news as a new subject of glory; and, turning bravely towards his people, "Let us go, my friends," said he; "this will be a thing never before seen, two battles in one day."

It was not only his valour that made him worthy to be admired on this occasion; it was likewise his justice, moderation, and clemency. For his justice we may recount what follows.

He had debauched the daughter of an officer of Rochelle, a thing which had dishonoured that family

---

[1] "And we," answered Condé, "will show you that you have good juniors."—Martin's *History of France*, vol. x. p. 41.

and very much scandalised him among the Rochellers.
A minister, as the squadrons were almost ready to go
to the charge and the prayer was to be made, took
the liberty to remonstrate with him that God could
not favour his arms if he did not beforehand demand
pardon for that offence, repair the scandal by a public
satisfaction, and restore honour to a family he had
deprived of it. The good King humbly hearkened to
these remonstrances, fell upon his knees, demanded of
God pardon for his fault, and prayed all those who
were present to serve as witnesses of his repentance
and to assure the father of the maiden that if God
gave him the grace to live, he would repair as much
as possible the honour he had deprived her of. So
Christian a submission drew tears from all present,
nor were there any who would not have ventured
a thousand lives for a prince who so cordially inclined
himself to do reason to his inferiors.

Having thus overcome himself, God made him conqueror over his enemies; and who knows but that He
exalted him because he so Christianly humbled himself?
The enemy's army was wholly defeated, with the loss
of five thousand men, and all their cannon, baggage,
and ensigns. All their chief commanders were taken
prisoners, except two or three, among whom were the
Duke of Joyeuse, and Saint-Saviour his brother, who
were found dead on the field.[1]

That night, our conqueror, finding his lodgings full
of prisoners and wounded persons of the enemy, was
constrained to cause his bed to be carried to those of

[1] This was the battle of Coutras, fought on October 20th,
1587. The victors lost only about forty men.

Du Plessis Mornay; but the body of Joyeuse being laid forth on the table in the hall, he was forced to go to an upper room; and there, while he supped, were presented unto him the prisoners, fifty-six foot ensigns, and twenty-two standards and cornets.

It was a fair and glorious spectacle for this prince to have under his feet that enemy who had obtained from the Pope the confiscation of his territories; to see his table environed with so many noble captains, and his chamber tapestried with ensigns. But, to speak truly, it was much more agreeable to generous souls to see that, amongst so many subjects of vanity and pride, and in such just resentment of those bloody injuries done him (things which often transport the sweetest souls to insolence and cruelty), there could not be observed either in his words or countenance the least sign that might breed any suspicion that either his constancy or goodness were in the least altered; but, on the contrary, showing himself as courteous and humane in his victory as he had shown himself brave and redoubtable in fight, he sent back almost all the prisoners without ransom, restored their baggage to many, took great care of the wounded, and gave the bodies of Joyeuse and Saint-Saviour to the Viscount de Turenne, who was their kinsman. He dispatched the next morning his master of requests to the King, to entreat peace of him; from whence it was judged that so great a courage would overcome all its enemies, and that nothing would be capable to reverse his fortune whom so great a prosperity was not able to move.

He was, however, blamed for not having hotly

pursued his victory, and for having permitted that triumphant army to break up, not again employing it in some great exploit. It was believed, and there was much appearance for it, that he would not press things too forward for fear of too much offending the King, with whom he desired yet to keep some measures, hoping daily that he might reconcile himself to him, and return to court, where it was necessary he should be, that he might be in a condition to take the crown when Henry III. should die. In fine, were it for this reason or any other, he retired into Gascony, and from thence into Bearn, under pretext of some pressing affair, carrying with him only five hundred horse and the Count of Soissons, whom he kept near him in the hope of making him espouse his sister. The Prince of Condé returned to Rochelle, and Turenne to Périgord.

In the meantime that great army of Germans, having received many checks in several places—but especially at Auneau in Beausse, where the Duke of Guise slew or took prisoners three thousand horse, and afterwards at Pont de Gien, where the Duke d'Epernon took twelve hundred lansquenets and almost all the cannon—willingly hearkened to an agreement which the King caused to be proposed to them, and afterwards retired by Burgundy and the county of Montbeliard, but were still pursued farther in that county by the Duke of Guise.

Now began the year 1588, which all judicious astrologers had called the wonderful year, because they foresaw so great a number of strange accidents and such confusion in natural causes that they were assured that, if the end of the world came not, there would happen at least a universal change. Their prognostications were seconded by a number of prodigies which happened throughout all Europe. In France there were great earthquakes, along the river Loire and likewise in Normandy. The sea was for six weeks together disturbed with continual tempests, which seemed to confound both heaven and earth. In the air appeared divers fiery spectres, and on the 24th of January Paris was covered with so horrible a darkness that those who had the best eyes could scarce see anything at noonday without the help of lights. All these prodigies seemed to signify what soon after took place—the death of the Prince of Condé, the besieging of Paris, the subversion of the whole realm, the murdering of the Guises, and lastly, the murder of Henry III.

As for the Prince of Condé, he died in the month of March, at St. Jean d'Angely, where he then made his residence. Though there had been a secret jealousy between him and the King of Navarre, even to the making of two factions in their party, yet the King deplored his loss with an extreme grief, and, having shut himself up in his closet with the Count de Soissons, he was heard to utter great cries and say that he had lost his right hand. However, after his grief had a little evaporated he recovered his spirits, and, casting all his trust on Divine protection, came forth, saying, with a heart full of Christian assurance, "God is my refuge and strength; in Him alone I will hope, and I shall not be confounded."

It was truly a great loss for him. He had now to bear alone all the weight of affairs; and being deprived of this supporter, remained more exposed to the attempts of the League, who had now only to give a like blow to his person to remain conquerors in all their affairs. He had therefore just cause to fear their attempts. However, the Duke of Guise had a heart so noble and great that whilst he lived he would never suffer such detestable ways.

The confidence of the League increased wonderfully by the death of the Prince of Condé. They manifested this by extraordinary rejoicings, and declared it to be an effect of the justice of God and of the apostolic curses. The Huguenots, on the contrary, were in an extreme consternation, considering that they had lost in him their most assured chief, because they believed him firmly persuaded in their religion, but had not the same opinion of the King of Navarre. In effect, the confusion and disorder was so great amongst them that, to all appearance, had the League continued strongly to prosecute them, it might have soon ruined them. The King hated them mortally, and would willingly have consented; but he wished to manage things in such a manner that their destruction should not prove the aggrandising of the Duke of Guise and his own loss. But this duke, knowing his intentions, pressed him continually to give him forces to utterly exterminate the Huguenots, in whose ruin he hoped to involve the King of Navarre.

He had this advantage over the King, that he had acquired the love of the people, principally by two means—the first by his opposing himself to the new imposts, and the second by continually being at variance with the favourites, nor ever bending before them; whilst the doing of the contrary things had made the King fall into an extremely low esteem, and had likewise taken away the fervour of some of his servants' love. Here is an example.

The King had two great men in his council, Pierre d'Espinac, archbishop of Lyons, and Villeroy, secretary of state. The Duke d'Epernon, who was fierce and haughty, would treat them according to his proud humour. They grew exasperated against him, and thereupon changed their affection to the Duke of Guise's party, but without doubt still in their hearts remaining most faithful to the King and crown of France, as afterward well appeared, especially in the person of Villeroy.

In the meantime the King lived after the ordinary manner, in the profusions of an odious luxury and in the laziness of a contemptible retreat, passing his time either in seeing dances or in playing with little dogs, of which he had great numbers of all sorts; or else in teaching paroquets to speak, or in cutting images, or in other occupations more becoming an infant than a king.[1]

But the Duke of Guise lost no time. He daily made new friends, kept his old ones, caressed the people, testified a great zeal for the ecclesiastics, undertaking their defence against all who would oppress them, and everywhere appeared with the splendour and gravity of a prince, but yet without pride or arrogance. The Parisians were intoxicated with esteem for him; the greater part of the parliament and most of the other officers attended his functions, and testified to him the affection they owed to the service of the King.

There were an infinite number of people who had

[1] The nuncio of the Pope thus describes Henry III.: "Il est faible et luxurieux, il n'aura pas de posterité."

signed the League; and in the sixteen quarters or wards of Paris, when they could not gain the *quarteniers* or aldermen, they chose one of the most violent of the Leaguers to act in their behalf; by reason of which the people of Paris afterwards called the principal of this party and his faction the "Sixteen"—not that they were but sixteen, for their number exceeded ten thousand, but all dispersed through the sixteen quarters.

Now the King, principally incited by the Duke d'Epernon, resolved to punish the most forward of this Sixteen, who on all occasions showed themselves furious enemies of that favourite. By this means he thought to overthrow the League and absolutely ruin the credit and reputation of the Duke of Guise. He caused, therefore, some troops secretly to enter Paris, and gave them orders to seize on those persons.

The Duke of Guise being advised of it, posted from Soissons, where he then was, resolving to perish rather than lose his friends. Barricades were raised in the month of May,[1] even to the gates of the Louvre, and the King's troops were all cut to pieces or disarmed. The Queen-mother, according to her ordinary custom, acted as mediator; but the King, affrighted, and fearing to be put in durance, retired to Chartres (May 13).

The League by this becoming master of Paris, took possession of the Bastille, the Hôtel de Ville, and the Temple, and hanged the provost of the merchants and the city lieutenant. And at the same time they possessed themselves of Orleans, Bruges, Amiens, Abbeville, Montreuil, Rouen, Rheims, Chalons, and more than twenty other cities in several provinces, the people

[1] The 12th of May was called the "Day of Barricades."

everywhere crying, "Long live Guise!" "Long live the Protector of the Faith!"

The King, not without much reason, was extremely alarmed. The Parisians sent to him to Chartres to ask pardon, but withal they demanded the extirpation of heresy. All his friends increased his fears, none fortified his courage. In this distress he knew no securer way to shun that danger which threatened him than by essaying to disarm his subjects. To this end he sent one of his masters of the requests to the parliament, to let them understand that his absolute intention was to forget all that was past, so that everyone might return to his duty, and labour diligently for the reformation of the kingdom; to further which he found it convenient to assemble the States-general at the end of the year, where they might provide for the assuring a Catholic successor of the blood royal, protesting that he would observe inviolably all the resolutions of the estates, but that he would have them free and without faction, and that from that day all his subjects should lay down arms.

It much troubled the Duke of Guise to consent to the laying down arms, fearing lest when he was left defenceless he should remain at the mercy of his enemies, and particularly of the Duke d'Epernon. He therefore stirred up the Parisians by a famous deputation to demand the continuation of the war against the Huguenots and the expulsion of that duke. The King, after some resistance, granted both the one and the other; for he caused to be ratified in parliament an edict most advantageously favourable for the League, and most bloody against the Huguenots, and he bid adieu to the Duke d'Epernon, who retired into his government of Angoumois.

After this the Duke of Guise came to attend the King at Chartres, having the Queen-mother's word for his security, and both gave great assurances of his fidelity, and received all the testimonies he could wish of the affection of the King, insomuch that he made him head of the *gens d'armes* of France.

In the meantime the League gained the upper hand throughout all the provinces on this side of the Loire, and caused deputies for the estates to be elected at its pleasure. In the month of November the estates assembled in the city of Blois. It is not necessary here to recount all their intrigues. Finally the King, persuaded that they had conspired to dethrone him, caused the Duke of Guise and the Cardinal his brother to be slain in the castle,[1] and kept prisoner the Cardinal de Bourbon, the Archbishop of Lyons, the Prince of Joinville, who after the death of his father was called Duke of Guise, and the Duke of Nemours, brother by his mother to the first duke.

The Queen-mother, under whose pledge the Guises thought themselves in security, was so touched with the reproaches made her, and with the slightings of the King her son, who after this believed he had no more need of her, that she died with grief and vexation a few days after (January 5th, 1589), lamented by no person, not even by her son, and generally hated by all parties.

In truth, if ever there was an action ambiguous or

[1] The duke on the 23rd and his brother on the 24th of December.

problematical it was that of these murders. The servants of the King said that he was constrained to it by the extreme audacity of the Guises, and that, if he had not prevented them, they would have shaved him and shut him up in a monastery. But the ill repute in which he was held among all men, the general esteem these princes had acquired, and the odious circumstances of the murder, made it appear horrible even in the eyes of the Huguenots, who said that this much resembled the bloody massacre of St. Bartholomew.

Our Henry observed a wise neutrality in this *rencontre*. He deplored their death, and praised their valour; but he said that certainly the King had very weighty motives to treat them in that manner, and for the rest, that the judgments of God were great, and His grace threefold towards him, having avenged him of his enemies, and neither engaged his conscience nor his hand in it. For certain gentlemen having often offered themselves to him with a determined resolution to go and kill the Duke of Guise, he had always let them know that he abhorred such a proposition, and that he would neither esteem them his friends nor honest men if they harboured it in their thoughts.

His council, being assembled upon the receipt of this grave news, found that he ought not on this account to make any change in the conduct of his affairs, because the King, though he himself might be willing to it, dared not for some months speak of a peace for fear he should make it be believed that he had slain the Guises to favour the Huguenots; so that he continued the war and held several places.

In the meantime the progress of affairs opened out before him a pathway that led to the heart of the kingdom and to the court, which was the post he ought most to covet.

While Henry III. was amusing himself after the murder of the Guises in examining the acts of the estates at Blois, instead of mounting his horse and showing himself in those places where his presence was most necessary, the League, which at first had been astonished at so great a blow, regained its spirits. The great cities, and principally Paris, which were possessed with this madness, having had leisure to dissipate their amazement, passed from fear to pity, and from pity to fury. The Sixteen chose at Paris the Duke d'Aumale for their governor. The preachers and churchmen declaimed bitterly against the King; the people pulled down his arms wherever they found them and dragged them through the dirt. The parliament, who would have restrained these hostile demonstrations, were imprisoned in the Bastille by Bussy le Clerc, a simple protector, but very much esteemed among the Sixteen, and were forced, in order to regain their liberty, to swear to the League. When released from the Bastille, there were many who continued to hold the parliament at Paris; the others stole away, little by little, and went over to the King, who transferred the parliament to Tours, where they kept their session until the reduction of Paris, in the year 1594. These, without doubt, testified most fidelity to their King; but those who remained at Paris rendered him afterwards much greater service, as shall be observed in its place.

The widow of the Duke of Guise presented her

request to these to take information of the death of her husband, and demanded of the commissioners that action might be taken against those who should be found convicted of it. She received favourable assurances from the procurator-general, and they proceeded very far on this subject, even against the person of Henry III.; but I cannot say to what point, because the papers were taken from the registers of parliament when Henry the Great re-entered Paris.

We cannot sufficiently detest such revolts against a sovereign; but these examples ought to make him know that though he holds his power from on high, yet obedience depends on the caprice of the people, and that he ought so to carry himself as not to attract their hatred; otherwise, since men have the audacity to blaspheme God, why may they not have it to revolt against kings?

Whilst these things were progressing, Henry III. understood that Pope Sixtus V. had excommunicated him for the murder of Cardinal de Guise. This great fire in a little time set France in a blaze. The Duke of Mayenne, who was at Lyons making war against the Huguenots, being informed by a courier from Roissieu, his secretary (who prevented the King's departure from that city), came into his own government of Burgundy, assured himself of Dijon and of Provence, and thence passed into Champagne, where the people received him with open arms; afterwards to Orleans, which had already revolted, and to Chartres, which his presence stirred into action; and in the end he came to Paris. The Sixteen and many of his friends advised him to take the title of King, which would be given him by the council which the League had established ; but he refused, contenting himself with the title of Lieutenant-general of the Estate and Crown of France, which he took, as if the throne had been vacant. They likewise broke the seals of the King, and made others, whereon was engraven on one side the arms of France, and on the other an empty throne, and for inscription about it the name and quality of the Duke of Mayenne in this manner : " Charles Duke of Mayenne, Lieutenant of the Estate and Crown of France."

All France took part in this occurrence, and almost all the cities and provinces of the realm ranged themselves on the Duke of Mayenne's side. The King, fearful that he should be shut up in Blois, retired to Tours. There now remained only one way for him to defend himself against the many dangers that were ready to environ him, and this was to call to his assistance the King of Navarre, who had five or six thousand men, old soldiers, by whom he was well beloved. Yet he durst not do it, for fear of being deemed a favourer of heretics, or of incurring the blame of violating those edicts against the Huguenots he had so solemnly sworn to in the estates of Blois. He tried therefore all sorts of ways to appease the resentment of the Duke of Mayenne, offering him very advantageous conditions. But what assurance, said the Leaguers, can this duke have, his brothers being murdered in so perfidious a manner ? He therefore would not listen to any of the King's proposals, and Henry III. was constrained to turn his thoughts towards the King of Navarre.

This prince above all things desired a passage

over the river Loire. The city of Saumur was given to him, where he established, as governor, Du Plessis Mornay, who fortified the castle and made it the head of the Huguenot garrisons. Having afterwards from thence approached Tours, his old captains, through distrust of Henry III., hindered him from going to see that King, whom they feared, they said, lest in a time when treachery was so necessary to draw him out of that labyrinth wherein the action of Blois had involved him, he should buy his absolution at the price of the King of Navarre's life.

The Duke d'Epernon, who had returned to court to serve his master in his need, and the Marshal d'Aumont would have engaged him to it, and given him their word of honour; but his friends could not consent that he should expose himself to the faith of a prince who, as they believed, had not any. In truth their fears were just, and our Henry was without doubt possessed with them as well as they. However, after he had well considered that he acted now for the safety of France, for the service of the King, and to open to himself a way to defend that crown which appertained to him, he resolved to hazard all, and to resign himself absolutely to the holy guard of the Sovereign Protector of kings.

The city of Tours is situated, as it were, in an island, a little below the place where the river Cher mingles its stream with the Loire, having coasted that great river three or four leagues. The King of Navarre's people wished not that he should trust himself between these rivers, but that the conference should be held beyond the Cher. He almost alone was of an opinion contrary to them all; nevertheless, to content them, he was constrained to hold a council on the banks, and afterwards to permit his captains to pass first, as if to sound the ford. He passed after them, and arrived at Plessis les Tours about three o'clock in the afternoon, in a warlike habit, all dirty and worn by his cuirass, himself only having a cloak, all his people being in their doublets, and ready to take up their arms, that he might show the King he was not come to make his court to him, but to serve him well.

He went to meet the King, who heard vespers at the Minimes. The crowd of people was so great that they were a long time before they could join. Our Henry, being within three paces of the King, threw himself at his feet, endeavouring to kiss them; but the King would not permit him, but, lifting him up, embraced him with great tenderness. They repeated their embraces three or four times, the King calling him his thrice-dear brother, and he calling him his lord. There were now heard to echo the joyful cries of "Vive le Roi!" which had for a long time been silent, as if the presence of our Henry had given a new birth to the people's affections, which seemed to be extinct in regard to Henry III.

After the two kings had for some time entertained each other, our Henry crossed the river and went to lodge at the suburb of St. Symphorien; for he had been obliged to promise this much to the old Huguenots, who believed snares and traps were everywhere laid for him. But he who was urged forward by other motives, and who was endowed with that generous principle, "that we ought not to be too sparing of our lives when there is something to be gained which ought to be more precious than life itself to one of great courage," departed at six o'clock the next morning, without consulting his people; and, attended only by one page, crossed the bridge and went to pay a visit to the King. They entertained one another a long time in two or three conferences, in which our Henry displayed great capacity and judgment. Finally they resolved to raise a powerful army to assault Paris, which was the principal head of the hydra, and gave motion to all the rest—a thing easy for them to do, because the King expected great levies from Switzerland, whither he had sent Sancy for that purpose, adding that the design of the siege being published it would infallibly attract a great number of soldiers and adventurers, in the hope of a rich pillage.

The two kings having passed two days together, he of Navarre went to Chinon to cause the rest of his troops to advance, who hitherto had refused to mingle themselves among the Catholics.

During his absence, the Duke of Mayenne, who had taken the field, fell upon the suburbs of Tours, thinking to surprise the city and the King within it, according to some intelligence he had received. The combat was very bloody, and the duke's design was nearly successful, but after the first endeavours he lost all hope and retired from the contest.

Afterwards, the King's troops being wonderfully increased, they marched conjointly, he and the King of Navarre, towards Orleans, took all the little places thereabouts, and from thence descended into Beauce, and drew together all of a sudden towards Paris. All the posts round about it, as Poissy, Estampes, and Meulan, were either forced or obtained capitulation, "in which they desired no other security than the word of the King of Navarre, to which they trusted more than to all the writings of Henry III., so great a profession made he of keeping his word, even to the prejudice of his interests."

Let us consider a little the different state to which these two kings were reduced by their different conduct. The one, for having often broken his faith, was abandoned by his subjects, and his greatest oaths found no belief amongst them; and the other, for having always exactly kept it, was followed even by his greatest enemies. On all occasions he gave marks of his valour and experience in point of war, but above all of his prudence and of those noble inclinations he had to do good and to succour all. He was always seen in the most dangerous places, to accelerate labours, animate his soldiers, sustain them in sallies, comfort the wounded, and cause money to be distributed amongst them. He observed all, inquired into all, and would himself with the marshal of the camp order the lodgings of his soldiers. He observed strictly what was done in the army of Henry III., where, though he often found faults, he concealed them, out of fear of offending those who had committed them by discovering their ignorance; and when he believed himself obliged to take notice of them, he did it with so much circumspection that they could not find any reason to take it in ill part. He was never niggardly of giving praises due to noble actions, nor of caresses and generous deportment to those who came near him; he entertained himself with them when he had time to do it, or at least to please them with some good word that they still went away satisfied. He feared not at all to make himself familiar, because he was assured that the more men knew him the more they would esteem him. In fine, the conduct of this prince was such that there was no heart he gained not, nor no friend who would not willingly have become his martyr.

Paris was already besieged. The King lodged at St. Cloud and our Henry at Meudon, keeping with his troops all that lies between Vanvres to the bridge of Charenton. Sancy had already arrived with his levies of Swiss; and they laboured with orders to give a general assault, to the end they might gain the suburbs beyond the river. The Duke of Mayenne, who was in the city with his troops expecting those supplies the Duke of Nemours was to bring, was in great apprehension that he should not be able to sustain the furious shock that was preparing, when a young Jacobin of the convent of Paris, named James Clement, spurred on by a resolution as devilish and detestable as it was determined, smote King Henry III. in the stomach with a knife, from the effects of which he died on the morrow. If the frantic monk had not been slain upon the spot by the King's guards, many things might have been known which are now concealed.

Our Henry, being informed late in the evening of this mournful accident and of the danger in which the King was, went to his lodging, accompanied only by twenty-five or thirty gentlemen; and, arriving a little before the King expired, he fell on his knees to kiss hands, and received his last embraces. The King called him many times his good brother and legitimate successor, recommended the kingdom to him, and exhorted the lords there present to acknowledge him and not to disunite. Finally, after having conjured him to embrace the Catholic religion, he gave up the ghost, leaving his army in an astonishment and a confusion beyond expression, and all the chiefs and captains irresolute and agitated, according to their humours, fancies, or interests.

PART II

CONTAINING THE ACTIONS OF HENRY THE GREAT, FROM THE DAY HE CAME TO THE THRONE OF FRANCE UNTIL THE PEACE, WHICH WAS MADE IN THE YEAR 1598 BY THE TREATY OF VERVINS.

THE death of Henry III. caused an entire change in the aspect of affairs. Paris, the League, and the Duke of Mayenne were transported from a profound sadness to a furious joy, and the servants of the defunct King, from a fervent hope to see him revenged, to an extreme desolation.

This prince who had been the object of the people's hatred being now no more, it seemed that that hatred would cease, and by consequence the fury of the League relent. But on the contrary, not only all those who composed that faction, but likewise many others who had held it a crime to league themselves against Henry III., their Catholic and legitimate King, believed themselves in conscience obliged to oppose themselves against our Henry, at least till such time as he should return into the bosom of the true Church, a qualification they believed absolutely necessary for the successor of Charlemagne or St. Louis. So that if the League lost that heart which hatred gave it, it gained one much more specious, from a zeal for religion, and had likewise a most plausible pretext not to lay down arms till Henry should profess the religion of his ancestors.

It was very difficult to judge whether the time at which the death of Henry III. happened were good or ill for our Henry; for on one side it seemed that Providence had drawn him from the utmost parts of the kingdom, where he was like a banished man, and led him by the hand to the fairest portion of France, only to make known his goodness and virtue, and put him in a position to gain that succession, to which had he been absent he would never have been called; but on the other side, when the multitude of his powerful enemies which armed themselves against him are considered, the small treasure and few forces he had, the obstacle of his religion, and a thousand other difficulties, it could not be certainly judged whether the crown was ordained for him to enjoy or to fall upon his head and crush him to pieces; and there might be reason to say that if the course of events elevated him, it was upon a throne trembling on the brink of a precipice.

Whilst Henry III. was in his agony, our Henry had held many tumultuous councils in the same lodgings with those whom he esteemed his most faithful servants. As soon as he understood the King was dead, he retired to his quarters at Meudon and attired himself in the mourning purple. He was presently followed by a large number of noblemen, who accompanied him as much for curiosity as affection. The Huguenots with those troops which he had led presently swore allegiance to him, but this number was very small. Some of the Catholics, as the Marshal d'Aumont, Givry, and d'Humières, swore service to him until death, and that willingly, without desiring any conditions from him; but the greater part of the others, being either estranged by inclination or exasperated by some discontent, or else believing now to have found the time to sell their services, kept at a great distance, and held several little assemblies in divers places, where they formed a number of fantastic designs.

Each of these proposed to make themselves sovereigns of some city or some province, as the governors had done in the decadence of the house of Charlemagne. The Marshal de Biron, among others, would have had the county of Périgord, and Sancy asked the King not to refuse him. This proposition was very dangerous, for if he denied it he incensed him, and if he accorded his demand he opened the way to all others to make the like, and so the kingdom would be rent in pieces. It was only by his great wisdom and understanding that he could walk safely in so dangerous a path. He therefore charged Sancy to assure the marshal on his part of his affection, of which he would willingly in proper time and place give him all the marks a good subject could expect from his sovereign; but at the same time he furnished him with so many powerful reasons wherefore he could not accord what he desired, that Sancy, being himself first persuaded, found it not difficult to work the same effect on the spirit of Biron, whom he persuaded not only to renounce that pretension, but likewise to protest that he would never suffer any part of the realm to be dismembered, in favour of any person whomsoever.

We may without doubt conclude that the great Henry did reason acutely, and that he explained his reasons in the best manner, since he could on occasions so important persuade such able men against their own interests.

Biron, being thus gained, went with Sancy to assure themselves of those Swiss which Sancy had brought to the deceased King, but who, being of the Catholic cantons, made some difficulty to bear arms for a Huguenot prince, and that without a new order from their superior. As for the French troops of the defunct King, it was not so easy to gain them. The lords who commanded them, or who had their chiefs under them, had everyone divers designs; one would have one thing and the other another, according to their several interests or caprices.

There were five princes of the house of Bourbon; to wit, the old Cardinal de Vendôme, the Count of Soissons, the Prince of Conti, the Duke of Montpensier, and the Prince of Dombes his son, who instead of being his firmest prop, gave him no little inquietude; because there was none of them which had not his particular pretension, which proved to him a continual obstacle.

Many of the lords who were in the army were not very well intentioned, particularly Henry, grand prior of France, natural son to Charles IX. (afterwards Count of Auvergne and Duke of Angoulême), the Duke of Epernon, and Termes Bellegarde, who out of the fear they formerly had lest he should deprive them of the favour of their master, had opposed him on divers occasions. For the courtiers, as Francis d'O and Manou his brother, Vieuxchâtel, and many others, they knowing that our Henry detested their villainous debaucheries, and that he would not prove a person of so ill management as to lavish his revenues to supply their luxury, had no great inclination for him. Nevertheless, hoping to find things better, they resolved to declare in his favour; but with such conditions as should restrain and bridle him, and in some manner oblige him to depend on them.

For this purpose there met an assembly of some noblemen at the palace of D'O (a man voluptuous, prodigal, and therefore not very scrupulous, but who at present made conscience a cloak to render himself necessary), and there resolved not to acknowledge the King till he were a Catholic. Francis d'O, accompanied by some noblemen, had the assurance to carry to him the resolutions of this assembly, and added a studied discourse to persuade him to return to the Catholic religion; but the King, who had already passed over his greatest fears, made them an answer so mixed with sweetness and gravity, with spirit and reservedness, that, courageously repelling them without too severely taunting them, he testified to them that he desired to attach them to him, but that after all he feared not much the loss of them.

Some time after the nobility, after divers little assemblies, held a great one with Francis de Luxembourg, Duke of Piney. There many propositions being made, at last the Dukes of Montpensier and Piney subtly managed and steered the opinions of the most importunate to this resolution: That they would acknowledge Henry for King, upon these conditions: 1. Provided that he would cause himself to be instructed—for they presupposed that conversion must necessarily follow instruction. 2. That he should not permit the exercise of any but the Catholic religion.

3. That he should neither give charge nor employment to the Huguenots. 4. That he should permit the assembly to depute agents to the Pope, to let him understand and agree to the causes which obliged the nobility to remain in the service of a prince separated from the Roman Church.

The King had the knowledge of this resolution from the Duke of Piney. He thanked them for their zeal for the preservation of the State and the affection they had for his person, promising them that he would sooner lose his life than the remembrance of those good services they had rendered him, and readily granted them all the points they demanded except the second, instead of which he promised them to re-establish the exercise of the Catholic religion through all his territories, and to re-admit the ecclesiastics into the possession of their estates; and of this he caused a declaration to be engrossed, which, after all the lords and gentlemen of note had signed it, he sent to be confirmed by that part of the parliament which was at Tours.

There were many who signed it with some regret, and others who absolutely refused it, among whom were the Duke of Epernon and Louis d'Hôpital Vitry. This last, disturbed as it was said by a scruple of conscience, cast himself into Paris and gave himself for some time to the League; but first of all he abandoned the government of Dourdan, which the defunct king had given him. Such then were the maxims of persons of true honour in the civil wars, that in quitting one party, whichever it was, they quitted likewise those places they held, and returned them to those who had conferred them.

The Duke of Epernon, protesting that he would never be either Spaniard or Leaguer, and that his conscience would not permit him to stay with the King, demanded leave of him to retire to his government. The King, after having in vain endeavoured to retain him, gave him leave, with many caresses and praises; but so much was he in his heart troubled at his abandoning him, that it has been believed he cherished against him a secret resentment as long as he lived.

The Duke of Mayenne was not a little troubled in Paris what resolution he should take. He saw that all the Parisians, even those who had held to the party of the defunct King, had fully resolved to provide for the security of religion; but that, however, they would all have a King, contrary to some of the Sixteen, who imagined they might form a republic, and turn France into cantons, like to the Swiss; but those were neither sufficiently powerful in number, riches, nor capacity to conduct such a design. So that most of his friends counselled him to take the title of King; but when he went about to sound this proposition, he found that it was neither agreeable to the people, nor yet to the King of Spain, from whom he received, and was to receive, his principal support and means of subsistence.

Hereupon two other counsels were given him: the first, to accord willingly with the new King, who without doubt, in the position things were, would grant him most advantageous conditions; the other, that he should by declaration publish to the Catholics of the royal army that all resentments becoming extinct by the death of Henry III., he had no other interest than that of religion; that that point being of Divine obligation and concerning all good Christians, he summoned and conjured them to join with him to exhort the King of Navarre to return to the Church, upon which they promised to acknowledge him immediately as King; but if he refused to do it, they intended to substitute in his place another prince of the blood. This advice was the best; and indeed it was proposed by Jeannin, president of the parliament of Burgundy, one of the wisest and most politic heads of his council, and who acted in his affairs without tricks or stratagems, but with great judgment and singular honesty.

The Duke of Mayenne rejected equally both these advices, and took a third; to wit, causing the old Cardinal de Bourbon (who was at present detained prisoner by order of our Henry) to be proclaimed king, still reserving to himself the quality of Lieutenant-general of the Crown. He published afterwards several declarations, one of which he sent to the parliament, the other to the provinces and the nobility, inviting them to endeavour to deliver their King and defend their religion.

At the same time the King tried by divers negotiations, and caused him to be exhorted rather to seek his advancement by his friendship than by the troubles and miseries of France. But to this the duke answered that he had engaged his father in the public cause, and given oath to King Charles X. (for so they called the old Cardinal de Bourbon, who was named Charles), to whom, according to the sentiment of the League, the crown appertained, as to the nearest kinsman of Henry III. In the meantime he entertained plots and conspiracies in the royal army, where his emissaries from day to day debauched many persons, even of those whom the King believed most assured. There were many generous enough to resist the temptations of silver; but nothing was proof against the intrigues of the ladies of Paris, who cunningly attracted the gentlemen and the officers in the city, sparing nothing to allure them.

Knowing that there daily remained some caught in these snares, and having just reason to fear that those who returned, tempted by their mistresses, might bring back some pernicious designs; and the Duke of Nemours being upon the advance with his troops, to join with the Duke of Mayenne, the Duke of Lorraine being likewise to send his; and having cause to doubt his retreat might be cut off on all sides, the King found it convenient to decamp from before Paris.

But before he dislodged, he wrote to the Protestant princes to give them an account of what he did, and to assure them that nothing should be capable of shaking his constancy, or separating him from Christ; and he spoke at present according to his thoughts and conscience, not having any desire to change, which yet the ministers of his religion would not believe, but watched him so close on this subject that they became importunate.

It was certainly an unspeakable trouble which for three or four years continually he was forced to undergo, to hear on one side the exhortations of those people, and on the other the most constant remonstrances of the Catholics; for it was necessary that he should allay the distrust of the first and entertain the second with continual hopes of himself receiving instruction. How much prudence had he need of! how much patience! with how much judgment and policy must he manage such great differences! Certainly he could not do it without employing all the powers of his mind and experience. And he well knew how far it was necessary for a prince to have his mind happily exercised, and to be well instructed how to negotiate and speak well, and to be able when necessary to avail himself of his talent. Without doubt he might at present well praise those who, having had the care of bringing him up, had trained him in his youth to the management of affairs, to dealing with men, and to gaining their affections.

Those last duties he desired to render his predecessor served as a fair pretext for raising his siege before Paris. To put the late King's body in a place where the resentment of the Duke of Guise's creatures might not outrage it, he carried it to Compiègne, and laid it in the Abbey of St. Corneille, where he celebrated all the funeral ceremonies as honourably as the confusion of the time would permit. Not able to assist himself, because of his religion, he committed the care to Bellegarde and Epernon, the last of whom accompanied him thither, and then retired to Angoumois.

There were three advices given concerning the place to which he ought to retire when he raised his siege from Paris. The first was to repass the Loire and abandon to the League all the provinces on this side of it, because he could only maintain them with difficulty; the second, to re-advance along the Marne, and, seizing the bridges and cities, await assistance from the Protestant Swiss and Germans who had promised to come to him; and the third, to march down into Normandy, to assure himself of some cities whose governors were not yet engaged in the League, to gather the money received for taxes, and to accept the assistance from England which Queen Elizabeth had readily promised him, and which could not be long deferred.

He decided to adopt the last of these advices. Many of the nobles who accompanied him desiring some time to go and refresh themselves, he gave them leave. He sent a part of his troops into Picardy, under the command of the Duke of Longueville; another into Champagne, under Marshal d'Aumont; and with three thousand French foot, two regiments of Swiss, and twelve hundred horse only, which he kept with him, he descended into Normandy.

The Duke of Montpensier, who was governor there, came to join him with two hundred gentlemen and fifteen hundred foot. Rolet, governor of Pont d'Arche, a man of courage and spirit, brought him the keys of that place, demanding no other recompense but the honour to serve him. Emer de Chattes, a commendatore of Malta, did the same with those of Dieppe. After which the King approached Rouen, where he expected to have some intelligence.

This enterprise put him in extreme danger, but in revenge gave him a fair occasion to acquire glory in rescuing himself from so great a peril. See how it passed.

The Duke of Mayenne came to the succour of Rouen with all his forces, and passed the river at Vernon.

The King, much astonished, retired to Dieppe, and sent to the Dukes of Longueville and d'Aumont to return to him speedily with their forces. The Duke of Mayenne in the meantime seized all the little places about Dieppe, so as to completely invest the King. In fact, he shut him up so closely that if he had not amused himself by an untimely motion to go to Bins in Hainault to confer with the Duke of Parma, he had in that disorder dissipated the greater part of the King's little army. He had already caused a report to be spread through France, and had written with assurance to all strange princes, that he held the King of Navarre (so he called him) shut up in a little corner, from whence he could not get, except by yielding himself to him or leaping into the sea. The danger appeared so imminent, even to his most faithful servants, that the parliament at Tours sent expressly to him a master of requests, proposing as the only expedient they saw to save the state, to associate him and the Cardinal de Bourbon, his uncle, in the royalty, giving the conduct of civil affairs to the one, and of military affairs to the other. There were likewise the greater part of the captains of his army of opinion that, leaving his forces on shore, well entrenched in their posts, he should as soon as possible embark for England or for Rochelle, for fear that if he should longer delay it he might be shut up by sea as well as by land. To the proposition of the parliament he made answer that he had taken such good measures that the intrigues of the Duke of Mayenne could not deliver the Cardinal de Bourbon, as they apprehended; and the Marshal de Biron, so stoutly opposed those who counselled him to embark that they desisted.

It appeared soon after by the proof that the forces of the League, which were thrice as great as his, were not to be feared in proportion to their number; and that the more commanders they had, the less their power was to be feared. The King was lodged at the Château d'Arques, which is seated on a little hill, to stop the passage of the valley which goes to Dieppe. The Duke had formed a design to take this post by sea, by four or five renewed attempts; and on divers days he essayed to assault the suburbs of Polet, and four or five times was driven back. Our Henry daily did wonders, and exposed himself so much that once he thought he would have been surprised and encompassed by his enemies. At last the duke, having lost eleven days' time, and a thousand or twelve hundred men, raised the siege and retired into Picardy.

It was believed that he passed into this province lest the Picards, a free and honest people but very simple, should permit themselves to be surprised by the artifices of the agents of Spain, who would persuade them to cast themselves under the protection of the King their master.

It was observed likewise that what hindered the success of his enterprise at Dieppe, and which kept him two or three days without attempting anything at the time he ought to have done it, was the jealousy and contentions between the chiefs who accompanied him, particularly of the Marquis du Pont-à-Mousson, son to the Duke of Lorraine, of the Duke of Nemours, and of the Cavalier d'Aumale; for they, believing the capture of the King certain, or at least his flight assured, and disposing already of the kingdom as of their conquest, regarded one another with an eye of jealousy, and each formed designs in his head to have the better part of it. It was observed likewise that in one of these combats of Dieppe, the Duke of Mayenne, having at present some advantage, would have gained an entire victory if he had advanced but a quarter of an hour quicker; but, marching too slowly, he let slip that opportunity he could never redeem, which made the King, who well observed his fault, say, "If he act ever in that manner, I shall be certain always to gain the field."

I have recounted these particulars, because they make known the defects of that great body the League, and the true causes which hindered its progress, and reduced it to nothing. I find three principal ones.

The first was the distrust the Duke of Mayenne had of the Spaniards; for though he could not be without them, yet he could but regard them as his secret enemies; and they assisted him not for love of himself, but out of the design they had to profit themselves out of the calamities of France. And therefore when they saw that he concurred not with them for their ends, and that he thought only of his own advantage without theirs, they afforded him but feeble succour; in such manner they let him fall so low that when they would themselves have done it, they could not raise him.

The second was the jealousy of the chiefs, who never agreed among themselves. They thought more of crossing and ruining one another than of weakening their common enemy; and confounded themselves in such manner by their delusions and partialities that they were ever wanting in the greatest enterprises; whereas in the party of the King, there was only one chief, to whom all was reported, and by whose orders all passed.

The third was the heaviness and dulness of the Duke of Mayenne, who at all times moved slowly. His flatterers called this gravity. This defect proceeded principally from his nature; and was augmented not only by the mass of his body, great and fat beyond all proportion, and which in consequence required a great deal of nourishment and much sleep, but likewise from a coldness and a numbness which a certain malady had reduced to a habitude in his body. This malady he had contracted at Paris shortly after the death of Henry III., at which event, some say, the Duke would very unhandsomely rejoice.

King Henry IV. was not of the same temperament; for though he very much loved feasting and to divert himself with his friends when he had leisure, nevertheless, when engaged in affairs of war, or of any other nature, he never sat at table longer than a quarter of an hour, and never slept for more than two or three hours together; so that Pope Sixtus V., being well informed of his manner of living and that of the Duke of Mayenne, confidently prognosticated that the "Bearnais" (for so he called him, as all the Leaguers did) could not fail to have the better of it, since he lay no longer in bed than the Duke of Mayenne sat at table.

Officers and servants form themselves after the example of their masters. Those of the King were ready, cheerful, and vigilant; who executed his commands as soon as they came out of his mouth; who took care of all, and acquainted him with all. On the contrary, those of the Duke were slow, negligent, idle, and who, however pressing the occasion, would not lose anything of their ease and diversions.

It seemed to me that, for the better understanding of our history, it was necessary to observe these circumstances, which are absolutely essential and very instructive.

We have particularised at the end of Part I. who were the chiefs of the League, and how they held all the best cities and richest provinces of the realm. I should never end did I recount all the factions, fights, enterprises, and changes which happened in every province for the space of five or six years. We shall follow only the great events, and behold how the providence of God and the incomparable virtue of our Henry so drew France out of its labyrinth of miseries that the state and religion, which might have been destroyed by an irreparable war, were both miraculously saved, and flourished with as much happiness and glory as ever.

Though the Duke of Mayenne had retired from before Dieppe, yet the people were entirely persuaded that the King could not escape him; particularly the Parisians, whom the Duchess of Montpensier made believe—by couriers sent for this purpose, whom she caused to arrive from day to day—now that he yielded himself, now that he was taken, and at last that he was coming to Paris; so that there were even many ladies who hired windows in the street of St. Denis to see him pass by.

Whilst they amused themselves with these false reports, they were much astonished to understand that, having received a reinforcement of four thousand English, he was now upon his march, and coming directly to Paris. He had intelligence which promised him that if he could gain the suburbs, they would open for him a way into the city. He assaulted therefore those of St. Germain, St. Michael, St. James, St. Marceau, and St. Victor, and carried them unawares; but he could not gain the quarter of the University, as he hoped, because his cannon was not brought in time. About eight o'clock in the morning on All Saints' Day he entered the suburbs of St. James, where he found the people had no aversion to him, for he saw them not affrighted nor despairingly fleeing, but looking out of their windows to regard him, and crying, "Vive le Roi!" He used his advantage with a great moderation. He forbade all sorts of violence or plunder, and gave orders that divine service should be continued, so that his people peaceably assisted at it with the burgesses, whilst he, having mounted the steeple of St. Germain, attentively considered what was being done in the city.

That evening, the Duke of Nemours having posted thither with the cavalry, and the Duke of Mayenne following the day after with his infantry, the King retired to Montlhéry; but beforehand he drew up his army in battle array in the sight of Paris, and kept them for four hours under arms, to make known to the Parisians the weakness of their chiefs.

After this Estampes, Vendôme, Le Mans, and Alençon, unable to sustain his presence and arms, surrendered to him; and in the way things were going, and in the manner the chiefs of the League defended themselves, he would without doubt have reconquered the whole realm in less than fifteen months, if he had not wanted money. This defect alone retarded the course of his prosperity. The ransoms imposed on cities reduced by force, all that he could borrow, and the money he could raise by taxes, did not half suffice to keep his troops in a body. For this reason he was constrained for four or five years' space to make war in an extraordinary manner. When his troops had served some months, and consumed besides their pay all they had foraged in their quarters, he sent them home, as well to refresh them as to preserve their country from the invasions of the League. In like manner when the volunteer gentlemen had spent the money they brought from other homes, he gave them leave to return, to endeavour to furnish themselves for another campaign, inviting them by his example to retrench the superfluous expense of clothes and equipage, and otherwise treating them with so much civility and courtesy that they never failed him on the most pressing occasions, for they returned as soon as possible, serving him, as we may say, each his quarter.

In the meantime he fell suddenly upon Normandy, and almost entirely reduced it; took the cities of Dompfort, Falaise, Lisieux, Bayeux, and Honfleur—this last by a very bloody siege. After his return from thence he took likewise Melun, on the Seine, seven leagues off Paris, and laid siege to Dreux.

At the news of these conquests, the Duke of Mayenne was obliged, for the sake of his reputation, to come forth out of Paris, to assemble his troops, and to receive, contrary to his inclination, fifteen hundred lancers and five hundred carabineers from the Duke of Parma, governor of the Low Countries. These forces were commanded by the Count d'Egmont.

After this duke had regained several little places which inconvenienced Paris and the country adjacent, he crossed the Seine, by the bridges of Mantes, to succour Dreux, imagining he might do it without hazarding anything. The King, as soon as he had advice of his advance, raised his siege, but with the intention of fighting him, and with this object he drew up his forces at Nonancourt, on the river Eure.

Two things principally impelled him to this resolution of giving him battle: The one, because, wanting money, he could not long keep his troops together, and had he led them into Normandy he would unprofitably have spent all the revenue of that province, which alone he valued above all others he held. The other, because he perceived so great a rejoicing throughout all his army, who seemed to leap for joy when they were told they were about to attack the enemy, demonstrating by their outward appearances that a day of fighting would be unto them as a day of feasting.

The Duke of Mayenne was not of opinion that he ought to engage his fortune and honour to the hazard of one day, especially considering the valour of the King's forces in comparison with his, the great experience and incomparable courage of that prince, and with all this, his good fortune, which had already gained so great an ascendency over his that he believed he could no better overcome him than by avoiding encounters with him. But the reproaches of the Parisians; the instances of the legate whom the Pope

had sent to support the interests of the League; the
Spanish cabal, who on whichever side fortune turned
itself, promised themselves great advantages from this
battle; and, lastly, the shame of having lost more than
forty places in six months without having endeavoured
to succour any of them, led him perforce to the relief
of Dreux; and when he was near it, the false news
he had that the King was retiring towards the city
of Verneuil au Perche, and the bravadoes of the
Count d'Egmont, who boasted himself able with his
troops alone to defeat the army of the King, caused
him to pass the river Eure, over the bridge of Ivry,
with extraordinary diligence.

To speak the truth, both the King and he were
equally surprised—the King to discover that he had
so soon accomplished his object, and the Duke to see
that the King, whom he believed to have taken the
way towards Verneuil, was coming directly towards
him. But now neither could withdraw if they would,
but must necessarily come to a battle, which happened
on the 14th of March, near the town of Ivry.

The histories describe at large the description of
the field of battle, the order of both armies, the
charges which the battalions and squadrons on both
sides made, and the faults of the chiefs of the League.
We shall therefore say nothing but what concerns the
person of our prince.[1]

---

[1] There was little order in the action: on one wing, the Germans
of the League behaved ill and yielded; on the other, the royalists
were beaten, but Biron rallied them with reinforcements. The
combat was decided by the central force of either army, the Count
d'Egmont leading the Spaniards, and Mayenne the gentlemen of
his party against the King. The Leaguers were marshalled too

His rare intelligence, his wonderful genius, and his indefatigable activity in the art of war were all admired. It was wondered how he could give so many orders without perplexing his intellect, and with as little confusion as if he had been in his closet; how he could so perfectly arrange his troops; and how, having observed the enemy's design, he could in a quarter of an hour change the whole order of his army; how during the fight he could be everywhere, take notice of everything, and himself give orders, as if he had had a hundred eyes, and as many arms, the noise, confusion, dust, and smoke augmenting rather than troubling his judgment and knowledge.

The armies being ready to attack each other, he lifted up his eyes to heaven, and joining his hands, called God to be witness of his intention, invoking His assistance, and praying that He would reduce the rebels to an acknowledgment of him whom the order of succession had given them for their legitimate sovereign. "But Lord," said he, "if it pleaseth Thee to dispose otherwise, or that I should be of the number of those kings whom Thou dedicatest to Thy anger, deprive me of my life with my crown; consent that I may this day fall a victim to Thy holy will; let my death deliver France from the calamities of war, and my blood be the last that shall be shed in this quarrel."

closely together. Henry's squadron got among them, and a sanguinary *mêlée* ensued. The King was reported to be killed, but soon showed his white plume in the path that he had promised. Egmont was slain, Mayenne's standard-bearer fell by Henry's own hand, and the army of the Leaguers was routed and driven from the ground.—Martin's *History of France*.

Immediately after, he caused his helmet to be given him, on the top of which he had a plume of three white feathers; and having put it on, before he pulled down his visor, he told his squadrons: " My companions, if you this day follow my fortune I shall likewise follow yours. I will overcome, or die with you. Let me only conjure you to keep your ranks; and if the heat of the combat make you quit them, think at once of rallying—it will be the gain of the battle. You may do so between those three trees which you see there on high, on your right hand (they were three pear trees); and if you lose your ensigns, cornets, or banners, lose not the sight of my white feather, which you will always find in the road to honour and victory."

The result of the battle having been for a long time uncertain, was in the end favourable to him, the principal glory being due to himself alone; so much the more because he charged most impetuously on that formidable body commanded by the Count d'Egmont, and having entered that forest of lances with his sword in his hand, rendered them useless and constrained them to resort to their short arms, by which he had a great advantage, because the French were more agile and active than the Flemings; so that in less than a quarter of an hour he had pierced them, dispersed them, and put them to rout; this being the chief cause of his winning the battle.

Of sixteen thousand men which the duke had, there were scarce four thousand saved. There remained over a thousand horse on the field with the Count d'Egmont, four hundred prisoners of note, and all the infantry, for the lansquenets were all cut to pieces. They took all his baggage, cannon, ensigns, and cornets—to wit, twenty cornets of cavalry, the white cornet of the duke, the colonel of the German horse, the great standard of Count d'Egmont, and sixty colours of foot.

The Duke of Mayenne acquitted himself with great valour, and many times endeavoured to rally his troops; but in the end, for fear of being encompassed, he retired towards the bridge of Ivry, and having crossed it, caused it to be broken down to stop those who pursued him, and so escaped to Mantes, thence to St. Denis, and afterwards to Paris. A great part of the fugitives took the same way with him, others took that of the plain and reached the city of Chartres.

The King having engaged himself during the retreat among a squadron of Walloons, was in great danger of his person, so that his army for some time believed him dead; upon which the Marshal de Biron, accustomed to speak freely to him, and who had taken no part in the fighting, but had been posted with a body of reserves to prevent the rallying of the enemy, could not refrain from saying to him, "Ah, Sire, this is not just; you have this day done what Biron ought to do, and he only what the King ought to have done."

This remonstrance was approved by all those who heard it, and the principal chiefs took the liberty to entreat the King not to again expose his person, but to consider that God had not destined him to be a musketeer, but to be King of France; that all the arms of his subjects ought to fight for him, but that they would all become lame and benumbed should they lose the head which gave them motion.

His valour this day outshone that of the greatest of his chieftains. But besides that, his clemency, his generosity, and his courtesy added a wonderful splendour to his fair actions; and the manner with which he used his victory was a certain proof that he gained it by his conduct rather than by fortune.

He chose rather to deal mercifully with the battalions of Swiss than to cut them to pieces, as he might have done. He restored to them their ensigns, and caused them to be escorted back into their own country by his emissaries, by which he gained the affection of five little Catholic cantons.

He had no greater desire in his heart than to make his subjects know that he desired to spare their blood, and that they had to do with a mild and merciful king, and not with a cruel and implacable enemy. He caused to be proclaimed in the rout, " Save the French, and let your blows fall on the stranger." He had mercy upon all those who demanded quarter, and saved them as much as he could from the hands of the soldiers flushed with victory. He treated the prisoners, particularly the gentlemen, not only with humanity, but likewise with courtesy; and he loaded with honour, praises, and thanks all the nobility who had fought for him, sharing with them the honour of the day, and giving them embraces as earnests of those recompenses they might expect from him when he should be in power.

I cannot forget one action which he did of wonderful goodness, and which was of marvellous efficacy in drawing to him the hearts of his officers and gentlemen. Colonel Thische, or Theodoric of Schomberg, commanding some troops of German horse, had been enforced the evening before the battle by the clamours of those brutes to demand of him those arrears which were due to them; and to represent to him that except upon these conditions they would not fight. The Swiss and Germans of that time used often to act so, of which history furnishes us with a hundred examples. The King, much incensed at such a demand, answered him, "How, Colonel Thische! is this done like a man of honour, to demand money, when you ought to receive orders for the battle?" The colonel retired, much confused, without making any reply. On the morrow the King, having arranged his troops, remembered he had ill-treated him; and thereupon, pressed by an impulse which could find no place but in a generous soul, went to seek him and told him, "Colonel, you see we are engaged in an occasion which permits us no long stay; but it is not just that I should take away the honour of so brave a gentleman as yourself. I declare therefore that I acknowledge you as being an honest man, and one incapable of committing anything unworthy."

This said, he cordially embraced him; and the colonel, with tears standing in his eyes, with tenderness answered him, "Ah, Sire, by restoring me that honour you had deprived me of, you deprive me of my life; for I should be unworthy if I did not this day lay it down for your service. If I had a thousand, I would willingly lay them all down at your feet."

In short, he was slain on this occasion, as were many other brave gentlemen.

I will recount yet another worthy action, which may admirably demonstrate how our Henry spared neither civilities nor caresses to gentlemen who served him well. At night, when he supped at the castle of Rosny, being informed that the Marshal d'Aumont came to render him an account of what he had done, he went forth to meet him; and having straightway embraced him, carried him into supper, and made him sit at the table, with these obliging words: "That there was great reason he should be at the feast, since he had so well served at his nuptials."

The terror was so great in Paris after the loss of this battle that if the King had gone directly thither, there is no doubt but that they would have received him without much difficulty. Some said that it was the Marshal de Biron who diverted him, fearing that afterwards, not having more need of him, he should consider him less. Others thought that it was the Huguenot ministers and captains that dissuaded him, because they feared lest he should make arrangements with the Parisians with regard to religion; and therefore they counselled him rather to gain this great city by famine, which the Marquis d'O, at present superintendent, pressed very strongly, to the end that the King, taking it in this way, might treat it as a conquered city, draw thence great treasure, seize the rents of the Hôtel de Ville, making bankrupt the burgesses for the debts of the King, which were very great.

The widow of Montpensier, one of the principals

of the League, who was accustomed to amuse the
people with false news, could not dissemble the mischief
of the loss of this battle but by saying that "truly
the Duke had lost it, but that *the Bearnais* was dead."
The burgesses believed it for five or six days; and this
was enough to restrain their first fears, and to gain
time to give orders and send to levy assistance on all
sides.

After the battle the King, having stayed some days
at Mantes on account of the great rains, retook the
field, and took Lagny, Provins, Montereau, and Melun,
without listening to the propositions of truce made to
him by Villeroy. After having in this march attempted
to take the city of Sens with little success, he came
to block up Paris, and took all the posts and castles
about it, where he lodged garrisons of horse to scour
the country.

The Duke of Mayenne was not therein; he had left
the Duke of Nemours as governor, and had gone to
meet the Duke of Parma at Condé on the Escaut, to
demand of him some assistance in his necessity. He
was in great trouble, and in a just fear of losing Paris,
whether he relieved it or whether he permitted it to
be taken; and that the rather because he saw well that
if he brought in the Spanish assistance the Sixteen
would take that opportunity to again raise themselves
up, and possibly out of despite to him place Paris
under the Spanish yoke; for this Sixteen was embit-
tered against him, because he had broken up their
council of forty, which bridled his authority, and that
to show himself absolutely averse to a republican
government, which they would have introduced, he

had created another council, a keeper of the seals, and four secretaries of state, with whom he governed affairs, without calling them except when he had need of money.

Besides this trouble there happened to him another subject of inquietude, this being the decease of the old Cardinal de Bourbon, who died at Fontenay, where he was guarded by the Lord de la Boulay. He had reason to fear lest his death should give cause to the Spaniards and to the Sixteen to demand the creation of a king, and that they would press him so much that in the necessity he had of their aid he should be obliged to suffer it. In fact, this was the first condition which the agents of Spain proposed in the treaty they held with him to give him assistance; and he, from the fear of displeasing them, testified that he ardently wished the convocation of the estates to elect a king, and transferred the place of their assembly from the city of Melun, where he assigned it, to Paris; that is to say, from a city which he had lost to one in which he was besieged. In the meantime he employed his friends with the parliament and at the Hôtel de Ville so as to keep to himself the quality of Lord-general, which being continued to him, he avowed that he feared nothing so much as the estates, and endeavoured with all his might to hinder them, which, to speak truth, completed the ruin of his party.

Paris being blocked up, the legate (Cardinal Caëtan) and the Sixteen forgot nothing that might encourage their people. They consulted their Faculty of Theology, and obtained what resolutions they pleased against him they named the Bearnais. They caused many both general and particular processions to be made, and the officers renewed their oath of fidelity to the Holy Union, as they called the League.

At the same time the Duke of Nemours took great care to put the city in a position of defence; and the burgesses, being for the most part persuaded that if the King took it he would establish preaching and abolish the mass, were possessed with an extreme ardour, and contributed all that was demanded, either of their purse or labour, towards its fortification.

There is no finer passage in the history of that time than the relation of this siege—the orders which Nemours gave in the city, the garrisons he established in divers quarters, the sallies he made for the first month, the inventions he used to animate the people, the endeavours and divers practices of the King's friends to bring him into the city, the negotiations held on one side and the other to essay a treaty; how provisions diminished, how they sought means to make them last, how, notwithstanding all their economy, the famine was extreme; and how in the end that great city, being within three or four days of utterly perishing, was delivered by the Duke of Parma.[1]

I shall observe only some particulars very memorable. There were in Paris when it was besieged only two hundred and thirty thousand persons, and among these were nearly thirty thousand of the people of the country round about, who had there sought refuge, and nearly one hundred thousand of the ordinary inhabitants had left the city; so that in those times

---

[1] Alexander Farnese, Duke of Parma, born 1546, killed in 1592.

there were no more than three hundred thousand souls in Paris.

The King was made to hope that as soon as the Parisians had for seven or eight days seen the granaries and markets without bread, the butcheries without meat, the ports without corn, wine, and other commodities with which the river is accustomed to be covered, they would take their chiefs by the throat and force them to treat with him; or at least, if a seditious humour did not so soon prompt them to it, famine would force them in fifteen days. In fact, they had but five weeks' victuals, but they managed them carefully; and those who had advised the King knew not well the people of Paris, for they are wonderfully patient, nor is there any extremity they are not capable to suffer, provided they have those who know how to lead them, and principally when it is a question of their religion. It cannot be read without astonishment how blind was the obedience and how constant the union of that fierce and indocile people for four whole months of horrible losses and miseries. The famine was so great that the people ate even the herbs that grew in the ditches. Dogs, cats, and hides of leather were food, and some have reported that the lansquenets, or foot soldiers, fed upon such children as they could entrap.

The Huguenots, ravished with delight to hold that city blocked up which had done them so much mischief, insisted strongly in the King's council, and not only cried it there themselves, but caused it to be cried aloud among the soldiers, that it should be assaulted vigorously, and that in six hours it would become a desolate thing. But the good and wise King did not follow those passionate counsels; he knew well that they would take parts by force, that they might murder all in revenge of the massacres of St. Bartholomew. And moreover he considered that they would thus lay a city desolate, the ruin of which, like a wound struck in the heart, might possibly prove mortal to all France; that he would in one day dissipate the richest and almost the only treasure of his state, and that no person would be benefited by it except the simple soldiery, who, becoming insolent by so rich a booty, would either overwhelm themselves in their pleasures or abandon him.

Those who had charge of the victualling of the city committed a great error in not sending forth the numerous poor and useless mouths. The scarcity augmenting, they sought, too late, means to remedy it; but not finding any, they sent messengers to the King to gain his permission to allow a certain number to depart, who, hoping for his grace, were already assembled near the gate of St. Victor, and had taken leave of their friends and neighbours with those regrets which rend asunder the hearts of even the most insensible.

The King was so good and merciful that he granted this favour; but some of his council opposed it so strongly that, for fear of displeasing them, he was at first constrained to send back those miserable people. His clemency, however, could not, for any long time suffer their violence; for having heard from many who, fearing death less than famine, had leapt from the walls, the pitiful state of the city, and they having truly represented to him what they had beheld of their terrible privations through the incredible obstinacy of the Leaguers, he was so overburdened with grief that the tears started from his eyes; and having turned himself away to conceal his emotion, he heaved a great sigh, with these words: "O Lord, thou knowest who are the causes of this; but give me the means to save those whom the obstinate malice of my enemies would cause to perish."

In vain did the most adverse of his council, and especially the Huguenots, represent to him that these rebels merited no favour; he resolved to open a passage to the innocent. "I wonder not at all," he said, "that the chiefs of the League or the Spaniards have so little compassion on those poor people—they are only tyrants; but for myself, who am their father and their King, I cannot bear the recital of these calamities without being touched to the bottom of my soul, or without ardently desiring to remedy them. I cannot hinder those whom the fury of the League possesses from perishing with it; but for those who implore my clemency, and who are only guilty of the crimes of others, I will stretch forth my arms to them." This said, he commanded that they should permit those miserable people to depart. There were some who crawled, and others who had to be carried. There came out at this time more than four thousand, who all with great and unanimous shouts cried, "Long live the King!"

After that day, since they knew it offended him not, the captains who kept the guards daily permitted great bands to escape, and likewise had the boldness to send victuals and refreshments to their friends and to their former hosts, and particularly to the ladies; for Paris being the common country of the French, there are few people who love it not, and who have not there some gage of friendship which forbids them from procuring its loss and utter ruin.

After the example of the captains, the soldiers took the liberty of conveying to them meat, bread, and barrels of wine over the walls, receiving in exchange some rich goods at an exorbitant price, and making themselves brave at the expense of the merchants, which these in some manner were constrained to tolerate, because the others had no money wherewith to pay them. This made Paris stand out nearly a month longer than it would have done; but it is almost impossible but that this should always happen on such occasions, as has been seen not so long since. God be pleased for ever hereafter to preserve France from such great ills!

After all, the King knew certainly that that great city could not long subsist; and he desired to gain absolutely their hearts, in order that he might undermine the very foundations of the League. For this reason he combated their obstinacy with an excess of indulgence. He gave passports to the scholars, not being able to refuse the requests of their parents who were with him; afterwards to the ladies and to the ecclesiastics; and in the end to those who had shown themselves his most bitter enemies.

However, to hasten a little the chiefs of the League in coming to a capitulation, it was agreed in his council that he should render himself master of the suburbs. On the evening of the 27th of July he caused them all to be assaulted at once. They were forced in less than an hour, and all the gates blocked up, his soldiers having first fortified their quarters and thrown down the houses nearest the ditch.

By this last action he took the Parisians by the throats, and pressed them so that they could scarcely breathe; their chiefs by reason of which apprehending that neither their defences, exhortations, nor fear of punishments would be capable to retain them any longer, concluded after ten or twelve deliberations to enter into conference with the King, not out of a cordial intention to treat with him, but only to spin out things to such a length that they might give time to the Duke of Mayenne to make an attempt to succour them.

They received intelligence from that duke twice every week, and each time he promised them that he would be with them with a powerful army in five or six days. Having fed them with these hopes for five or six weeks, he advanced in the end to Meaux, where Vitry was governor, and from thence gave them some greater hopes of relief. He was, however, too weak to hazard it.

The Duke of Parma, who had orders from Spain to join with him and not to spare anything for the relief of Paris, came with great unwillingness. He feared lest during his absence the council or cabinet should appoint a successor in his government, and that he should lose more in the Low Countries than he should gain in France. However, he received commands so express that he was constrained to obey. He departed therefore from Valenciennes on the 6th of August, and arrived at Meaux on the 22nd. He brought along with him only twelve thousand foot and three thousand horse, but artillery and ammunition for an army thrice as great, and fifteen hundred waggons of provisions to revictual Paris.

He was without doubt the greatest captain among strangers of the age in which he lived for all exploits which depend on profound reason and judicious conduct. He had so well laid his plans, so well taken his measures by the most exact maps of the country, and so well meditated on all that could befall him and all that he could do, that he felt himself assured of success.

Those who were about the King had always made him believe that this duke would not leave the Low Countries, and said that if he did, he would not be able to raise a sufficient force to march into the heart of France, or if he raised any great army, he would not arrive in time to deliver Paris. The King suffered himself to be a little carried away with these false reasons; but when he understood that he was marching in this manner, he began already to fear that which happened; and the danger appeared so much the more because he had less foreseen it. In these apprehensions he was well content to renew the negotiation with the Duke of Mayenne, who on his side feigned to desire a truce more than ever, in order that he might keep him occupied, for fear he should assault Paris by force, and also to sustain the Parisians with the hopes of their final delivery, for the famine made them despair so much that it was no longer in his power, with all his inventions, to restrain them from surrender for more than five or six days at most.

When the Duke of Parma was within two days' journey of Meaux, he caused it to be signified to the

King that the Duke of Mayenne could no longer treat except conjointly with him. At first the council of the King was much astonished and in a great irresolution, not knowing what to do. It was without doubt a great blow for the King, and a notable diminishing of the reputation of his arms, to raise a siege which had lasted four months; and it must needs be a great displeasure to this prince, who was brave and glorious, to raise it on the eve of the taking of that great city, the reduction of which would have been a mortal wound to the League.

He had, therefore, but one course to take, but which was without doubt very hazardous; nevertheless, the King resolved upon it. This was to leave a part of his troops in the suburbs, and choose a place of battle, where the rest of the army might engage with the Duke of Parma, and thus avoid the necessity of raising the siege. To this effect, the King, confirmed in it by the advice of La Noue, Guitry, and Du Plessis Mornay, left only three thousand men on the side of the University, and put the rest of his army in battle array in the plain of Bondy, which was between Paris and the Duke of Parma.

But the Marshal de Biron, disapproving absolutely that counsel, prevailed so far that it was resolved to advance to Chelles with intention to give battle. It was not known whether he gave this advice from jealousy, because he had not given the first counsel, or because it seemed to him too dangerous to remain so near Paris, from whence there might sally fifteen or sixteen thousand men on the day of battle to charge them behind. However this be, his authority was so great among the men of war, and it was so dangerous just then to contradict that hot spirit, that they were forced to believe him, and absolutely raise the siege and encamp at Chelles.

The Duke of Parma seeing that, and judging it not convenient to fight, intrenched himself readily in a marsh so well that he feared not to be forced. He boasted, likewise, that the King should not in that position be able to force him to discharge one pistol; and yet that he would take a city then in sight, and open a passage on the river to send provisions into Paris. Indeed he executed to the letter what he had said. It was not in the power of the King to oblige him to fight; and he took Lagny on the Marne, whilst the King was not able to relieve it. Thus Paris was effectually delivered, receiving on the morrow a very large number of boats laden with all sorts of provisions. Yet their joy was not equal to their comfort, for their too long misery had in such manner weakened their bodies and depressed their courage that they were not capable of any sentiments of rejoicing.

The troops of the Duke of Nemours, having regained heart by the food abundant, sallied daily with the most courageous of the burgesses, and cut off all provisions from the King's camp in such manner that there being a little scarcity amongst them, sickness began to multiply, and the gentlemen who had flocked thither out of the hopes of a battle began to grow impatient; which the King seeing, assembled his council to seek some remedy for these straits. He found that throughout his whole army there were very ill dispositions, and that he had better retreat than expose himself to greater affronts. But being loth to quit the enterprise of Paris, he tried in passing to carry it by storm on the University side, between the gates of St. James and St. Marceau; which having done in vain, he retired to Senlis, and thence to Creil. In the end, not being able to do better, he took Clermont and Beauvais, which threatened Senlis and Compiègne. Afterwards he put one part of his troops in the towns about Paris, sent another into the provinces to confirm them in their obedience, and kept with himself only a flying army.

As soon as he had retired, the Dukes of Parma and Mayenne spread their troops over the Brie. Parma, instantly solicited by the Leaguers, besieged Corbeil. He thought to take it in four or five days, but he lay before it a whole month, through the Duke of Mayenne's fault, who, either out of neglect or jealousy, furnished him with ammunition only in small quantities. So that, seeing his army much diminished, and the rest giving themselves up to all sorts of license after the example of the French soldiers, he returned to Flanders much discontented with the conduct of the French nation, whom he had found, as he said, "inconstant and volatile, full of jealousies and divisions, insatiable and ungrateful." His vexatious melancholy surely made him say so.

Before his departure he heard with displeasure of the loss of Corbeil which had cost him so much. Givry, governor of Brie for the King, regained it in one night by storm, and the League, despite all their endeavours, could not prevail upon the Duke of Parma to stay in France till they had retaken it. He left them only eight thousand men of his, promising to return in the spring with a greater army, and counselling them in the meantime to dally with the King by treaties of peace until the next campaign—a counsel which the Duke of Mayenne was not unwilling to follow, and which kept many towns to his party which were ready to abandon him.

The expedition of the Duke of Parma into France retarded much the affairs of the King, but did not advance those of the Duke of Mayenne. On the contrary, it embroiled them, and begat those dispositions which in the end ruined them. For the Duke of Parma, knowing the defects of the Duke of Mayenne, represented to the council of Spain that he was not a proper person for the advancement of their interests, being both too weak and having too little authority to keep in unity so great a party; too jealous, too slow, and too idle to attend to all things; and that therefore it was necessary that the King of Spain should take care of the League, and become absolute master of it, and that to this effect he should gain the ecclesiastics and the people of the great cities, who having a great desire to see the form of the government changed, because under the last kings it had been very oppressive to the people, would be easily induced either to join the cities together in the form of cantons, or to make a king whose power should be so limited that he could never weaken them, either by taxes or by arms, as the two last kings had done.

Therefore the King of Spain finding this plan the more agreeable to his designs, and thinking by it to change France into a republic, or make a king who should be dependent upon him, considered no longer the Duke of Mayenne so much as he had done and assisted him but weakly, but endeavoured to create factions among the great cities, and particularly that of the "Sixteen" of Paris, not sparing any money; so that many believed that had he expended such great sums in raising armies he might have conquered a good part of the realm.

Now our Henry, understanding his designs, laboured on his part to frustrate them. And first, as to the Duke of Mayenne, he flattered him with kindnesses and much good treatment, which he did for two ends; to wit, to try to win him over, and likewise to render him more suspected by the Spaniards. He likewise endeavoured to augment in him the disgust he already had for that nation, and withal promised him great advantages if he would come to terms with him. By these means he gradually restrained him, cooled his ardour, and hindered him from carrying things to extremities. And as for the people, knowing that it was the ill-government of his predecessor which had altered their affections and had furnished them with the pretext and occasion of the League to raise their passions, he omitted no diligence nor kindness which might bring them to their duty.

This good king considered that to cure a disease it is necessary that the causes be taken away, and that to this purpose he had only to correct and sweeten the ill-humours which had put the state into this extremity. What he had seen of it had likewise made him know that three things principally had rendered his predecessor odious and contemptible.

The first was his softness and faint-heartedness, which made him, instead of employing those fair talents which God had given him to rule in his state and act in the functions of a king, neglect to apply himself, and not take sufficiently to heart the conduct of his affairs, but addict himself wholly to his pleasures. As if royalty, which is the greatest and most eminent of all things here below, were only a vain diversion, or as if God had made kings only for the love of themselves, and not for His glory and the common good of men.

The second was his ill-management and the waste of his revenues, which obliged him to seek extraordinary and oppressive means to exact money. Now he had not only consumed his revenues by his own extreme profuseness and by the immense gifts he made to his favourites—a thing which made the people desperate—but much more by his negligence, because he would not give himself the trouble to take knowledge of or watch over those to whom he intrusted their administration, who, forgetting that they were only his dispensers, became prodigal in a thousand foolish expenses, and distributed them to their creatures, as if they had been their private property.

The third was the little belief they had in his faith; his manner of acting with his subjects was too subtle, too fine, and too clouded, so that he had always this misfortune, they were in continual distrust of him, and his words and actions seemed false, and they thought they did prudently in believing quite contrary to all he would have them believe.

Now our Henry, having known that these ill ways

had conducted his predecessor to a precipice, resolved, as much from the inclination to do good as from good policy, to follow paths quite contrary.

First, he would show to the League, who disputed the sceptre with him, that he was worthy to carry it; and therefore he acted continually, not only in the field and in matters of war, but in his cabinet by his deliberations of important affairs, by his negotiations, by the order and distribution of his revenues, by his dispensation of his charges and employments, by his knowledge of the principal laws, the order and policy of his realm, and, in fact, in all his actions, like one who contents himself, not with the name of a king, but who would be one in reality. He would have faithful ministers, but would have no companions. He committed to them the care of his affairs in such a manner that he still remained the absolute master and they the servants. He loved them tenderly, as it was just, and used a great familiarity with them, but yet permitted them not to be wanting either in submission or respect. If he took their counsel it was in the form of advice, and he obliged them much oftener by reason to follow his than he followed theirs. He honoured them with his graces and with benefits, but in proportion and measure; he gave them not all to one alone, nor to two or three, but, like a common father, distributed his rewards to all those he judged worthy. And he desired them to receive them from his hands, and not from others, for he knew that to give and do good is the most glorious attribute of sovereignty, which ought not to be communicated to any person.

In the second place, he took most particular care

to cause his revenues to be well administered, to which four motives obliged him. The first, because he was naturally, though not covetous, yet a good manager, and one who hated profuseness. The second, because he loved his people, and would spare them as much as he possibly could; for he made it a matter of conscience the drawing money out of their purses except upon most necessary occasions, and therefore he never kept near him any of those blood-suckers of the court, who draw all to their coffers and who never care from whence it comes so that they have it. The third, because the necessity he had often been in had made him know the value and need of money, and that it was good to manage it well because hard to recover. And the fourth, because not having been brought up ignorant in affairs, as too often princes are, he had been well informed that the greatest part of those ills which had afflicted France proceeded from the ill administration of public moneys. And therefore among all the cares he took to govern well his states, he had none greater nor more continual than that of ordering well his revenues and of keeping them in order. The superintendents had confused and entangled them into a hundred thousand knots, so that they could neither be loosened nor distinguished; and they so acted that the management of the revenue, as a treasurer of that time said, was a kind of black art, where nothing could be seen, so that the goods of the prince and the blood of the poor people remained entirely at their discretion.

The revenues were at this time under the care of a Norman gentleman named Francis d'O, who had been superintendent since the time of Henry III. This man, to speak the truth, was horribly prodigal in all sorts of expenses. His profuseness rendered him more ingenious and more subtle in finding out new inventions to grasp the substance of the people, even to their very marrow, and to perplex more and more the order of the revenues, in order that it might, not be discovered what spoil he made. Now though the King knew him for such as he was, nevertheless, because he had a strong cabal with the minions and servants of the defunct Henry III., who acted the parts of zealous Catholics, he was obliged to allow him to remain in that charge, expecting when his affairs were in a better state to be able to give a check to his insatiable covetousness. He little by little himself gained knowledge of the management of his moneys, and quietly introduced some changes, now by one means and then by another, so that he knew in time how to bridle him, and simplified things in such a manner that he could take but little in comparison with what he had done before.

It would be superfluous to relate with what nobleness and what freedom our Henry acted with all the world. We may see through the whole course of his life that his very enemies had more confidence in his word alone than in the writings of all others. He used much prudence in all his conduct, but never practised deceit, cunning, nor artifice. The prudent man never walks but by ways straight and virtuous, and the cunning man, on the contrary, by paths crooked and evil. The prudent man can only be generous and good, whilst the other can only be base, deceitful, and unworthy. Now, it is certain that all the life of this great King was nothing but generosity, goodness, sweetness, and clemency, and that he had a natural inclination to oblige all sorts of persons, at least with kindnesses, embraces, and sweet words, when he had no other means. He acknowledged the smallest services when he could do it; he showed himself easy and affable to all the world, familiar to his soldiers, compassionate to the country-people, so that he would often excuse himself to them, when occasion offered, for the evils they suffered, protesting that he was not the cause of them, but ardently desired that peace which Jesus Christ recommended to Christians, and that it was his enemies who forced him to make that war, which of himself he detested as the source and fountain of all crime and misery. There appeared in his countenance a certain gaiety, in his discourse a vivacity and particular grace of spirit, and in all his actions a resolution and promptitude which contented the most disaffected and animated the most indifferent. Though he was yet a Huguenot, he spoke with respect of the Pope and of the ecclesiastics, treated the noblemen and gentlemen as his companions, and flattered them with the glory of being the right hand of his state and the upholders of the crown upon his head. He scarcely knew what vengeance was; his great heart was without any gall; he pardoned injuries, and likewise easily forgot them, so long as he knew that those who had committed them had repented and were disposed to do good, or at least to do no more ill. It was with these arms rather than with the sword that he vanquished his bitterest enemies, that he forced the most obstinate and envenomed hearts to love him, and that of the most passionate Leaguers he made his most faithful servants, esteeming it a procedure agreeable to the grandeur and goodness of a sovereign not to lose those he might gain, and to withdraw men from their vices rather than see them sink under them. It may thus be seen how he followed ways quite contrary to those his predecessor had taken.

After the departure of the Duke of Parma, the two parties, that of the King and that of the League, remained some time in great weakness, and both were equally tormented with the mischief of divisions and jealousies; but with this difference, that those of the King's party were extinguished by his good conduct and those of the League daily increased.

There was great jealousy between the Duke of Nemours and the Duke of Mayenne, brothers by the mother's side. Nor was it less between the Duke of Mayenne and the Duke of Lorraine; and much greater between the latter and the Spaniards, who raised a thousand annoyances against him by means of the Sixteen, for as he could not suffer them for companions they could not suffer him as master, but desired above all things that the League had another chief than he.

In the party of the King there were likewise three or four factions. The first, of the rigid and obstinate Huguenots, who did not desire the King to speak of permitting himself to be instructed, threatening to abandon him if he thought of it, and for this purpose observing him continually, and, as it were, counting all his footsteps. The second, that of the Catholics, who were zealous, or who feigned to be so; these endeavoured to draw him from the Huguenots, and murmured when he either gave them charges or employments or éntertained them particularly. The third was that of the servants and courtiers of the late King, whom the bearing of our Henry displeased, because he did not give them all they wished and did not permit himself to be led by their fancy. These were for the most part atheists and libertines; nevertheless they conspired with the Catholics, and caused much inquietude to the King.

Of these two last factions joined together was a third party formed; Charles, Cardinal de Bourbon, who was called Cardinal de Vendôme whilst the old Cardinal de Bourbon lived, was the chief of it. This prince, vain and ambitious, imagining that the crown would be conferred on him if his cousin Henry IV. were excluded, stirred up the Catholics to press his conversion, from the belief he had that the conscience of that King and his affairs not being yet disposed, he could not hearken to it, and would in consequence, by these heedless shifts, be taken for an obstinate heretic, and oblige the Catholics to abandon him, and afterwards turn on his side. This faction was the most dangerous affair that our Henry ever had to deal with, though he seemed to despise it, and called those who were of it *les Tiercelets*, or the Thirdlings. It did not come to the light with an unmasked face, nor ever openly separate itself from the other; yet because of this it was the more to be feared. But it produced in the end this good, that he was constrained to permit himself to be instructed and thus wrought to his conversion.

As for the Huguenots, when they saw that he lent

an ear to the Catholic doctors, they consulted among
themselves, in order that they might entangle him so
that he could not escape them, and were of opinion
that they ought earnestly to solicit Queen Elizabeth
and the Protestant princes of Germany to send him
great forces, by whose help they believed they might
overcome the League, after which there was no need
of his conversion, and in the meantime they would
continually keep him, as it were, besieged by those
strange forces. Therefore, Elizabeth, who was zealous
for the Protestant religion, interested herself very
strongly in the cause of this King, generously assisted
him, and strenuously solicited the German princes to
concur with her.[1]

At the same time the Huguenots pressed him with
all their might to grant them an edict for the free
exercise of their religion. They pursued their object
so strongly that he was forced to accord it them, and
they sent it to the parliament sitting at Tours, but
they could never get it confirmed by them except with
these words: "By proviso only"—the parliament thus
showing as much enmity to this false religion as they
did to the factions of the League.

During this time Pope Sixtus V. died (August 27th,
1590), leaving in the treasury of the Church five millions
of gold which he had hoarded up. He was much dis-
gusted with the League, and stretched forth his arms as
much as he could to our Henry to recall him into the

---

[1] Elizabeth is said to have demanded the restitution of Calais
as the price for her services, but Turenne gave her to understand
that Henry would ruin his cause by agreeing.—Martin's *History of
France.*

Church, whilst the League endeavoured to shut the gates against him that they might exclude him from his royalty. To Sixtus V. Urban VII. succeeded, who held the seat only thirteen days; and to Urban succeeded Gregory XIV., who, being of a violent spirit and a Spaniard by inclination, zealously embraced the League, as we shall see hereafter.

I silently pass over divers enterprises made by one party and the other. The Parisians made one upon St. Denis. The Cavalier d'Aumale, one of their chiefs, whom they called the "Lion Rampant of the League," was killed in the midst of the city when he had made himself almost master of it. The King on his side made another attempt upon Paris. It was called the "Battle of the Flour," because he was to surprise the city under pretext of a convoy of flour or meal carried thither; but it was discovered, and obliged the Duke of Mayenne, upon the vehement cries of the Sixteen, to receive four thousand Spaniards into the garrison, which retarded for more than a year the reduction of Paris.

It is necessary to understand that neither party having sufficient money to keep their armies continually on foot, they only made war at intervals. When they had been together three months they retired, and then assembled again, and, according as they were stronger or weaker, made their attacks.

The King, having drawn up his army, besieged the city of Chartres, where La Bourdaisière commanded. There was but a small garrison within; yet the siege was long, difficult, and bloody. Its length formed a pretext to the third party for carrying on a number of dangerous intrigues, but the taking of the city repressed them for some time. The King restored the government of Chartres to Chiverni, chancellor of France, who had held it before the League seized it.

After this the Duke of Mayenne, who saw that he was in no very good state, following the counsel of the Duke of Parma, renewed a conference for peace, which ended without doing anything, and the Princes of Lorraine and the principal chiefs of the League then held a general assembly at Rheims. It was resolved that, being altogether too weak to resist the King and being in want of money, they should unite themselves more firmly with Spain than they had formerly done; and to this effect they dispatched the president Janin to Philip II. This president was a man of great ability, and a good Frenchman, who laboured for the League and for the Duke of Mayenne, but who would save the state by saving the religion; so that while endeavouring to win over the Spaniards, he would not serve them or procure their advancement. Yet we cannot doubt but that as he had his ends, they likewise had theirs, and that they designed to make good their expenses incurred for the League out of the kingdom of France.

The Spaniard had in this undertaking the assistance of the new Pope Gregory XIV., who pressed on even more swiftly and more fervently than he; for without having regard either to the letters which M. de Luxembourg, afterwards Duke of Piney, wrote to him on the part of the princes and Catholic lords who were in the King's party, or to the submissions and three humble remonstrances made him by the Marquis of Pisani, who

was there at Rome deputed from them, he strenuously
embraced the party of the League, entered into correspondence
with the Sixteen, receiving letters from
them and writing to them; and, what is more, he
prodigally wasted that treasure which Sixtus V. had
heaped up to raise an army of twelve thousand men,
giving the command to Count Hercules Sfondrato, his
nephew, whom he made expressly Duke of Montmarcian,
to authorise him the more by this new title. He accompanied
this army with a monition or bull of excommunication
against the prelates who followed the King, and
sent it by Marcelin Landriano, his nuncio, with a great
quantity of silver to the Sixteen, to be distributed among
them and the chiefs of the cabals in the great cities.

The parliament at Tours having heard of this
monition, caused it to be torn by the hand of the
common scavenger, and issued a decree against the
nuncio. That at Paris, on the contrary, annulled that
decree, as being, they said, ordered by persons without
power, and commanded that the Holy Father and his
nuncio should be obeyed.

After all, these bulls produced no great effect at
present, and the Cardinal de Bourbon strove in vain
to make the assembly of the clergy which was held
at Chartres declare against the decree at Tours. Nor
did the army of the Pope do any great exploits, but
was almost entirely dispersed before it could render
any service.

The same fate did not await those troops the King
had caused to be raised in Germany by the Viscount
de Turenne. They served the King well in his affairs,
and gained him notable advantages. As a recompense

he honoured this lord with the staff of Marshal of France, to render him the more capable to espouse Charlotte de la Mark, Duchess of Bouillon and sovereign lady of Sedan, who, although a Huguenot, had been eagerly sought after, both by friendship and force, by the Duke of Lorraine, who desired to marry her to his eldest son, the Marquis du Pont. The King made this match to oppose a man to the Duke of Lorraine, who helped to sustain the League. The new marshal soon justified the King's favour by having among other fair exploits surprised Stenay the night preceding his nuptials.

The King had another great captain in the Dauphinate, this being Lesdiguières, who held that country, having reduced the city of Grenoble, and who saved Provence for him, which the Duke of Savoy thought of seizing and dismembering from the crown. This duke being son-in-law to Philip II., King of Spain, the power of his father-in-law had raised his ambition and courage and made him forget that constant affection which his predecessors have almost continuously had for France, inasmuch as they have considered themselves much honoured to be pensioners to our kings. But the conduct and valour of Lesdiguières made him repent of all his high designs, especially by the battle of Esparon de Palières and of Pont-Charra, where that duke sustained as much loss as confusion.

About this time our Henry conceived a passion for the fair Gabrielle d'Estrées, who was of a very noble house; and that passion, by degrees, grew so strong that whilst she lived she held the principal place in his heart, so that after having had by her three or four children, he had almost resolved to marry her, though he knew not how to do it, except by hazarding great troubles and very dangerous difficulties. Having taken the city of Noyon, he gave the government of it to Count d'Estrées, father of this fair one, and shortly after gave him likewise the post of grand master of the artillery, which had been held by John d'Estrées in the year 1550.

Not long after the siege of Noyon he heard of the escape of the Duke of Guise, who, after many other attempts, had, in broad daylight, got out of the castle of Tours, where he had been imprisoned since his father's death. The news at first no less touched the King than it surprised him. He feared this great name of Guise, which had given him so much trouble; and he feared lest this young prince should re-engross the love of the people, which his father had possessed to so great an extent. He was troubled to have lost such a pledge, who might have served him in many things. However, after he had meditated a little, his apprehensions diminished, and he told those who were about him that he had more reason to rejoice than to be troubled, for it must perforce happen that either the Duke of Guise must take his party—and if he did so he would treat him as his parent and kinsman—or that he must cast himself into the League; and then it would be impossible that the Duke of Mayenne and he could continue any long time without contending and becoming enemies.

This prognostication was very true. The Duke of Mayenne having seen those rejoicings which all the

League testified at this news, the bonfires made in the great cities, the thanks which the Pope caused publicly to be rendered to God, and the hopes which the Sixteen conceived of seeing revived in this prince the protection and qualities of his father, whom they had idolised—the Duke of Mayenne, I say, seeing all this, was filled with a very powerful jealousy; and though he sent him money, with entreaties that they might have an interview, yet notwithstanding he did not look upon him as a new reinforcement, but rather as a new subject of inquietude and trouble to himself.

This young prince immediately knit himself in firm bond with the Sixteen, and promised to place himself under their protection. By this means, and by the help of the Spaniards, they were emboldened so much that they resolved to get rid of the Duke of Mayenne, not ceasing to cry down his conduct among the people. I have been assured that there were some amongst them who wrote a letter to the King of Spain, by which they cast themselves into his arms, and entreated him, if he would not reign over them, to give them a king of his race, or to choose a son-in-law for his daughter, whom they would receive with all obedience and fidelity. They decided, besides this, to make a new form of oath for the League, which excluded the princes of the blood, in order that they might oblige all suspected persons who would not swear a thing so contrary to their thoughts to depart out of the city, and to abandon their goods to them. By this artifice they drove away many persons, among others, the Cardinal de Gonde, bishop of Paris, whom they had begun to hate, because, with some clergy of the city, he honestly endeavoured to dispose the people in favour of the King.

There remained nothing now but to dissolve the parliament, who watched them day and night, and stopped their undertakings. They had condemned a man named Brigard because he had correspondence with the royalists; and the parliament having pardoned him, they were so incensed that the most passionate, by conspiracy amongst themselves and by their private authority, having caused those of their faction to take arms, went to seize on the persons of the president, De Brisson, and of De Larcher and Tardiff, councillors, whom they carried prisoners to the Châtelet; and after some formalities, one of the League pronounced against them the sentence of death, in execution of which they caused them all three to be hanged at the window of the chamber (November 15th, 1591), and on the morrow to be carried to the Grève,[1] to the end that they might move the people in their favour; but the greater part abhorred so damnable an outrage, and even the most zealous of the party remained mute, not knowing whether they ought to approve or blame it.

Yet there were some of these Sixteen found so determined as to go farther. They said they must finish the tragedy, and rid themselves of the Duke of Mayenne if he came to Paris, he being at present at Laon; that after that they might assure to themselves the city, elect a chief who should be dependent upon them, re-establish the Council of Forty which that duke had

---

[1] Formerly the public place of execution in Paris.

abolished, and demand the union of the great cities. And certainly there was some appearance that, having the Bastille, of which Bussy was governor, and having the common people and the garrison of Spaniards for them, they might render themselves masters of Paris, and afterwards treat at their pleasure, either with the King, the Duke of Guise, or the Spaniards; but they wanted resolution. In the meantime the Duke of Mayenne, having been two days in doubt whether he should come to Paris, because he feared they would shut the gates against him, at length came with a warlike attendance; and feeling that the parliament durst not attempt to take steps to punish these people, he resolved, whatever might happen, to chastise them himself, and thereupon, without legal formalities, condemned nine to death. They could only catch four, whom he caused to be hanged in the Louvre; the other five saved themselves by escaping to Flanders. The most remarkable of these five was Bussy le Clerc who had been constrained to yield the Bastille to the duke's people. He was known to be leading a miserable life in the city of Brussels; yet still he preserved his hatred for the French, even to the last gasp, which he breathed forth a little before the last declaration of war between the two crowns.

This terrible blow having quite quelled the faction of the Sixteen, the duke made four presidents of parliament, there being then none at all, for De Brisson had alone remained, the rest being gone to Tours. But he demonstrated by this that he did not well understand his own interests, for, in my opinion, it is impossible that the parliament and the nobility should remain separate from the King for any length of time; nor can the force of a party opposed to royalty consist but in two things: to wit, the people or the soldiery.

As soon as the King had received the aid of England and that of the Protestant princes of Germany, he besieged the city of Rouen. This was one of the most memorable sieges of that time. Villars, a provincial gentleman, who was governor, did wonderful actions. The Duke of Parma came to his assistance, having for that purpose joined the Duke of Mayenne; but Villars, who feared that they would not come in time, and likewise that the Duke of Mayenne would deprive him of his government if allowed to enter his city with a force superior to his own, endeavoured to relieve himself, and by a sally, which might almost be called a battle, drove the besiegers a good distance from the walls. The dukes seeing that, and that he was no longer pressed, retired, and Parma lodged his troops about Rue in Ponthieu. But two months after, Villars wanting victuals, and the courage of the burgesses slackening, he was constrained to write to the dukes asking them to make haste to come and relieve him. The dukes, on receipt of so pressing a request, reassembled their troops in one day, recrossed the Somme, and, marching without baggage, came more than thirty leagues in four days, though they had on their way four rivers to cross.

Having arrived within a league of Rouen, they drew up in battle array in a valley on the side of Dernetal. The King, who had gone to Dieppe, finding on his return his army too much weakened to resist those within and without, raised the siege, to his great discontent, and having waited at a league's distance for twelve months in battle array, he afterwards retired to Pont de l'Arche. It was held by many that had they pursued him he could only with difficulty have shunned a battle. But the Duke of Mayenne, either on account of the jealousy he had of the Duke of Parma, or for other reasons, was obstinately of opinion that it was necessary to take Caudebec, to open the mouth of the Seine, and bring provisions to Rouen. The Duke of Parma was forced to yield to his advice. They took Caudebec in twenty-four hours; but Parma was wounded in the arm with a musket-shot, and some days after the Duke of Mayenne fell sick, so that both generals were at one time in their litters.

In the meantime, in five or six days, the army of the King increased by three thousand horse and six thousand infantry, which flocked to his assistance from the adjacent provinces, so that he was stronger than his enemies by nearly five thousand men. Now that fortune had turned he went after them, and shut them up near Yvetot, cutting off all provisions from them, so that they were obliged to dislodge by night and encamp near Caudebec. The two generals being still in bed and their troops very much amazed, the Marshal de Biron beat up one quarter, and in the end defeated their light horse. The King's infantry prepared at the same time to charge the Walloon foot, which without doubt, in the fear they were in, would have demanded quarter; but Biron called them back, for fear, he said, lest they should engage themselves between two quarters of the enemy. It was believed he did this that he might not finish the war, where he had the principal command. And we have a sufficient proof of it at another time.

The Baron de Biron, his son, who was likewise afterwards marshal, having demanded of him five hundred horse and as many dragoons to go and invest the Duke of Mayenne, who was as it were in a trap, the father, seeing that this enterprise was infallible, regarded him with an angry look, told him swearing, "How now, villain, wouldst thou have us sent to plant cabbages at Biron."[1] From hence we may know how wars come to be of such continuance, it being to the interest of their chiefs to prolong them, because they find in them their advantage in the same manner as lawyers do theirs in retarding a process.

Some days after the Duke of Parma, being recovered, called to mind all those inventions and stratagems which he had learnt by a long experience and by profound meditation to extricate himself from his difficulties. He found in the end no other way than to pass the river and retreat in all haste towards Paris. For this purpose he caused two forts to be built, directly opposite to each other, on the banks of the Seine, with redoubts which commanded the water, and greater ones on the outside, which looked towards the army of the King. Under the protection of these forts he succeeded in passing, one dark night, all his baggage, cavalry, infantry, and artillery over bridges of boats, covered with planks which he had had sent from Rouen, whilst the King, who had perceived it too late, could not hinder him. As soon as he had crossed he took his march by the plains of Neufbourg, and made such haste that in four days he arrived at Charenton, not having been

---

[1] A French proverb, as to say, "Wouldst thou have me ruin my own fortune?"

able to sleep (as he himself avowed afterwards) till he had come into Brie.

Afterwards he led back his troops to the Low Countries covered with glory, having for the second time made a great king raise his siege when there was least apparent likelihood of it, and having in his sight, deceiving his vigilance and diligence, crossed a great river, or rather arm of the sea, without his being able to assault him.

This action was so gallant that our Henry could not refrain from wondering at it, esteeming it more glorious than the winning of two battles, acknowledging that the chief work of a great captain was not so much to fight or overcome as to do what he desires without hazarding a combat.

We must not forget how, the first time that the Duke of Parma advanced to the relief of Rouen, the King went to meet him with a part of his army as far as Aumale, so as to hinder him in passing that little river, as well as take notice of him; and how, with four or five hundred carabineers only, he stopped for a long time all the enemy's army by three or four vigorous charges. The Duke of Parma did not believe that the King was there, not judging that he would hazard his person in so dangerous a post and with so few forces; but as soon as he knew he was present he caused all his carabineers to give the charge, sustained by his light horsemen. The King seeing his men so pressed made two vigorous charges, during which they drew forth the greater part of the baggage out of the town; but all the body of the duke's cavalry coming on, the King lost many of his men, and himself ran great danger of being slain or taken prisoner; but God permitted him to be only wounded by a pistol shot in the loins, which would have been mortal if the bullet had had more force, but it pierced only his clothes and his shirt, and somewhat grazed the skin. His valour and his good fortune both equally contributed to draw him out of this peril, and to bring, after so sharp a check, both his person and what remained of his troops into safety.

The Duke of Parma admired this action, but praised the courage which our Henry had testified more than his prudence; for when he was asked what he thought of this retreat, he said, that indeed it was very gallant, but for his part he would never bring himself into a place where he should be forced to retire. This was tacitly to say that a prince and a general ought to secure themselves better. And so all the King's faithful servants came the same evening to entreat him to spare his person, on which the safety of France depended. And the Queen of England, his most faithful friend, prayed him to preserve himself, and at least keep within the duties of a great captain, who ought only to come to blows himself in the last extremity.

After the raising of the siege of Rouen the greater part of the King's army passed into Champagne in pursuit of the Duke of Parma, and laid siege to the city of Epernay and took it. The Marshal de Biron was killed by a cannon shot, which carried away his head as he was viewing the place (July 26th, 1592). His eldest son, who was named the Baron de Biron, as great a captain as the father and much loved by the King, was shortly after honoured with the same office of Marshal of France; but he lost his head somewhat less gloriously than his father.[1]

The Duke of Mayenne and the Duke of Parma having parted ill satisfied with one another, it was not difficult to renew the conferences between the former and the royalists. However, things were not yet ripe. There were some seeds sown, which for some time after brought forth fruit, for the King consented that he would within six months permit himself to be instructed by those means which might not wrong either his honour or his conscience. He gave leave likewise to the Catholic lords of his party to depute some of themselves to the Pope, to let him understand the duties he applied himself to, and to entreat him to add his authority, and that in the meantime peace should be daily treated of.

The Duke of Mayenne and his party demanded very advantageous conditions; but they could not well be rejected, for, to speak the truth, many things at this time did much trouble our Henry. That which most of all perplexed him was that the Duke of Mayenne, violently pressed by the instances of the Pope and the King of Spain, by the remonstrances of those great cities which supported his cause, and likewise by the necessity of his affairs, had called the States-general to Paris to proceed to the nomination of a king.

Now this nomination would have been the undoubted ruin of France, and would possibly have caused the absolute expulsion of our Henry; for there was much appearance and likelihood that all the Catholic potentates of Christendom would have ac-

[1] He was decapitated at the Bastille on July 31st, 1602.

knowledged that king whom the estates had elected, that the clergy would have done the like, and that the nobility and people, who only followed our Henry because he had the title of King, would not have scrupled to quit him for another to whom the estates had granted it.

To the end, therefore, that he might hinder this mortal blow, he wisely decided to propose a conference of the lords of his party with these pretentious estates. The Duke of Mayenne was well content with this expedient, because he saw well that the King of Spain desired that he who was elected should espouse his daughter, Isabella Clara Eugenia, and thus the election could not fall upon him, since he was married and had children; but likewise, out of fear lest they should hearken to an acknowledgment of our Henry, he secretly stirred up some divines to say that this conference with a heretic was unlawful; and by virtue of this advice he wrought in such manner that the estates agreed they would not confer with him, either directly or indirectly, touching his establishment or the doctrine of the faith, but that they would confer with the Catholics among his party, for the good of religion and the public repose.

The legate, knowing well what this would come to, endeavoured with all his power to hinder the effect of this decision of the estates, but in the end he was constrained to lend his hand to it. The conference was then decided on, and the deputies of both sides assembled at the borough of Surênes, near Paris.

The estates were assembled in the month of January, in the year 1593, and sat in the great hall of the Louvre. There were a few noblemen, a great following of prelates, and a sufficient number of deputies of the third estate, but for the most part creatures of the Duke of Mayenne or paid by the King of Spain. This prince, desiring at any price to have the crown for his daughter, intended to send a powerful army into France, which should hasten the resolutions of the estates; but happily for our Henry, the incomparable Duke of Parma was dead, and the Spaniard had not in the Low Countries any captains capable of great things. The Count of Mansfield was given the command of the troops, and the Duke of Mayenne went to meet him. They retook Noyon, but that was all. Afterwards they melted away and became so weak that, not daring to pass any farther, they returned into Flanders, where Prince Maurice of Nassau found them sufficient employment.

During the siege of Noyon the young Biron, upon whom the King had recently bestowed the office of admiral, surrendered by the Duke of Epernon in exchange for the government of Provence, had besieged Selles in Berry, so as to take that thorn out of the foot of the city of Tours. The King, perceiving that this paltry town took him too long a time, had called him thence to go and relieve Noyon, which, however, he was afraid to attempt. These little disasters wonderfully encouraged the hearts of the King's enemies, cooled his friends, and emboldened the faction. The third party, who had kept under cover, now began to move, and likewise a report spread that there were some Catholics who had conspired to seize the person of the King in Mantes, under pretence of snatching him out of the hands of the Huguenots, and carry him to mass whether he wished it or not. He was so much alarmed at it, or feigned to be so, that he took the field, gathered together his surest friends, and caused the English forces to come and lodge in the suburbs of Limay.

At the same time the Duke de Feria, ambassador from the King of Spain to the States-general, arrived at Paris. He presented to them a very civil letter on the part of his master, and made them a long speech, in which he exhorted them to expedite the naming of a king, offering them all assistance both of men and money. In fact, the King of Spain passionately desired the choosing of one, because, as we have said, he wished to give him in marriage his daughter Isabella, whom he dearly loved.

It was therefore now time that our Henry should either publish to the world that he would persevere in his religion without wavering, in which case he must resolve on a war of which possibly he might never see the end, or that he should return into the bosom of the Catholic Church.

The Leaguers who favoured Spain feared above all things this change, which would take from them all pretext; the good Catholics ardently wished it—they only feared lest his conversion should be feigned; the rigid Huguenots endeavoured to divert him, threatening him with the judgments of God if he abandoned, they said, the Evangelical truth. But all politicians, both of the one and the other religion, counselled him not to delay it. They told him that of all canons, the canon of the mass would prove best to reduce the cities of his kingdom; they besought him to avail himself of it, and to their prayers they added threats of abandoning him and of withdrawing from his service, being wearied with consuming themselves in his interests for the caprice of some obstinate preaching ministers, who hindered him from embracing the religion of his predecessors.

Besides these human motives, God, who is never wanting to those who seek Him with submission, cleared his understanding with His holy light, and rendered him capable to receive the saving instructions of the Catholic prelates. This resolution taken, he immediately gave notice of it to the deputies of the League in the conference of Surènes. It cannot be imagined how great was their astonishment, nor how the Duke of Mayenne was surprised, for they least of all expected to hear this news.

The Spaniards and the legate, having advice that he was about to turn convert, pressed the estates more vehemently to elect a king; and seeing that the French would not accept of any but one of their own nation, they proposed that their King should name a French prince, who should reign wholly and individually with the Infanta Isabella.

When the parliament understood this, and that the estates were not averse to this proposition, that great body, though captive and dismembered, remembering its ancient vigour, ordained that remonstrances should be made to the Duke of Mayenne, that he should maintain the fundamental laws of the state, and that he should hinder the crown, the lieutenancy of which was committed to him, from being transferred to strangers;

moreover, declaring null all treaties made or about to be made which should be contrary to the law of the state.

It was suspected that this decree was made by collusion with the Duke of Mayenne; but Villeroy, the greatest statesman of the kingdom, gave testimony on behalf of the parliament that it took the counsel from himself, "Having no other motives than those of honour and duty, as persons who would choose rather to lose their lives than be wanting either of the one or the other, by conniving at the overthrow of the laws of the realm, of which by their institution they are protectors, and obliged to maintain them by the oath given them at their reception." These words are all very memorable.

The vigour of this decree made all those good Frenchmen who were in Paris, and in the estates, take heart; and at the same time the taking of Dreux, which the King's army forced, caused great astonishment among the most ardent of the Leaguers. Nevertheless the Spaniards did not cease to pursue their design. The Duke of Mayenne, thinking to stop their course, made excessive demands before any progress should be made towards the election of a king; but that they might come to their point they granted him all, and in the end they declared that their King would name to the estates the Duke of Guise, to whom he would give his daughter in marriage, together with all forces necessary to assure him of the crown, if they found it convenient to give him their suffrages and elect him.

Never was man more astonished than the Duke of

Mayenne when he saw that he would be constrained to obey his nephew and that his authority must end. His wife, yet more impatient than he, could not refrain from making her spite and jealousy apparent, and rather than suffer that they should confer the crown on this young prince, she counselled her husband to make peace with the King at any price whatsoever. He was, in fact, resolved to do anything rather than raise his nephew above himself, and therefore he employed all sorts of means to hinder him, and to this purpose concluded a truce with the King, notwithstanding the opposition of the legate and the Spaniards.

In pursuance of this truce, the King came to St. Denis, where he met many prelates and divines, under whose guidance he caused himself to be instructed. An historian reports that the King caused a conference to be held before him between the divines of the two Churches, and, hearing a minister grant that one might be saved in the religion of the Catholics, his Majesty broke silence, and said to the minister, "How? do you agree that one may be saved in the religion of these gentlemen?" The minister answering that he doubted it not, provided they lived well, the King very judiciously replied, "Prudence advises that I should be of their religion and not of yours, because being of theirs I may be saved both according to their opinion and yours, but being of yours I can be saved only according to your opinion and not according to theirs. Prudence therefore teaches me to follow the most assured." And thus, after long instructions, in which he desired thoroughly to be cleared of all his doubts, he abjured his error, made profession of the

Catholic faith, and received absolution in the abbey of St. Denis, in the month of July, 1593, by the ministry of Renaud de Beaune, archbishop of Bruges.

That evening the whole country between Paris and Pontoise was ablaze with bonfires; and a great number of Parisians who had flocked to St. Denis to see this ceremony brought back a good report and filled the whole city with esteem and affection for the King, so that they called him no longer Bearnais, but absolutely King.

The estates of Paris did not sit long after this. The Duke of Mayenne dismissed the deputies, who for the most part returned ill satisfied to their provinces, which served not a little to dispose them to render themselves obedient to their legitimate sovereign.

There remained now no other pretext to the League except that the King had not received absolution from St. Peter's chair, that therefore he was not yet within the bounds of the Church, and that they could not acknowledge him until he had entered at the great gate. He had sent the Duke of Nevers to Rome to negotiate this affair with the Pope, who was very much incensed that the prelates of France had taken upon themselves to absolve him, though they had absolved him but provisionally (*ad cautelam*); for he said that he alone had authority to restore a relapsed person, as having the only sovereign power to bind and to loose; and for this reason he appeared so enraged that he could not be appeased until he saw the party of the League quite overthrown.

Now since the life and actions of the King made it appear that his conversion was not feigned, the

League, having no other valuable pretext, was dug up, as we may say, by the very roots, so that before the end of the year it fell to the ground, and there remained to it only a very small number of places in the uttermost parts of the realm, the other chiefs not being willing to follow to the end the fortunes of the Duke of Mayenne. This prince was very irresolute, and knew not what he ought to do, as much by reason of his natural slowness as of the reluctance he had to quit the sovereign authority which he had in his hands, and out of fear likewise of not finding safety with the King.

In the meantime Vitry, desiring to be the first to return unto his obedience, as he had been the first to depart from it, brought back the city of Meaux. The Count of Carces delivered that of Aix in Provence. Lyons surrendered of itself, which the Duke of Mayenne partly caused by having endeavoured to make himself master of that city and so snatch it from the Duke of Nemours, his brother on the mother's side, who intended to establish a small sovereignty in that country. That he might accomplish his design, he had by secret contrivances made the burgesses rise against that young prince, so that they, having seized his person, had made him a prisoner in the castle of Pierre-Encise. But he found that in this he laboured more for the King than for himself; for the burgesses who had imprisoned the Duke of Nemours, fearing lest the brothers should agree among themselves to their prejudice, treated secretly with Colonel Alfonso d'Ornano, lieutenant-general for the King in the Dauphinate, and being well fortified, took the white flag, and cried,

"Vive le Roi!" La Châtre likewise returned to its duty, with the cities of Orleans and Bruges. The reduction of Paris happened on the 22nd of March. The parliament, the provost of the merchants, and the sheriffs, having disposed of this great city, received the King, despite the vain endeavours of some remnant of the faction of the Sixteen. The Duke of Mayenne had gone to Picardy, and Brissac, to whom he had confided the government of Paris for some months past, having taken it from the Count of Belin, broke faith with him, believing he owed it rather to the King than to him.

The King had shortly before this caused himself to be anointed at Chartres, with the cruse of St. Martin of Tours. The city of Rheims was still in the hands of the League, but he would no longer defer his coronation, because he knew that that ceremony was absolutely necessary to confirm to him the affection and respect of his people.

It was almost a miracle how, there being four or five thousand Spaniards engarrisoned in Paris and ten or twelve thousand disaffected persons remaining of the cabal of the Sixteen, who all cruelly hated the King, he could nevertheless render himself master of it without striking a blow or without shedding blood, except that of five or six mutineers who came into the streets to call the citizens to arms. His troops having by intelligence seized on the gates, ramparts, and public places, he entered triumphantly into the city by the new gate, by which Henry III. had unhappily fled six years before, and went directly to Notre-Dame to hear mass and cause the "Te Deum" to be sung. Afterwards he returned to the Louvre, where he found his officers, and his dinner ready, as if he had always remained there.

After dinner he gave the Spanish garrison a safe-conduct and a good convoy to conduct them as far as the tree of Guise in all security, for so those who brought them into the city had desired. The garrison departed about three o'clock on the day of his entrance, with twenty or thirty of the most obstinate Leaguers, who chose rather to follow strangers than obey their natural prince. He desired to see them depart, and watched them passing from a window by the gate of St. Denis. They all saluted him with their hats very low and with a profound inclination, and he returned the salutes of their chiefs with great courtesy, adding these words: "Commend me to your master; go now in peace, but return no more."

The same day that he entered Paris the Cardinal de Pelleve, archbishop of Sens, an ardent Leaguer, expired in his palace of Sens. The Cardinal of Placenza, legate from the Pope, had safe-conduct to return home, but he died by the way. Brissac for recompense had the staff of marshal, and a place as honourable counsellor to the parliament, a favour very rare in that time. D'O was replaced in his government of Paris, which he had had under Henry III.; but he did not enjoy it long, dying soon after. That part of the parliament which was at Tours was recalled, and that which was at Paris re-established (for it had been interdicted), and both reunited to serve conjointly the King.

By noon of the day on which our Henry entered,

Paris was everywhere peaceable. The burgesses in a moment grew familiar with the soldiers, the artificers worked in their shops; in a word, the calm was so profound that nothing interrupted it but the ringing of the bells, the bonfires and the dances which were made in all the streets even till midnight. It is certain that that which caused this joy and wonderful tranquillity was the great opinion which the people had conceived of the generous goodness of this prince, and the commands he gave for the orderly government of his soldiers.

There were two actions which he did on the day he entered Paris worthy of observation, proceeding from an admirable justice, goodness, and policy.

The first was that he suffered the baggage of La Noue, one of his principal officers, to be arrested by the sergeants on his entry into Paris for the debts of his father contracted in his service; and when La Noue complained to him of this insolence, he answered publicly, "La Noue, you must pay his debts, for I pay likewise those of mine." But after that he took him apart and gave him some precious stones to give to his creditors instead of the baggage which they had seized. Was there ever a finer example of wonderful goodness and strict justice?

The second was that the same evening he played at cards with the Duchess of Montpensier, who was of the house of Guise, and one of the most vehement Leaguers of the party. What could be more politic?

After this reduction of Paris, the other cities and their governors hastened likewise to conclude their treaties. Villars made his for Rouen, thus gaining to himself the government in chief of this city and bailiwick, as well as that of the country of Caux, with the office of admiral, which he was to take out of the hands of Biron, who became Marshal of France with twelve hundred thousand livres in cash, and sixty thousand livres of pension. At the same time, or shortly after, Montreuil and Abbeville in Picardy, Troyes in Champagne, Sens, Riom in Auvergne, Agen, Marmande, and Villeneuve d'Agenois rendered themselves obedient, and their governors had all they could demand of the King. The city of Poitiers and the country thereabouts yielded likewise by means of its principal magistrates; and the Marquis of Elbeuf, governor of the League, seeing that he could not hinder the revolution, permitted himself to be drawn in with them, and made his peace with the King, who left him the government of that province.

In the meantime Count Mansfield entered into Picardy to endeavour to sustain the League, which was in a very low condition, and took La Capelle. The King, in revenge, laid siege to Laon, and made it capitulate, notwithstanding all the endeavours of the Duke of Mayenne to relieve it.

Balagny, with his city of Cambray, likewise renounced the League and promised service to the King. He had called himself sovereign of this city, and had held it from the time that Henry III.'s brother (the Duke of Alençon) had usurped it from the Baron of Inchi, who in the great rebellion of the Low Countries had quitted the obedience of Spain to join his party. In like manner, the cities of Beauvais and Peronne renounced the League, as did likewise that of Amiens, shaking off the yoke of the Duke of Aumale, there remaining to that party in all Picardy only Soissons, La Fère, and Ham. And, what was even more important, the Duke of Guise shook off the Duke of Mayenne, and brought the cities of Rheims, Vitry, and Mezières unto obedience to the King, who in recompense gave him the government of Provence, from which he was obliged to withdraw the Duke of Epernon, because the people, the parliament, and the nobility had taken arms against him.

The Duke of Lorraine likewise, who negotiated his peace by the intervention of Bassompierre, concluded it on the 26th of November. But neither the example of this duke, chief of the house of Lorraine, nor the general dissolution of that party, could induce the Duke of Mayenne to withdraw himself from that danger wherein he was about to be overwhelmed. He could not abandon that fair title of Lieutenant-general of the Crown, but flattered himself with the hope that the assistance of Spain might again give his affairs the upper hand. He retired into his government of Burgundy, because that remained yet most true to him, though to keep Dijon he was forced to cut off the head of the mayor and another citizen, who had laboured to reduce it to the King's service.

Now, since it was the Spaniards who maintained him in his obstinacy, and who made war against the King in his name, it was proposed and agreed in the council to attack them in open war, in order that, being employed in their own country, they might lack the desire and leisure of coming to disquiet the King in his; for they not only assaulted him by force of

arms and by practices which encouraged the people in rebellion, but they wished to take his life, and endeavoured to murder him by base and execrable means. They contrived or favoured many conspiracies against his sacred person, which were, however, discovered. The two which made most noise were that of one Peter Barrière and that of John Castel.

The first was a soldier, aged about twenty-seven, who, being discovered at Melun in the year 1593, as he sought the opportunity to deliver his detestable blow, was condemned to have his right hand burned, holding the knife with which he would have struck the King, and afterwards to have his flesh torn off with redhot pincers, and to be broken on the wheel alive.

The second was a young scholar, aged about eighteen, son of a merchant draper of Paris, who kept a shop in front of the palace. This villain, about the end of the year 1594, having thrust himself with the courtiers into the chamber of the fair Gabrielle, where the King was, would have struck him with a knife in the belly, but by good fortune, the King then bowing to salute someone, the blow chanced on his face only, piercing his upper lip and breaking a tooth. It was not discovered at once who had struck the blow; but the Count of Soissons seeing this young man affrighted stopped him by the arm. He impudently confessed that he had given the blow, and maintained that he was right in doing it. The parliament condemned him to have his right hand burned, his flesh torn off with redhot pincers, and afterwards to be torn in pieces by four horses. This detestable youth showed no sign of pain, so much had they imprinted in his spirit that he would offer a sacrifice acceptable to God by taking out of the world a prince relapsed and excommunicate. The father of this miserable villain was banished, his house in front of the palace demolished, and a pyramid erected in its place.

The Jesuits under whom this miscreant had studied were likewise accused of having instructed him in this pernicious doctrine; and they having many enemies, the parliament banished the whole society out of the kingdom on the arrest of their scholar. Yet these fathers were not wanting, notwithstanding that the times were contrary to them, in attempting to sustain their honour, but wrote many things to justify themselves against the charge. And truly those who were not their enemies did not at all believe the society culpable, so that some years after the King revoked the decree of parliament and recalled them, as we shall mention hereafter.

The success of the war waged against Spain was of another kind to that which the King maintained against the League, which made it apparent that it is a far different thing to assault a stranger equal in strength, over whom nothing is to be gained but by force of arms, than to have to do with rebellious subjects in one's own country, where intrigues and rumours prolong the strife.

This year the cities of Beaune, Autun, and Aussonne returned to their obedience. Those of Mâcon and Auxerre had returned the year before. The city of Dijon followed their example, and fortified itself against the castle which Biron went to besiege. But in the meantime the Constable of Castile descended with a great army of Milanese into Burgundy by the French county, and passed the Saône at Gray with the Duke of Mayenne.

The King, who had gone into that country, had the boldness to advance as far as Fontaine-Française. Here it was that with only 1500 men he made head against that great army, and did an exploit of war scarcely imaginable. Villars-Oudan and Sanson, two of the principal officers of the enemy's army, charged furiously on his troops; Villars charged a body commanded by the Marshal de Biron, and Sanson another by the side of it. They made them both give way and retreat, flying within sight of the King. It was reported that Villars knowing he was there, so powerful is the name of king, durst not assault him, but retired on the left hand. But Sanson was not so happy; for the King having with him only one hundred horse, but all chosen gentlemen of note and mounted to advantage, with his sword in his hand, mingled with the enemy and cut them to pieces. Sanson in endeavouring to rally his people lost his life, but won no small honour.

The King was in such great danger in this fight that he himself said that on other occasions wherein he had been engaged he had fought for victory, but that in this he had fought for his life.

Having therefore made the Constable by this encounter see in what manner he was to act, he so much lowered his courage that he durst attempt nothing, but shortly afterwards retired. The Duke of Mayenne likewise despairing at such ill success, and no longer knowing where to hide his head, had resolved to retire to Sommerive in Savoy, from whence he would send to demand a safe-conduct into Spain to give an account of his actions to King Philip II. But the goodness of the King took care to divert him from this precipice, and to open to him means of reconciliation. He, to this effect, sent for Lignerac, his confidant, assured him of the good-will he always had for the duke, testified to him that he pitied him, that he would be always disposed to receive him into his favour, and that he would permit him to retire in safety to Chalons-sur-Saône until they could conclude a treaty of peace.

The duke accepted this favour; and having understood that the Pope was disposed to receive the King into the Church, he craved a general truce for the rest of his party.

The greater part of the King's council, who considered the delays and artifices which he had for six years employed, having begun fifty treaties without ever concluding any, advised the King to grant him no respite but to pursue him to the utmost. But the prudence and goodness of the King conformed not with this sentiment, because he was not ignorant of two maxims, which are most true ones; the one, "that kings may always, when they please, reduce the most rebellious to their duty;" the other, "that it is very dangerous to reduce great persons to despair," especially persons of the quality of the Duke of Mayenne. And for these reasons, acting on his own opinion and contrary to the advice of his council, he granted him a truce. The events which followed demonstrate well that this sage prince had more knowledge than all his ministers, and how prejudicial it would have been to his interests to do the contrary.

In the meantime, of those three cities which we have said remained to the League in Picardy; to wit, La Fère, Ham, and Soissons, the governor of the first, named Colas, had delivered it to the Spaniards, and D'Orvilliers had done the same with Ham. However, this last they did not retain long, for D'Humières, one of the bravest gentlemen of those times, came, and at the same hour so hotly assaulted it that, after a long and bloody defence, they were hewn in pieces; but D'Humières was killed, and more than two hundred brave gentlemen with him.

This loss so much excited the indignation of the loyal French against the Leaguers that the greater part of the latter fled in despair to the Low Countries and to Spain, where they found at first a favourable reception and good employment, by which they did very great mischief to France. Amongst others was a valiant captain named Rosny, who, imagining that they would extend their utmost rigour to those who, not being governors, had no places to buy their peace with, resolved to make war so well that either the Spaniards should have cause to recompense him or the King to redeem him.

He it was who inspired the Count of Fuentes with the design of besieging Cambray after he had forced Cattelet, and who persuaded him to facilitate this great enterprise by taking Dourlens first, in order that the French might not bring an army to relieve it. It was likewise by his counsel that Fuentes went to meet the Duke of Nevers, the Marshal de Bouillon, and Admiral

Villars, who came to the relief of Dourlens; that he fought them, and defeated them with a great slaughter of the French nobility, and caused Villars, one of the bravest men of his time, to be slain in cold blood. Afterwards returning to Cambray, he took it by famine, and despoiled Balagny of his pretended principality.

But news most important and long expected comforted the King for these two great losses of Dourlens and Cambray, which was that he received information that the Holy Father, passing over all those difficulties which the Spaniards formed, had granted his absolution on the 16th of September, by the negotiation and persistency of D'Ossat and Du Perron, advocates in the court of Rome, who were afterwards, upon his recommendation, honoured with cardinal's caps.

After this, the Duke of Mayenne, having no longer hopes of holding out, resolved to sue for peace. It was very late, and he could not well expect to be treated otherwise than with the utmost rigour, if the generosity of the King had not been greater than the duke's obstinacy. It is most true that the fair Gabrielle, very well disposed to those who asked his favour, and being at present in hopes to create to herself friends and supports with regard to the marriage of the King, to which she aspired, did not a little assist to obtain a most favourable understanding. Certainly the terms of the edict and the conditions which the King granted him are so honourable that no subject ever had greater advantages from any King of France; but they would have been greater if before his party had been so much ruined he had treated for those great cities which yet held him as their chief, and which by this means he might still have kept firm to his interests.

Some time after he came to Monceaux to salute the King, who, seeing him coming along an alley where he was walking, advanced some paces towards him with all alacrity and good countenance possible, and straightway thrice embracing him, assured him that he esteemed him so absolute a man of honour that he doubted not his word, treating him with as much freedom as if he had always been his most faithful servant. The duke, surprised with his goodness, said at his departure that it was now only that the King had completely vanquished him. And he afterwards as well performed the duty of a most faithful subject, as the King showed himself a good prince and an exact observer of his word.

At the same time that this duke had concluded his treaty and obtained an edict from the King which confirmed it, the Duke of Nemours, his brother by the mother's side, and who was called the Marquis of St. Sorlin whilst the brave Duke of Nemours his elder brother was living, by means of his mother became likewise reconciled to the King, and brought to his obedience some little places which he yet held in Lyonnais and Forez.

His elder brother, one of the most noble and generous men ever known, died the year before of a strange malady, which made him vomit through his mouth and through all his pores, even to the last drop of his blood. Whether this malady happened to him through his extreme grief when he was shut up in the castle of Pierre-Encise at hearing of the surrender of

Vienne, which was his surest retreat, or whether it were caused by a sharp and scalding poison, reported to have been given him by those who feared his resentment, he died without being married, and his younger brother, of whom we are now speaking, was father to those Messieurs de Nemours whose deaths we mourned not long since.

The Duke of Joyeuse, who, after the death of his younger brother, slain in the battle of Villemur, near Montauban, had doffed his attire of capuchin to become chief of the League in Languedoc, and had maintained the city of Toulouse and the neighbouring countries in his party, took likewise this opportunity to make his submission, and obtained very favourable conditions, by the influence of Cardinal de Joyeuse, his other brother; amongst other things he was given the staff of marshal of France. The Lord of Boisdauflin received the same recompense, though he had no more than two little places in Maine and Anjou: to wit, Sable and Château-Gontier, the King granting him this good treatment rather in consideration of his person than his places.

All were now submissive, with the exception of the Duke of Merceur and the city of Marseilles. This city was governed by Charles de Casaux, the consul, and by Louis d'Aix, the provost, or judge. As these two men were upon the point of delivering it up to the Spaniards, a burgess named Libertat, with a band of his friends, caused the inhabitants to rise against them, and having killed Casaux and driven out Louis d'Aix, placed it in complete submission to the King.

As for the Duke of Merceur, the King granted him

a prolongation of the truce, because he was not able just then to go and dispossess him of the rest of Brittany, being much hindered by the siege of La Fère, which he conducted in person, and where he had made but little progress in three or four months. Moreover, it happened when he least expected it that the Archduke Albert, who commanded the Spanish army, incited by the counsels of Rosny, of whom we just now spoke, fell upon Calais, and that Rosny, who was a great captain, having first taken the forts of Risban and Nieule, the Spaniards forced the place on the 24th of April, and put all to the sword. Shortly after the King took La Fère, which surrendered for want of provisions. The Spaniards having made the treaty, would accept no hostages from him, saying that they knew he was a generous prince and of good credit, a testimony so much the more glorious for him because it came from the mouth of his enemies.

The grief which he felt for the loss of Calais was redoubled by that of the cities of Guinez and Ardres, which were likewise taken by the industry and valour of Rosny, who would have done many similar exploits if, happily for France, he had not been killed some months after at the siege of Hulst, near Ghent.

Now the news of these four or five great losses, sustained one upon the other, cast some terror into the hearts of the people, and the emissaries of Spain sowed new seeds of dissension in their spirits, to that end availing themselves of all sorts of pretexts, but above all, of that of the oppression of the people. This was indeed great, but it was caused by the pillages of war and by the necessity of affairs rather than by the King's fault, who had no greater desire than to procure the ease of his subjects, as we shall see.

This cast him into a great affliction and trouble, because he had no treasure to continue the war, and he foresaw by the murmurs already excited that if he crushed the people more he should raise against himself a new tempest. In this trouble, he had recourse to that great remedy to which it is customary to resort when France is in danger; that is, the convocation of the estates; but because the pressing necessity gave him no time to assemble them in a full body, he called only the chiefs of the peers of his estate, of the prelates, and of the nobility, with the officers of justice and of the revenues.

He desired that the assembly should be held at Rouen, in the great hall of the abbey of St. Ouen, in the midst of which he was seated in a chair elevated in form of a throne, with a cloth and canopy of state. On each side of him were the prelates and lords; behind, the four secretaries of state; beneath him, the first presidents of the sovereign courts and the deputies of the officers of justice and of the revenues. He made his overtures to them in a speech worthy a true king, who ought to believe that his greatness and authority consist not only in an absolute power, but in the good of his state and the safety of his people.

"If I accounted it a glory," said he to them, "to pass for an excellent orator, I should have brought hither rather good words than good-will; but my ambition tends to something higher than well-speaking; I aspire to those glorious titles of Redeemer and

Restorer of France. Already, by the favours of Heaven, by the counsels of my faithful servants, and by the sword of my brave and generous nobility (from which I distinguish not my princes, the quality of gentleman being the fairest title we possess), I have delivered it from slavery and ruin. I desire at present to restore it to its former power and to its ancient splendour. Participate, my subjects, in this second glory, as you have participated in the first. I have not called you hither as my predecessors have done, to force you blindly to approve my will. I have caused you to be assembled to receive your counsels, to believe them, to follow them, and, in a word, to put myself in guardianship under your hands. This is a desire which seldom possesses kings grey-haired and victorious like myself; but the love I bear my subjects, and the extreme desire I have to preserve my state, makes me find all things easy and honourable."

The assembly, moved even to the bottom of their hearts by such tender words, laboured with affection to find the wherewithal to continue the war; and to this effect they ordained that one year's payment of all officers' salaries should be gathered, and that for two years only there should be imposed one sou per pound on all which entered into walled cities, excepting only corn, which is the nourishment of the poor. This last resort caused much trouble in the provinces beyond the Loire. But Rosny,[1] whom the King had some months before made superintendent, no less able than faithful, as we shall show elsewhere, joined to this stock a

[1] Marquis of Rosny, the celebrated Sully, born 1560, died 1641.

great sum of money which the receivers had diverted, and which he caused to be returned to the King's coffers.

In the meantime the King of Spain, finding the forces both of his body and mind diminishing by a languor which afterwards degenerated into a horrible malady, feared lest his weakness should cause revolts in his countries so distant from one another. Moreover, he had expended his revenues, and passionately desired to give the Low Countries to his dearest daughter Isabella; and for these reasons had made known to the Holy Father that he desired peace, and his Holiness had sent the general of the Cordeliers to dispose him more particularly to it.

But now, when some progress was made in it, there happened an accident which retarded it for more than a year. Hernand Teillo, governor of Dourlens for the Spaniards, being notified of the little care which the burgesses of Amiens took in the guard of their city, surprised it one morning about nine o'clock when they were at mass, it being Lent time, having caused the gate to be blocked with a cart laden with nuts, of which a sack was purposely spilt to amuse the soldiers of the guard. This troublesome news astonished the King so much the more because he was at present rejoicing and diverting himself at Paris. He had given orders that all important packets should be brought directly to him and not to others, and that they should bring him them at all hours whatsoever, so that being in a profound sleep after attending a ball a courier came to awaken him to tell him of this accident.

He immediately leapt out of bed and sent for three

or four of his greatest confidants to consult with them. They all judged that it happened at a very unfortunate time, because the Duke of Merceur was powerful in Brittany, the rest of the factions being yet concealed under their ashes, the Huguenots making cabals or secret councils, and the consternation of Paris being very great, for it beheld itself by this means become a frontier. But the heroic courage of the King, whom so many perils could not terrify, was not startled by this; on the contrary, he resolved to encounter it at once and go immediately to invest Amiens before the Spaniards were longer settled in it.

His greatest captains were not of this mind; but, notwithstanding that, he, who had greater knowledge and more constancy than them all, undertook it courageously, not so much, said he, on account of his expectation of succeeding by human means as of the confidence he had in God, who had always done him the grace to assist him.

And in truth it may be said that God assisted the King more visibly on this occasion than He had ever done. For he discovered many conspiracies against his person, particularly one amongst the religious orders, whom an agent of the King of Spain, as it was said, would have induced to kill him; and also very dangerous cabals which the money of the same king upheld at Paris, which observed all his actions, and had designed one day to seize his person at his castle of St. Germain-en-Laye.

Moreover, his people answered as they ought to his paternal affection, not denying him anything that he demanded to hasten the siege; and all the Leaguers, desiring to testify to him their thankfulness for all his goodnesses, served him so faithfully and vigorously on this occasion, whilst others wavered and kept their stations, that he was obliged to say that he acknowledged that the greater part of that people hated not his person, but only the Huguenot religion.

The siege was for some time difficult and doubtful, and if the King of Spain had employed all his power, the King could never have succeeded in it. But the King of Spain had become very melancholy; he desired only repose, and cared no more for conquests, so that he gave not any of those assistances which the archduke demanded. The archduke ceased not, however, to use his greatest endeavours to raise the siege. He presented himself before the quarter of Longpré with very great forces on a day when he was not expected, which put the French into so great a fear and disorder that had he known how to avail himself of the occasion, and had he not lost time in consultation, he would have put those three thousand men into the city, as he had intended.

The King, on returning from hunting, found a general fear throughout his army, and likewise some of his principal officers quite daunted. In so great a danger neither his heart nor his head failed him; he dissembled his fear, gave orders with coolness, and showed himself everywhere with a cheerful countenance, and with discourses as resolute as after a victory. He made his forces nimbly draw into the field of battle, which he had chosen three days before, eight hundred paces from the lines. From this place, having considered the excellent order of the Spanish army, the little assurance of his, and the weakness of his posts, which he had not had leisure to fortify, he was a little moved, and doubted of the success of the day. When leaning on the pommel of his saddle, with his hat in his hand, and lifting up his eyes to heaven, he uttered these words with a loud voice: "O Lord, if it be to-day Thou wilt punish me as my sins deserve, I offer my head to Thy justice; spare not the culpable, but, Lord, for Thy holy mercy's sake, take pity on the poor kingdom, and smite not the flock for the offence of the shepherd."

The wonderful efficacy of these words cannot be expressed; they were in a moment carried through the whole army, and it seemed as if some virtue from Heaven had given courage to the French.

The archduke, therefore, finding them resolved and in good countenance, durst not pass further. Some other attempts he afterwards made which did not succeed, and he retired by night into the country of Artois, where he dismissed his army. At length Hernand Teillo, being slain by a musket shot, the besieged capitulated, and the King established as governor in the city the Seigneur de Vic, a man of great order and exact discipline, who by the royal command began to build a citadel there.

At his departure from Amiens, the King led his army to the very gates of Arras to visit the archduke; he remained three days in battle array, and saluted the city with some volleys of cannon. Afterwards, seeing that nothing appeared, he retired towards France, ill satisfied, he gallantly said, with the courtesy of the Spaniards, who would not advance so much as one pace to receive him, but had with an ill grace refused the honour he did them.

The Marshal de Biron served him extraordinarily well at this siege; and the King, when he had returned to Paris, and the citizens had given him a reception truly royal, said to them, showing them the marshal, "Gentlemen, see here the Marshal de Biron, whom I do willingly present both to my friends and to my enemies."

There remained now no appearance of the League in France, except the Duke of Merceur, yet keeping a corner of Brittany. The King had often granted him a truce, and offered him great conditions, but he was so intoxicated with ambition to make himself duke of that country that he found out daily new fancies to delay the concluding of peace, imagining that time might afford him some favourable revolution, and flattering himself with I know not what prophecies, which assured him that the King should die in two years.

At last the King, wearied with so many excuses, turned his head that way, resolving to chastise his obstinacy as it deserved. The duke would certainly have been lost, if he had not been advised to save himself by offering his only daughter to the elder son of the fair Gabrielle d'Estrées, Duchess of Beaufort.

His delegates could at first obtain nothing else but that he should immediately depart from Brittany, and give up those places which he held, which done, his Majesty would grant him forgiveness for all his past misdeeds, and receive him into his favour. But the King being of a tender heart, and desiring to advance his natural son by so rich and noble a marriage, granted him a very advantageous edict, which was verified in the parliament, as all those of the chiefs of the League were. This arrangement was made at Angers, the contract of marriage signed at the château, and the betrothal celebrated with the same magnificence as if he had been a legitimate son of France. He was four years old and the maiden six.

The King gave him the duchy of Vendôme, by the same rights that other dukes hold them, which the parliament verified, not without great repugnance, and with this condition, that it should be no precedent for the other goods of the King's patrimony, which by the laws of the realm were considered as reunited to the crown from the time of his coming to it.

From Angers the King passed into Brittany. He stayed some time at Nantes, and from thence went to Rennes, where the estates were held. He passed about two months in this city in feasts, joys, and diversions; but yet ceasing not to seriously employ himself in hastening the expedition of many affairs. For it is to be observed that this great prince employed himself all the mornings in serious things, and dedicated the rest of the day to his diversions; yet not in such manner that he would not readily quit his greatest pleasures when there was anything of importance to be done; and he still gave express orders not to delay the notification to him of such things.

He abolished a great many superfluous garrisons in this country; suppressed many imposts which the tyranny of many persons had introduced during the war; disbanded all those pilfering troops which laid waste the land; sent forth the provosts into the country against the thieves, who were in great number; restored justice to its authority, which license had weakened; and gathered four millions, of which the estates of the country of their own free-will levied eight hundred thousand crowns. So he laboured profitably for those two ends which he ought most to desire; to wit, the ease of his people and the increase of his treasures, two things which are incompatible when a prince is neither just nor a good manager, or lets his money be managed by others without taking diligent care of his accounts.

Thus was a calm of peace restored to France within itself, after ten years' civil war, by a particular grace of God on this kingdom, and by the labour, diligence, goodness, and valour of the best king that ever was. And in the meantime a peace was earnestly sought for between the two crowns of France and Spain. The two kings equally wished it: our Henry, because he passionately desired to ease his people and to let them regain their forces after so many bloody and violent agitations; and Philip, because he found himself drawing to the end of his days, and that his son Philip III. was not able to sustain the burden of a war against so great a king.

The plenipotentiaries of one side and the other had been assembled for three months in the little city of Vervins, with the papal nuncio. Those of France were Pompone de Bellièvre and Nicholas Brûlard de Sillery, both councillors of state, and the last likewise president of the parliament, who, acting agreeably and without jealousies, determined on the most difficult articles in very little time, and, according to the order they received from the King, signed the peace on the 2nd of

May. On the 12th of the same month it was published at Vervins.

It would be too long to insert here all the articles of the treaty; I shall say only that it was agreed that the Spaniards should surrender all the places they had taken in Picardy, as well as Blavet, which they yet held in Brittany; that the Duke of Savoy should be comprehended in this treaty, provided he delivered to the King the city of Berry, which he held in Provence; and for the marquisate of Saluces, which that duke had taken from France towards the latter end of the reign of Henry III., that it should be remitted to the judgment of the Holy Father, who was to decide that controversy in a year.

The publication of the peace was made on the same day through all the cities of France and the Low Countries, with such great rejoicings that the report of them spread to the utmost bounds of Christendom; but none were more truly pleased than our Henry, who was accustomed to say that, it being a thing barbarous and contrary to the laws of nature and Christianity to make war for the love of war, a Christian prince ought never to refuse peace if it were not absolutely disadvantageous to him.

PART III

BRIEFLY CONTAINING WHAT HENRY THE GREAT DID AFTER THE PEACE OF VERVINS, MADE IN THE YEAR 1598, UNTIL HIS DEATH, WHICH HAPPENED IN THE YEAR 1610.

HITHERTO we have followed the fortune of our Henry through ways craggy and intricate, over rocks and precipices, during times very troublesome and full of storms and tempests. Now we are about to trace it through paths more fair, in the sweetness of calm and quiet peace; where, however, his virtue slept not in his repose, but appeared always active; where his great soul was employed without ceasing in the true functions of royalty, and where, in fine, among his diversions, he made his most necessary and most important duties his principal pleasures.

In the two first parts of his life which we have seen he was by constraint a man of war and of the field; in this last a man of counsel and a great politician, but in both invincible and indefatigable.

The true duty of a sovereign consists principally in protecting his subjects. He must both defend them against strangers and repress the factions and attempts of rebels. It is for this purpose that he has the power of arms placed in his hands, and that it is advantageous to him to perfectly understand the mystery of war. But that comprehends but a part of his functions, and we may truly say that it is neither the most necessary nor the most satisfactory, for besides being able to manage his wars by his lieutenants, who doubts him to be the most happy prince that governs his affairs in such a manner that he has no need of his sword, but is powerful enough to distribute justice, punish the wicked, and to honour and reward deserving men; to confer graces and recompenses, to keep good order, and conserve the laws; to maintain his provinces in tranquillity, sustain his reputation and greatness by his good conduct, inform himself often and diligently of all that passes, make himself feared by his enemies and esteemed by his allies; and, like a sovereign, himself to preside at his council, listen to ambassadors and answer them; to settle great affairs by treaty and negotiation; to watch incessantly, so as to prevent all ill, and deprive wicked persons and enemies of their power to hurt; to encourage commerce and the study of sciences and the fine arts; to make his kingdom rich, flourishing, and abundant; to fetch wealth from all quarters of the earth; but, above all, to procure the glory and service of God, so that his kingdom may be as a paradise of delights and a harbour of felicity? These are, in my opinion, employments worthy of a powerful king, a Christian and wise king, who, being the shepherd of his people (as Homer often calls the great King Agamemnon) ought not only to know how to drive away the wolves —I mean, make war—but likewise understand how to manage his flock, preserve them from all diseases, and fatten and multiply them.

The peace being proclaimed, to the incredible joy of the French, Flemings, and Spaniards, it was solemnly sworn by the King on the 21st of June, in the church of Notre Dame, on the Cross and the holy Evangelists, in the presence of the Duke of Arscot and the Admiral of Arragon, ambassadors sent by the King of Spain for that purpose; and afterwards Cardinal Archduke Albert, governor of the Low Countries for that King, swore it on the 26th of the same month, in the city of Brussels, the Marshal de Biron assisting, whom our Henry had newly honoured with the dignity of duke and peer, confirmed in parliament, as much in order to bestow more splendour upon that embassy as to recompense those great services which that lord had rendered him in his wars.

In this voyage the Spaniards spared neither caresses nor praises of this new duke, to inspire him with pride and vanity, and intoxicated him to such an extent with a good opinion of himself, that he took it into his head that the King owed him more than he would ever be able to give him, and that if his valour were not sufficiently honoured in France, he would find someone elsewhere who would set a higher value upon it. This afterwards produced very ill effects.

Many among the French, who were unacquainted with the pitiful state of the King of Spain and of his affairs, could not comprehend why this prince had bought the peace at so dear a rate as the surrender of six or seven strong places, and amongst others, Calais and Blavet, which might be called the keys of France. On the contrary, the Spaniards, who saw that their King was dying, that his treasury was exhausted, the

Low Countries shattered to pieces, Portugal and his estates in Italy on the point of revolt, and his son, a good prince in reality, but who was fond of repose, were astonished that the French, having so bravely retaken Amiens, and reunited all their forces after the treaty with the Duke of Merceur, had not pressed farther into the Low Countries, seeing that in all appearance they might either have conquered them, or at least made breaches in them. The King answered that if he had desired peace, it was not because he was weary of the hardships of war, but to give leave to afflicted Christendom to breathe; that he knew well, from the position in which things were, that he might have derived great advantages, but that God often overturns princes in their greatest prosperity; and that a wise man ought never, out of the opinion of some favourable event, to be averse to a good accord, nor rely too much upon the appearance of his present happiness, which may change by a thousand unexpected accidents, it having often happened that a man who is thrown down and wounded has killed him who wanted to make him beg for his life.

It was known in a little time that King Philip II. had more need of the peace than France, for his sickness increased. He suffered, for twenty-two days continually, from a perpetual bloody flux: and a little before his death four abscesses formed in his breast, from which proceeded a continual swarm of vermin, which all the attention of his officers was unable to check.

In this strange sickness, his firmness was wonderful; nor did he abandon the reins of government until his last breath, for he took care before his death to arrange the marriage of his son with Margaret, daughter of the Archduke of Gratz; and also that of his dear daughter Isabella with the Cardinal Archduke Albert, of the same blood as herself, giving him for dowry the Low Countries and the county of Burgundy, on condition of its reversion if he died without issue.

He had already signed the articles of peace; but his mortal sickness would not permit him to take the oath to it with the same solemnities as the King and archduke had done. Philip III., his son and successor, acquitted himself of this obligation on the 21st of May, 1601, in the city of Valladolid, and in the presence of the Count of Rochepot, ambassador of France.

The license of wars having for many years permitted mischiefs with impunity, there were still to be found a great number of vagabonds, who believed it was still allowed them to take the goods of others at pleasure; and there were others who thought they had the right to do themselves justice by acts of violence, not acknowledging any laws but force. This obliged our wise King to begin the reformation of the state by the re-establishment of public security. To this effect he forbade the carrying of firearms to all persons of whatever position, upon pain of the confiscation of their arms and horses, and a fine of two hundred crowns for the first offence, and death for the second; permitting anyone to arrest those who carried them except his light-horsemen, his *gens d'armes*, and his bodyguards, who were allowed to bear them only when they were on service.

To the same purpose, and to ease the country of

the multitudes of the military, he dismissed not only the greater part of his new troops, but likewise reduced by half his old ones. He reduced the companies of orderlies to a very small number, and abolished the guards of the governors of the provinces and lieutenants of the King, being unwilling to suffer anyone besides himself to have that glorious mark of sovereignty about their persons.

The wars had spoiled all commerce, reduced cities to villages, villages to old ruins, and lands to deserts; nevertheless the tax-collectors constrained the poor husbandmen to pay taxes for those fruits they had never gathered. The cries of these miserable people, who had nothing but their tongues to complain with, touched to the quick so just and so good a King, that he made an edict by which he released them of all they owed him for the time past, and led them to expect he would ease them more for the future.

Moreover, having understood that during the troubles a large number of false nobles had been created, who were exempted from the tax,[1] he commanded that they should be sought out; nor did he confirm their usurpation for a money consideration, as has sometimes been done, to the great prejudice of other persons

---

[1] *Taille.* Besides the personal services which the *corvée* constituted, the serfs owed to their lord presents in money and in kind. The ancient name given to the pecuniary fine was that of *cens*. From the thirteenth century it was replaced by the word *taille*, which seems to have had for origin the custom that the collectors of the said tax had of marking upon a piece of wood the sum received. In many instances the extent of this charge on the serfs was in proportion to the good pleasure of his master. But in some instances the extent of the charge was regulated each year in advance, and was then called *taille abonné*.

liable to taxation, but he insisted that the tax should be reimposed upon them, to the end that by this means they might assist the poor people to bear a good part of the burden, as being the richer.

He desired with much affection to do good to his true nobility, and repay them those expenses they had been at in his service; but his coffers were empty, and moreover, all the gold in Peru would not have been sufficient to satisfy the appetite and luxury of so many people. For King Henry III. had by his own example and that of his favourites, raised expenses so high that lords wanted to live like princes, and gentlemen like lords, for which purposes they were forced to alienate the possessions of their ancestors, and change those old castles, the illustrious tokens of their nobility, into tinsel, gilding, retinue, and horses. Afterwards, when they were indebted beyond their credit, they fell back either upon the King's coffers, demanding pensions, or on the backs of the people, fleecing them by a thousand robberies. The King, wishing to remedy this disorder, declared very stoutly to his nobility that he desired them to accustom themselves to live every man on his means, and that, for this purpose, he would be well content, since they now enjoyed peace, that they should go and see their country houses and make their estates yield a good return. Thus he eased them of the great and ruinous expenses of the court, by sending them back into the provinces, and made them understand that the best capital they could have was that of good management. Moreover, knowing that the French nobility prides itself upon imitating the King in all things, he showed them by his own example how to do away with all superfluity of clothing, for he ordinarily wore a grey cloak with a doublet of satin or taffeta, without slashing, lace, or embroidery. He praised those who were clad in this manner, and laughed at the others, who carried, he said, their mills and their woods and forests on their backs.

About the end of the year he was seized with a sudden and violent sickness at Monceaux. All France was affrighted; his life was despaired of, and the rumours which spread nearly revived the factions; but in ten or twelve days he was on foot again, as if God had only sent him this sickness to reveal to him what evil intent there still was in the kingdom, and to give him the satisfaction of feeling, through the sorrow of his people, the pleasure of being loved.

At the height of his illness, he spoke to his friends these beautiful words: "I do not at all fear death, for I have faced it in the greatest dangers; but I avow that I am unwilling to leave this life until I have restored this kingdom to that state of splendour which I have proposed to myself, and until I have testified to my people, by governing them well and easing them of their many taxes, that I love them as if they were my children."

After his recovery, continuing in his praiseworthy design of putting his affairs in order, he came to St. Germain-en-Laye to settle the items of expenditure of his household, as well as for the guard of frontiers and garrisons, maintenance of forces, artillery, naval affairs, and many other charges. He had then in his council (as we may say we have at present) very great men, and most experienced in all sorts of matters; but he still showed himself more able and more enlightened than they. He examined and discussed all the particulars of his expenditure with a judgment and a clearness of spirit truly admirable, and he retrenched and cut off all that was possible, retaining only what was necessary. Amongst other things, he cut down the superfluous expenses of the tables in his house, not so much that he might spare himself, as to oblige his subjects to moderate their prodigality in eating and drinking, and to hinder them from ruining their whole houses by keeping too great kitchens. And thus, by the example of the King, which is always of more force than the laws or correction, luxury was soon converted into economy, very necessary for the state.

He had chosen for his council very able and faithful ministers, such as Chiverny, Bellièvre, Sillery, Sancy, Jeannin, Villeroy, and Rosny. I speak not here at all of his great military advisers, as the Marshal de Biron, Lesdiguières, governor of Dauphiné, the Duke of Mayenne, the Constable of Montmorency, the Marshal de la Chastre, the Marshal d'Aumont, Guitry, La Noue, and many others, of whose services he did not avail himself in the administration of state affairs, though he often conversed with them, and by way of compliment sometimes communicated to them things of consequence, asking their advice.

The Chancellor de Chiverny, who had been raised to this office in the reign of Henry III., was a man cold, deceitful, and calculating, but, as his enemies said, he was a much better practitioner than councillor of state.

He died the year following, and in his place the King appointed Pompone de Bellièvre, a man perfectly accomplished in the knowledge of the rights and interests of France, and a most expert negotiator, as he well showed in the treaty of Vervins. He was old when the King gave him this charge, and therefore said himself that he only entered upon it to go out of it. He induced the King to issue a severe edict against duels; he established very good order in the council, and ordained that none should be received as "master of requests"[1] who had not been ten whole years in one of the supreme companies, or sixteen in other of the subordinate seats.

Nicholas Brûlard de Sillery, president of the Cap in the parliament of Paris, who was his son-in-law, and who had been his companion at Vervins, was of a gentle, easy, and affable disposition, but one which saw further ahead than people believed. It has been said that the public never saw any emotion either in his countenance or discourse.

Harlay-Sancy was a man free, bold, and dauntless, who feared no person when it was a question of the service of the King; but he was rather abrupt, and spoke to him too freely, as may be seen by what he said concerning Madame Gabrielle, who knew how to return it to him.

As for Jeannin, president of the parliament of Burgundy, and Villeroy, chief secretary of state, they had both taken part with the League, and yet very

---

[1] *Maître des requêtes:* formerly a magistrate who reported on a man's petition before the King's Council; now one who draws reports before the Council of State on all state affairs.

profitably served both the King and France, having in what they did striven only for the defence of the Catholic religion, and not out of a spirit of faction. They had hindered the Spaniards from encroaching upon this realm, and the Duke of Mayenne from throwing himself completely into their arms, as his despair had often inclined him to do. They agreed both in this point, that they loved the state and royalty passionately and that they had great judgment, but, in other respects, their temperaments were very different.

Jeannin was an old Gaul, who desired to manage his affairs by ancient forms, according to the laws and ordinances ; a good lawyer, firm and resolute, who went directly towards his end, and who knew no subtle turnings and windings, but entirely loved the public good.

Villeroy was one of the wisest and most adroit courtiers that was ever seen. He had a clear and unprejudiced mind, which would unravel with an incredible facility the most embroiled affairs, and explain them agreeably and intelligibly, and directed them as he pleased. He was wonderfully active withal, and most excellent at finding expedients, taking his business by so sure a hold that it was difficult for it to escape him.

The King often conferred with these councillors, as they were still called, and not ministers, as they have been called since. He spoke to them of his affairs, sometimes to be instructed, and sometimes to instruct them, which he did either in his study, or walking in the gardens of the Tuileries, Monceaux, St. Germain, and Fontainebleau. He discoursed often with them apart, summoning them one after another; and he did this either to oblige them to speak to him with more liberty, or not to tell them all together what he only wished to tell to some particularly, or for some other reason which without doubt was due to good policy. He said that he found none amongst them who satisfied him like Villeroy, and that he could dispatch more business with him in an hour than with the others in a whole day.

As for Maximilian de Béthune, Baron of Rosny, and afterwards Duke of Sully, he had been brought up with the King in the Huguenot religion, and the King had recognised his capacity and affection in divers affairs of consequence, but above all, that he had a genius for the good management of finances, and that he had all the qualities requisite for that purpose. In fact, he was a man of good order, exact, a good manager, and a man who kept his word; neither prodigal nor ostentatious, nor inclined to vain follies or expenses, play, banquets, or any other vanity not becoming to a man entrusted with such an employment. Moreover, he was vigilant, laborious, expeditious, and one who dedicated almost his whole time to his affairs and little to his pleasure; and withal, he had the gift of piercing into the very bottom of matters, and unravelling those twistings and knots with which financiers, when they are not trusty and faithful, endeavour to conceal their deceits.

We have already told how the King desired above all things to provide for economy in the management of his revenues, and the reasons for which he had been obliged to leave Francis d'O in the position of superintendent. After this man was dead, he gave that office to five or six persons, whom he believed both capable and honest men; he was persuaded that he would be better served by them than by one alone, imagining that they would serve as checks and controllers of one another. But quite the contrary happened; everyone threw the blame upon his companion; nothing was advanced, and if any of them wanted to act, the others did not fail to cross him by their jealousies, so that they only agreed in this point, that everyone looked that his salary was well paid him, which cost the King six times as much as if he had had only one superintendent, whilst he drew no profit from this multitude.

When he discovered that so many people only confused his finances, he returned them again into the hands of one man, and this was Sancy. But a short time after, finding him more proper for other employments than that, he gave him Rosny for a companion, afterwards making Rosny alone superintendent.

Rosny, before he entered upon this office, had provided himself with all the knowledge necessary to acquit himself well of it; he knew perfectly all the revenues of the kingdom, and all the expenses which were necessary. He communicated all he knew to the King, who on his part had likewise studied all these things so thoroughly, that a hundred crowns could not be laid out but he would know whether it were well or ill employed. As it is to the advantage of an unfaithful steward that his master should be ignorant and make no inspection into his affairs, so it is of a true and faithful servant that he should be well instructed, and clearly see them, in order that he may know how worthily to esteem his services.

Besides, his temperament agreed perfectly well with that of the King. When he trusted him with his revenues, he desired him that he would never take even a bottle of wine or the smallest present without telling him. And when Rosny did tell him of it, he immediately consented to it, and likewise was so glad that, in serving him well, he found his reward, that oftentimes he added gifts of his own, to give him courage to serve him still better and better. But Rosny never received them till they were duly ratified in the chamber of accounts, so that all the world might know the liberality of the King towards him, and that he might not be reproached with making use of his favour to drain his coffers.

Under the administration of this superintendent, the first law which the King made concerning affairs of this nature was the immutable constancy of their ordering, which was never to alter, after it was once agreed and concluded on; for as the most desperate things are by good order redressed by a firm and decided manner of action, so the best established and most assured become dispersed under a light head, which does, undoes, and does again without ceasing, and which on the morrow revokes what it commanded to-day.

Rosny soon gave indubitable proofs of his capacity, for having visited only four generalities,[1] he in a short

[1] A general place for receipt of revenues, of which there are twenty in France, viz.: Paris, Rouen, Caen, Nantes, Tours, Bruges, Poitiers, Agen, Toulouse, Montpellier, Aix, Grenoble, Lyons, Dijon, Chalons, Amiens, Orleans, Limoges, Soissons, and Moulins.—Translator's Note.

time got in a million and half of money which was in arrear; and after the capture of Amiens by the Spaniards he readily found money to raise a great army and furnish the expense of the siege, so that he was one of the principal instruments in the recovery of that great city.

It is well to take notice of an expedient which, amongst others, he discovered to hinder the pilferings of the tax-gatherers, for that is necessary at all times. He knew that there were some persons in the King's council who were in collusion with the *traitants*[1] and farmers, and who caused the farms and duties to be adjudged to the council at a low price, and often caused them to be given to them at a great reduction. To hinder, therefore, these people from eating the cake amongst them, he stopped the hands of the general farmers, forbidding the under-farmers to pay them anything, but themselves to bring the money of their under-farms into the exchequer. He doubled by this means the revenues of the King, for the under-farms and under-rents were found to be greater by almost two-thirds than the general rents and leases.

The members of the council and the collectors at first exclaimed loudly against his conduct; they laid snares everywhere for him, and caused him a thousand troubles; but in time he brought them to reason. Likewise all those who had no right to demand anything of him, and who ceased not to importune him when they could get nothing from him, stormed against his hardness; but he cared not for their idle

[1] The farmers of certain branches of the revenue under the old French monarchy.

wrath; he only wished legally to pay the debts of the King, and readily to pay what was ordained for good ends, for he did not know what it was to be asked a hundred times for that which was truly due.

We have lingered somewhat the longer on this point of the revenues, because it is the most important of all; that by which all things are done, and without which nothing can be done, on which depends either the ease or the oppression of the people and the good or ill success of all designs or enterprises.

Our Henry at the same time would have liked to take care for the reformation of the clergy, which in truth was in great disorder, as well in temporal matters —its goods having been usurped during the wars by the Huguenots and wicked Catholics—as in spiritual, the greater part of both prelates and pastors being as ignorant as depraved; but he could not yet apply suitable remedies. The necessity to which he was driven, of recompensing those who had well served him, constrained him to tolerate abuses, and even to commit them, disposing of benefices as formerly Charles Martel had done; for he gave them to unfit persons, to married men, to soldiers, to children, and even to women, to compensate them for the loss of their husbands killed or ruined in his service.

I have not attempted to excuse this fault; for there can never be any lawful reason given for the prostitution of the goods of the sanctuary to the use of the profane, or employing the treasures of the Cross in other services than that of the altar. I know well that many ecclesiastics themselves act otherwise, but who doubts these people to be worse than those Jews who played at dice upon the holy robe of Jesus Christ?

About the end of this year, the general assembly of the clergy was held at Paris, and it drew up a remonstrance to the King, by which the prelates prayed him to cause the Council of Trent to be published in France; not to charge his conscience with the nomination to bishoprics, abbacies, and other benefices having the charge of souls; not to give any laymen the right to draw upon benefices; not to permit churches and holy places to be profaned as they then were, but to see that they were repaired and Divine service re-established.

As regards the Council of Trent, it must be understood that it was received in France as affects those Articles concerning the faith, but not generally as to those which concerned policy and discipline, because it seemed to many that these last were for the most part contrary to the liberty of the Gallican Church and the rights of the King. For which reasons, whatever endeavours the zealous have made, they could never bring about its reception, the parliaments having always strongly opposed it.

To the harangue of the clergy, the King eloquently answered, but in few words, that he acknowledged what they had said concerning the nomination of benefices was true, but that he was not the author of that abuse. That having come to the crown during the flames of a civil war, he had run wherever he beheld the greatest fire to extinguish it. That, now that he had peace, he would endeavour again to raise up those two pillars of France, to wit, piety and justice. That, God willing, he would restore the Church to as good an estate as it was in the time of Louis XII.

"But," said he, "contribute, I pray you, on your side; let your good examples as much incite the people to do good as they have been heretofore diverted. You have exhorted me to my duty, and I exhort you to yours; let us emulate one another in this. My predecessors have given you fair words, but I with my grey jacket will give you good deeds. I am all grey without, but you shall find me gold within. I will see your note-books (*cahiers*) and answer them as favourably as I possibly can."

All his prudence and all his address were not too much to teach him to govern himself so that both the Catholics and Pope might be content with his conduct, and the Huguenots have no cause to be alarmed or form themselves into cantons. His duty and his conscience inclined him to the assistance of the first; but reasons of state, and the great obligations he had to the last did not permit him to make them despair. To keep, therefore, a necessary balance, he granted them an edict more ample than the preceding one. It was called "The Edict of Nantes," because it was concluded the year before (April 13th, 1598) in that city whilst he was there. By this he granted them all liberty for the exercise of their religion and likewise liberty to be admitted to charges, hospitals, and colleges, and to have schools in certain places, and the right of preaching everywhere; and many other things, of which they were afterwards deprived by reason of their rebellions and other misdeeds.

The parliament strongly opposed it for more than a year; but in the end, when they were made to understand that not to accord security to the Huguenots, who were both powerful and quarrelsome, would be to kindle war afresh in the kingdom, they confirmed it.

On the other hand, to quiet the Pope, who might be annoyed at this edict, the King showed him all possible manner of respect, and strenuously embraced his interests, as appeared in the affair of Ferrara, in the years 1597 and 1598.

This duchy is a fief male of the holy see, with which the Popes had formerly invested the lords of the house of Est, with provision for its reversion in default of legitimate male issue. Alphonso d'Est, second of that name, and last duke, died in the year 1597, without children, and had left great treasures to Cæsar d'Est, bastard of the first Alphonso, his kinsman. He had done all he possibly could to obtain the investiture of the duchy on this bastard, who, although not able to obtain it, nevertheless took possession of it after the death of the second Alphonso, resolving to maintain it by force of arms. Clement VIII. was obliged to make war against him to dispossess him. The princes of Italy took part in the quarrel, and the Dukes of Guise and Nemours were upon the point of undertaking the defence of Cæsar, whose near kinsmen they were, being the sons of Anne d'Est, daughter of Hercules II., Duke of Ferrara, and Madame Renée de France, Anne in her first marriage having espoused Francis, Duke of Guise, and, in her second, James, Duke of Nemours. The King of Spain likewise secretly favoured Cæsar, not desiring that the Pope should grow greater in Italy by reacquiring that duchy. But Henry the Great was not backward in taking this occasion to offer his sword and his forces to the Holy Father. The allies knowing this were extremely disheartened, and Cæsar was constrained to come to a compromise with the Pope, to whom he surrendered all the Duchy of Ferrara. There remained to him only the cities of Modena and Reggia, which the Emperor maintained to be fief of the Empire, and of which he gave him the investiture, from whence come the present Dukes of Modena.

If the fervour which the King testified on this occasion for the interests of the holy see sensibly obliged the Pope, the care which he daily took to bring back the Huguenots into the bosom of the Church was no less agreeable to him. He acted to this purpose in such a manner that, from day to day, many of the greatest understanding and the best quality were converted. But what was more important was his taking the young Prince of Condé from the hands of the Huguenots, who had kept him diligently at St. Jean d'Angely ever since the death of his father, which happened in the year 1587, and brought him up in the false religion, with great hope of making him one day their chief and protector. The King, considering that it would be both prejudicial to the safety of the young prince and to his own interests to leave him longer there, knew so well how to gain the chief men of the party that they suffered him to be brought to court; and he gave him as tutor John, Marquis of Pisani, a lord of rare merit and of wisdom without reproach, who forgot not to instruct him well in the Catholic religion and in the truest sentiments of honour and virtue. He was then but seven or eight years old. When he reached his ninth year the King gave him the government of Guienne, loving him tenderly and cherishing him as his presumptive successor.

During this time of peace nothing was spoken of but rejoicings, feasts, and marriages. That of the Infanta of Spain, Isabella Clara Eugenia, and of the Archduke Albert, was solemnised in the Low Countries, and that of Madame Catherine, sister of the King, with Henry, Duke of Bar, eldest son of Charles II., Duke of Lorraine, at Paris.

Catherine was forty years of age, and more agreeable than fair, having one leg a little short. She was very clever, loved learning, and knew much for a woman, but was an obstinate Huguenot. The King feared lest she should marry some Protestant prince, who by this means might become the protector of the Huguenots, and be like another king in France. For this reason he gave her to the Duke of Bar; thinking, moreover, to gain more credit among the Catholics by allying himself with the house of Lorraine. Before this he had used all possible means to convert her, even to the employment of threats; but not being able to succeed, he said one day to the Duke of Bar, " My brother, it is you who must vanquish her."

There was some difficulty about the place and the ceremony of celebration of this marriage; the duke wanted it performed at the church, and the princess by a Huguenot minister. The King found a middle course. He caused it to take place in his closet, whither he led his sister by the hand, and commanded his natural brother, who had for about two years been Archbishop of Rouen, to marry them. This new archbishop at first refused to perform the ceremony, alleging the canons were against it, but the King representing to him that his closet was a consecrated place, and that his presence supplied the want of all solemnities, the poor archbishop had no longer the power to resist him.

This marriage being made for the good of the Catholic religion, it seemed that the Pope should have been content. Nevertheless, not willing to suffer an ill that a good might come of it, he declared that the Duke of Bar had incurred excommunication for having without the dispensation of the Church contracted a marriage with a heretic; nor could the duke, whatever entreaties he made, obtain absolution. It was necessary for God to lend His hand. This princess died three years after with sadness and melancholy at seeing herself live in a discontented manner with her husband, who daily pressed her to turn Catholic.

Besides the solemnities of these marriages, many other things engaged the attention of the court. Two notable changes — one of the Duke of Joyeuse, the other of the Marchioness of Belleisle — caused it astonishment.

The Duke of Joyeuse, who had quitted the habit of capuchin to become chief of the League in Languedoc, one day, without saying anything to anybody, retired to his convent at Paris, and resumed the habit. A few days after there was much astonishment at seeing him whom they had seen the week before dancing at balls, as one of the most gallant, preach in the pulpit in that habit of penitence. It was said that the holy exhortations of his mother, who from time to time reminded him of his vow, and some ambiguous words which the King had thrown out in conversation with him, made him think that he could no longer live in the world either with safety of conscience or with honour.

The Marchioness of Belleisle, sister to the Duke of Longueville, and widow of the Marquis of Belleisle, eldest son of the Marshal de Retz, having received some secret annoyance, renounced likewise the world, and went and shut herself up in the convent of the Feuillantines at Toulouse, where she took the veil and ended her days.

After this news came to the court that Phillipin, bastard of the Duke of Savoy, was killed in a duel by the Seigneur de Créquy, of whom it might be without flattery said that he was one of the most gallant and bravest men of his time. The history of this combat may be found written in so many places, and is yet so firm in the memory of all those who wear swords, that it would be superfluous to recount the details.

The chase was now the King's ordinary diversion. It is recounted that while hunting in the forest of Fontainebleau, accompanied by many lords, he heard a great noise of horns, huntsmen, and dogs, which seemed to be a long way off, but all at once approached them. Some of his company who were twenty paces in front of him saw a great black man among the bushes, who alarmed them so much that they could not tell what became of him; but they heard him cry out to them with a frightful voice, "M'attendez-vous," or, "m'entendez-vous," or, "amendez-vous"; that is, "Do you expect me?" or "Do you understand me?" or else, "Amend yourselves." The woodmen and country people thereabouts said that it was no extraordinary thing, for they had often seen this black man, whom they named the "Great Hunter," with a pack of hounds which hunted at full cry, but never did any harm.

Numberless accounts are told in all countries in the world of like illusions in regard to such hunters. If we give any credit to them, we may believe them either to be the tricks of sorcerers, or of some evil spirits to whom God gives permission to convince the incredulous, and make them see that there are substances apart from and a Being above man.

Now if prodigies are signs, as some have said, of great and awful events, it may be believed that this presaged the strange death of the fair Gabrielle, which happened some days after (April, 1599). The love which the King had for her, instead of being extinguished by enjoyment, had become so strong that she had ventured to demand of him that he should acknowledge his fault and legitimatise his children by a subsequent marriage; and he was not able absolutely to refuse her this grace, but entertained her still with hopes.

Those who love the glory of this great King can with difficulty believe that he would have done such an action, which without doubt would have caused a low opinion of him, and levelled against him his people's hatred. However, it was to be feared that the allurements of this woman, who had found his weakness, added to the flattery of the courtiers whom she had almost all gained either by presents or kindnesses, might engage this poor prince to a dishonour. And without dissembling, he had his soul too tender towards ladies. He was master of all his other passions, but he was a slave to this; nor can his memory be justified from this reproach, for although admirable in all other parts of his life, he ought not to be imitated in this.

In the meantime Gabrielle, still flattering herself with the hope of shortly becoming his wife, in consequence of those hopes he himself had given her, managed so well that she obliged him to demand of the Pope commissioners to try the divorce between him and Queen Margaret. The King, in order that he might find favour with the Holy Father, and render him more favourable to his intentions, caused it to be said secretly, by Sillery, his ambassador, that he would marry Marie de Medicis, his niece, sister to the Duke of Florence, for whom nevertheless it was believed that he had not then any desire.

And the Pope, whether he distrusted his intention, or whether he saw that Queen Margaret did not encourage it, protracted the business, and returned only ambiguous answers. It was likewise said that being one day much pressed by the Cardinal d'Ossat and by Sillery to give consent to their master, or else, they said, he may go further, and espouse the duchess, he was so astonished at these words that he immediately remitted the conduct of this affair to the hands of God, and commanded a fast throughout the city of Rome, while he himself prayed asking God to inspire him with what should be best for his glory and for the good of France; that at the end of his prayer he cried out in ecstasy, "God hath provided!" and that a few days after there arrived a courier at Rome, bringing news of the death of the duchess.

In the meantime the King grew impatient at these

delays; and it was to be feared lest resentment at being neglected should cause the same inconveniences to him as formerly to Henry VIII., King of England, or lest by the counsel of some flatterers, forcing the goodness of his nature, he should be persuaded to rid himself of Queen Margaret by whatever means he could.

Gabrielle was at that time great with her fourth child, when the feast of Easter approaching, and the King desiring to perform his devotions for that holy season far from all object of scandal, he sent her to Paris, accompanying her just half-way. She with no small grief parted from him, recommending to him her children with tears in her eyes, as if she had some secret presentiment, telling him that she should never see him again.

At Paris she lodged in the house of Zamet, the famous treasurer. After having dined with him, and heard *Ténèbres*[1] at St. Anthony's (being Holy Thursday), on her return, while walking in the garden, she was struck with apoplexy of the brain. The first attack of it having passed, she would no longer stay in that house, but caused herself to be carried to that of Madame de Sourdis, her aunt, near St. Germain l'Auxerrois. All the rest of that day and the morrow she suffered from swoonings and convulsions, of which she died on the Saturday morning.

The causes of her death were variously related; but, however, it was a happiness to France, since it deprived the King of an object for which he was about to lose both himself and his estate. His grief was as

---

[1] A service in the Roman Church used three days before Easter, and called *les trois jours de ténèbres*.

great as his love had been; yet he, not being one of those feeble souls who please themselves in perpetuating their sorrows and in bathing themselves in their tears, not only received consolation, but sought it, although still preserving for the children, and particularly for the Duke of Vendôme, that affection he had borne the mother.

All good Frenchmen earnestly desired that so good a king might leave legitimate children. They dared not press him to take a wife who would bear him children so long as Gabrielle lived, for fear lest he should espouse her, and for the same reason Queen Margaret would not give her consent to the dissolution of his marriage. But when Gabrielle was dead she willingly lent her hand to it, and herself addressed a request to the Holy Father to demand the dissolution, adducing two principal reasons for nullity. The first was the want of consent, for she alleged she had been forced to it by King Charles IX., her brother; the second was the proximity of kindred (they being related in the third degree), for which, she said, there had never been any valid dispensation.

In like manner the lords of the kingdom and the parliament besought his Majesty by solemn deputations that he would think of taking a wife, representing to him the inconveniences and the danger in which France would be if he should die without children. These deputations will not seem strange to those who know our ancient history, where it may be seen that neither the king nor his children married except by the advice of his barons, and this passed at that time almost for a fundamental law of the state.

The King, touched with these just supplications of his subjects, addressed his request to the Pope, containing the same reasons as that of Queen Margaret, and charged the Cardinal d'Ossat and Sillery, his ambassador extraordinary, whom he had sent to Rome to obtain the judgment of the Pope concerning the restitution of the marquisate of Saluces, to push on this affair instantly.

The cause having been reported to the consistory, the Pope gave commission to the prelates to judge it in France, according to the rights of that crown, which does not permit Frenchmen to be transported for such affairs beyond the mountains, whither it would be almost impossible to bring the necessary proofs and witnesses. These prelates were the Cardinal de Joyeuse, the Pope's nuncio, and the Archbishop of Arles, who, having examined both parties and seen the proofs produced on each side, together with the request of the three estates of the kingdom, declared this marriage null, and permitted them to marry whom they should think fit.

Queen Margaret, who for many years had left the King and voluntarily shut herself up in the strong castle of Usson, in Auvergne, had now permission to come to Paris, money given her to pay her debts, great pensions, the possession of the Duchy of Valois, with some other lands, and the right to retain the title of Queen. She lived for fifteen years longer, and built a palace near Pré-aux-Clercs, which was afterwards sold to pay off her debts and pulled down to build other houses. She was very fond of good musicians, having a delicate ear, and also of wise and eloquent men, because she was of a fine intellect and very agreeable in her discourse. For the rest, she was liberal even to prodigality, pompous and magnificent, but she did not know what it was to pay her debts. This is without doubt the greatest of all a prince's faults, because there is nothing so much against justice, of which he ought to be the protector and example.

The marriage being dissolved, Bellièvre and Villeroy (fearing lest the King should engage himself in new loves and be taken in those snares which the fairest of the court laid for him) persuaded him by many great reasons of state to fix his thoughts on Marie de Medicis, who was daughter to Francis and niece to Ferdinand, Grand Dukes of Tuscany.

The Cardinal d'Ossat and Sillery made known his intention to the Grand Duke Ferdinand, her uncle; and Alincourt, son to Villeroy, whom he had sent to thank the Holy Father for his speedy justice touching the aforesaid dissolution of his marriage, had orders to testify to him that the King, among all the daughters of the sovereign houses of Christendom, had found no princess more agreeable to him. The business was managed with so much activity and vigilance by the diligence of those who had undertaken it, that the King found himself finally engaged. The contract of marriage was signed at Florence by his ambassadors on the 4th of April, 1600, and Alincourt in seven days brought him the news to Fontainebleau. He was at that time assisting at the famous conference or dispute between David du Perron, Bishop of Evreux, afterwards Cardinal, and Philip du Plessis Mornay, at which truth nobly triumphed over falsehood.

The solemnities at Florence, the magnificence of the Grand Duke, the ceremonies of the affiancing and marriage of this Queen, of her embarking, her being convoyed by the galleys of Malta and Florence, and her reception at Marseilles, at Avignon, and at Lyons, have all been related elsewhere, and therefore I shall speak nothing of them.

Whilst the marriage was being arranged at Florence, the King, having a heart which could for no long time keep its liberty, became enslaved to a new object.

It is to be understood that Mary Touchet, who had been mistress to Charles IX., and whose son was the Count of Auvergne, had been married to the Lord d'Entragues, and had by him many children, amongst them a very fair daughter named Henriette, who was consequently sister on the mother's side to the Count of Auvergne. This Count was then about thirty years old, and she about eighteen.

It is but too well known that flatterers and cowardly sycophants ruin everyone in the courts of great men, and also corrupt their persons. It is these who sweeten the poison, who embolden the prince to do ill, who make him familiar with vice, who seek and facilitate occasions for it, and who act, as we may say, the part of Satan and the tempter. It is impossible to purge courts of these plagues; they insinuate themselves, in spite of the utmost endeavours, into the palaces of the great; they render themselves agreeable by new diversions, gain the ear by flattering praises, by pleasant and well-devised fables and great falsehoods; and when they have gained their entrance they envenom the hearts and poison the souls of the most innocent.

Our Henry, great prince as he was, had such people near him, who knowing his weakness as to women, instead of fortifying him against it and restraining him like true friends, spurred him forward as it were in his weakness, and made their fortunes from his faults. It was these who, by commending the beauty, the engaging ways, the wit, and the diverting and pleasant discourse of Mademoiselle d'Entragues, made him first have a desire to see and to love her. They could not have done a worse service to their master than this. She had certainly many charms, but she was no less clever and cunning. Her refusals and modesty did more and more provoke the King's passion. Though he was not prodigal, he caused a hundred thousand crowns to be taken to her at once. She refused them not, and reciprocally testified much love and impatience for so great a king; but she cunningly caused her father and mother to get in the way, and observe her so closely that she could not give him a good opportunity to speak to her.

She let him understand that she was grieved that she could not keep her word with him; that it was necessary to have the consent of her father and mother, for which on her part she would labour. Afterwards, after many delays and procrastinations, she told him that they could not be brought to so delicate a point, unless, if only to secure their consciences towards God and their honour towards the world, his Majesty would make her a promise of marriage; that she had no desire to use the document to his prejudice, and that if she did so, she knew well there was no official who durst challenge a man who had fifty thousand men of war at his command; but that these good people desired it should be so, and that he need make no difficulty to please their fancy, since he would be giving her but a little bit of paper in exchange for the most precious thing she had in the world. At last, she managed to work upon his mind so cleverly that he gave her a promise under his hand by which he agreed to espouse her in a year, provided that during that time she brought forth a male child.

All this intrigue may be seen in the memoirs of Sully, where he says that the King having led him alone into the first gallery of Fontainebleau, showed him this promise written under his hand, and demanded his advice. Instead of formally answering him concerning it, he tore it in two pieces. The King was quite astonished, and said angrily, "How! now I believe that you are a fool"; to which the other answered, "It is true, Sire, that I am a fool, and could wish I were more so, so that I alone in France were one." He also says that on his departure from the gallery, the King entered his closet and called for a pen and ink, and that he believed it was to write another. However this be, this promise caused much trouble afterwards, for the lady wished it to be made valid, as we shall relate.

At the same time that the King was endeavouring to obtain the dissolution of his first marriage at Rome, he also requested the Holy Father to decide the difference concerning the restitution of the marquisate of Saluces, the decision of which had been referred to him by the treaty of Vervins.

To understand this well, it must be known that this marquisate was a fief dependent upon the Dauphinate, which King Francis I. had seized by right of reversion, in default of heirs male in the succession of the lords that held it. Now, in 1588, during the assize of the estates of Blois, the Duke of Savoy, understanding that the League was becoming very strong in France, and that apparently that monarchy would be dismembered, snatched this marquisate without having any subject of quarrel; he only pretended to justify this unjust usurpation with the pretext that he seized it from fear lest Lesdiguières should possess himself of it, and by this means establish the Huguenot religion in the midst of his territories.

Seven years after, to wit, in the year 1595, when the King had gone to Lyons, after the battle of Fontaine-Française, the duke, who foresaw that the King would again take possession of this marquisate, proposed to him some arrangement concerning it. The King offered to give it to one of his sons, to hold it in faith and homage, with some other conditions, but the duke demanded it without any dependence, and so this negotiation was broken off.

The King's ambassadors treating on the general peace at Vervins urgently demanded the restitution of that fief. Those of the duke, who were present, alleged in favour of their master that the marquisate appertained to him as being a fief of Savoy, and that he had several essential titles to prove its dependency, which it was necessary to see in order to decide the difference with knowledge of the facts. Now it would have taken up too much time to have them sent from Savoy, and the

Pope's nuncio hurried on the peace, for fear lest during these delays some accident might happen to break it; so that, in order not to retard it, it was judged convenient to refer to the Pope the decision of this affair, on condition that he should terminate it in a year.

The French during that time earnestly solicited at Rome to have it decided. The Savoyards objected only through fear of losing their cause by default. Both sides produced their titles. Those of the French were the best, and, moreover, they had had peaceable possession for more than sixty years, which was more than sufficient to gain prescription. The year being expired, the Pope demanded of the King a further prolongation of two months to give in his sentence of arbitration, and that in the meantime the marquisate should be sequestrated in his hands. The King willingly consented, but the duke mistrusted that the Pope wanted to keep it for one of his nephews; and his ambassador having testified this mistrust, the Pope refused to meddle any further either with the gage or with the arbitration.

The duke imagined that his best way was to use delay, since it might happen that either the French King would grow weary of pursuing this business, or that some more important affair might divert his thoughts into another channel. Moreover, knowing that there were many disaffected persons who could not be cured of the opinion that the King was still in his heart a Huguenot, and among them many secret and dangerous enemies, so that no year passed without many conspiracies against his person, it was possible that in the end some of them might succeed. In fact, during that year there had been three discovered, of which the one that made most noise was that of a woman, who volunteered to the Count of Soissons to poison the King; but the count brought her to justice, and she was burned alive in the Grève.

In order, therefore, to gain time, he desired to come to France himself, having so good an opinion of his own cunning that he felt assured that he would obtain from the King the gift of this marquisate; or at least he intended to make such proposals, and to employ so many artifices that it would take more than a year to put them straight. He said that his ambassador had sent him word that he had heard the King say that if they were together they would soon decide this difference like friends, and it was this good word which had caused him to make this voyage. But many suspected, and with apparent reason, that he had a design to win over some of the King's council, to sound the disaffected and observe and awake discontent, to cast abroad seeds of corruption and division, and to renew such intrigues as he might have at court. Others imagined that he was discontented with Spain, because Philip II., having given the Low Countries as a dowry to his youngest daughter, had left to the eldest, wife of this duke, only a crucifix and an image of Our Lady. Moreover, he had indeed received some causes for displeasure at the hands of the ministers of Spain; and he spread abroad a report, whether it were true or false, that he had undertaken this voyage without communicating with Philip III., his brother-in-law. In fact, everyone judged according to his fancy; and possibly none divined his secret thoughts, there never having been a prince more close or less penetrable than he. And some said his heart was covered with mountains as well as his country, that is because he was hunchbacked and Savoy was mountainous.

He brought with him a train which well set forth his degree, for he had with him twelve hundred horse; but all his officers were clad in mourning, on account of the death of his wife, which many took as a bad omen. The King desiring to receive him according to his dignity, commanded all the cities to render him the same honour as if he were there in person.

He came to Lyons by the river Rhône, and was received by La Guiche, governor of that city. But the chapter of St. John would not give him the place of canon and count of that church, because he no longer possessed the county of Villars, by virtue of which the counts of Savoy had been at other times received. Added to this, he had not his titles, nor would he give time to prove his nobility, with which the chapter will not dispense in the case of anyone except the King.

From Lyons he came to Roanne, and descended by water to Orleans, afterwards coming post to Fontainebleau, where the King was. He arrived on the 20th of December, accompanied by seventy horse. To acquire confidence with the King, he complained loudly against the Spaniards, and disclosed, or feigned to disclose to him, his most secret thoughts, and a design he had to drive them out of Italy. He told him his friends, his means, and his information with regard to it, and he tried to make him believe that he was opening his heart to him; that he was an earnest

Frenchman, and desired to consult the interests of France without reserve. The King listened to him with attention, and thanked him for his good intentions; but after saying that, he finished thus: "I am of opinion that we should decide first those affairs between us, and then talk of others." Three days after, the King went to Paris, where they were to discuss more fully the subject which had brought the duke to France.

The beginning of the last year of the fifteenth century, that is, the year 1600, was celebrated for the centenary jubilee, which was opened at Rome. There were twenty-four thousand French at Rome, some moved by devotion, others by curiosity, among whom were a large number of Huguenots, who went to see the great ceremony. They were able to do it with all security, for during the great jubilee the Inquisition ceased at Rome, where at any time it was much less rigorous than in Spain. The Duke of Bar was in disguise at this jubilee. He went to demand license for his marriage, and absolution of the Holy Father. He obtained absolution in the manner related by Cardinal d'Ossat in his letters; but in spite of his submission he could not obtain the license, nor did he procure it till the death of Madame Catherine, his wife, three years later.

The beginning of this year saw the King and the Duke of Savoy live with so much familiarity, and so many proofs of friendship, that it might have been believed they had but one heart. The French courtesy and civility obliged the King to treat the duke with great honour, and the desire which the duke had of

obtaining from him the marquisate moved him to a
great complacency, and to seek all means to render
himself agreeable to so great a King. The court of
France declared that it had never seen a more perfect
courtier, the ladies a more pleasing gallant, and the
officers of the King and the great ones a prince more
liberal. He knew how to behave himself with the
King, so as neither to act as his companion nor his
servant; and if he wished to appear inferior to him
in grandeur, he endeavoured to be superior to him in
generosity and liberality. He gave with open hand,
even to the principal men of the court. The King
permitted them to accept his presents, and on his
side gave very large ones to the duke. He treated
him well, and made the chiefs of the court treat him
well also, every day providing him with some new
object of pleasure. Among other things, he desired
that he should see his parliament, which our kings
have usually shown to strange princes as a compendium of their greatness and the place where their
majesty sits with the greatest splendour. They went
together into the lantern[1] of the great chamber, where
they with great delight heard a very singular cause
pleaded, specially chosen, and the sentence or agreement pronounced by Harlay, first president, a person
so grave and so eloquent that all which came from
his mouth seemed to come from that of Justice herself.

There was no civility nor courtesy which the King
failed to show to the duke; but after all he would not
give way in regard to the marquisate. The duke tried

[1] A place which looked into the parliament-house, and I
suppose so called because they might see and not be seen.—
TRANSLATOR'S NOTE.

to gain his end by all means in his power; sometimes he offered to hold it in homage from the crown; sometimes he proposed that the King should share his great designs on the Milanese and on the Empire; sometimes he set before him the programme of a powerful league to destroy the Spaniards in Italy. But the King was too wise to be gulled by gilded shadows;[1] he answered that he had no ambition to conquer the possessions of another, but only to recover his own; that he would speak no further of this affair to the duke, as he considered they should refer it to their council. Therefore they named some representatives, who conferred together; but as those of the King insisted on the restitution of the marquisate, while those of the duke endeavoured to keep it for him, nothing was concluded.

Yet though all the duke's hopes of obtaining anything had vanished, he did not lose courage, but trusted to the intrigues he had renewed with some of the great ones of the court, and particularly with the Duke of Biron. Many believe that he began now to corrupt him, and that he entrusted this business to a gentleman of Burgundy, named Laffin, of the house of Beauvais la Nocle, the most pernicious and traitorous fellow that could be found in France, for he made a trade of carrying tales from one to another. The King knew him well, and often seeing him very familiar with Biron, he had the goodness to tell the marshal more than once, "Let not that man approach you; he is a plague, and he will ruin you."

[1] The French is, " Prendre le change," which is taken for flying out at a wrong deer like hounds of riot.

The duke knew that Biron loved the King, because he had raised him to the greatest dignities of his realm, and that the prince likewise honoured him with his good-will. It was therefore necessary to cause him to lose this affection before he would be able to render him capable of any evil design.

Biron was without doubt brave and valiant to the utmost, but so puffed up with his gallantry, that he could not suffer anybody to equal him. After the peace of Vervins, not having anything more to do, he continually boasted of his great deeds. According to his own words he had done everything, and he intoxicated himself so much with his own praise that he raised his own valour above the King's. He believed that Henry owed his crown to him, and so could refuse him nothing, and should be governed by him absolutely. These bravadoes displeased the King. He was annoyed that his subject should think that he equalled him in valour, but much more that he should have the presumption to hope to govern him, who had ten times more brains and good judgment than the marshal.

It is certainly a noble ambition, and not only well placed, but absolutely necessary for a king, to believe none of his subjects more worthy than himself. When he has not this good opinion of himself, he lets himself be governed by those whom he believes more able than himself, and by this means soon falls into captivity; therefore, though he may be deceived, he ought still to esteem himself the most capable person to govern in his whole realm. I may say rather that he cannot deceive himself in this, because there is no person more proper than himself, however ignorant he be, to rule his kingdom, God having destined this function to him, and not to others, and the people being always disposed to receive commands when they come out of his sacred mouth.

Henry the Great had therefore become greatly annoyed with the Marshal de Biron because of his vanity. The Duke of Savoy, praising one day the noble actions and great services of the Marshals de Biron, both father and son, the King answered that it was true they had served him well, but that he had had great difficulty to moderate the drunkenness of the father and the extraordinary whims of the son. The duke remembered his words, and caused them to be carried by Laffin to Biron, who, touched in his most sensitive part, was transported to a thousand extravagances; and having lost all respect, lost likewise his affection for the King. It has been suspected that he at once abandoned himself to all manner of wicked designs, and that he promised to enter into a league which the Duke of Savoy was about to make with the King of Spain, on condition that he gave him his daughter in marriage, and assisted him to make himself Duke of Burgundy.

After the Duke of Savoy had remained more than two months at the court of France, showing, as the proverb says, "A merry countenance at an ill game,"[1] and hiding his annoyance under an apparent joy, but not knowing how to return without shame nor to stay longer with advantage, the King, who did not wish to give him cause to say that he had treated him harshly, gave him to understand that if the marquisate was

[1] I.e., concealing his dissatisfaction.

so necessary to him, and that he could not restore it without great inconvenience, he would be content to take La Bresse in exchange. This condition seemed no less hard to the duke than that of the restitution of the marquisate. However, in order that he might have some pretext to retire with honour, he seemed not averse to it, and there were some articles drawn up which he professed were not disagreeable to him; but he demanded time to consider the alternative of the restitution or exchange, and to take the advice of the grandees of his duchy on so important a subject. The King, therefore, granted him for this purpose three clear months.

Shortly afterwards he took leave of the King, who conducted him to Pont Charenton, and instructed the Baron of Lux and Praslin to accompany him to the frontier. He returned by Champagne and Burgundy, from whence he entered La Bresse, and went to Bourg. They were very pleased to see him return safely, because they feared that he might be detained in France. Indeed there were some who counselled the King to keep him till such time as he should restore the marquisate; but the King, much offended at this proposition, answered angrily that they studied to dishonour him, but that he would rather lose his crown than incur the least suspicion of having broken his faith, even to the greatest of his enemies.

The three months being expired, and the duke not having fulfilled his promise, the King was annoyed, and pressed him to decide at once which course he would pursue. The duke found new delays, but promised daily to satisfy the King. In the meantime he communicated to the council of Spain the danger in which he was, pointing out that the loss of the marquisate would put him in such a position that he would not have the power to serve the Spaniards; that it would open the door to the French to trouble Italy; and that this tempest, after having laid waste his country, would fall upon Milan. The council of Spain apprehended well the urgency of the question, but, proceeding very slowly, were a long time before they decided to take action. At last the Count of Fuentes, governor of Milan, received instructions, two months later than he ought to have, to vigorously assist this prince. He therefore came to Milan, where, with two millions of gold which were ready, he began to make great preparations.

After the duke had in various ways protracted the negotiations for almost two months longer, the King, wearied with these delays, made preparations to bind this Proteus, who changed himself into all sorts of forms, and to force him to give a decided answer. He advanced to Lyons, whither he had sent his council beforehand. The duke, learning of his approach, had recourse to fresh stratagems. He sent to him three ambassadors, who conjointly proposed an arrangement, by which they declared that their master was ready to fulfil the treaty made at Paris, and that he promised to restore the marquisate; but the one who held the secret refused to sign the articles till the duke had first shown them to his council and signed them. By this trick the duke gained seven or eight days more; but the King, resolved to press him to a conclusion, still pursued him, discovered his subterfuge, and left him no further opportunity for delay. He was forced therefore to answer positively, and he promised to surrender the marquisate by the 16th of August.

Upon this assurance, the King caused Le Bourg-l'Espinasse, an old colonel of infantry, with the Swiss troops, to advance and take possession of the marquisate. As he approached the duke threw off his mask, and answered clearly that, according to the conditions proposed, war was not so hard to him as peace. Thereupon the King was obliged to come to what he had long foreseen, to wit, an open war. He declared it therefore on the 11th of August, but with these express terms, that he did it only to recover the marquisate, and without prejudice to the treaty of Vervins, which he desired to observe inviolably.

At the same time he gave information of this rupture to all the neighbouring princes, and made them understand the just reasons he had. This great King knew well that among Christians the breach of peace is extremely odious, and that without reasons which thoroughly convince our spirits, we ought never to trouble the public tranquillity.

The King at that time was at Grenoble, where he had, to begin this war, only three or four companies of ordnance.[1] Some proposed that he should order his regiment of guards to advance. He answered, that he would not send them from him, that they were the Tenth Legion, which never fought without Cæsar.[2] But in a short time the French nobility and adventurers

---

[1] *Compagnies d'ordonnance:* certain privileged companies, quite independent of any regiment.

[2] Julius Cæsar would never let the Tenth Legion fight except with him.

flocked to him on all sides, as if to a marriage or a ball.

The Marshal de Biron, though still disaffected, having gathered some troops, laid waste the country of Bresse in many places. With his cannon he forced the city of Bourg; but the citadel defended itself better, and proved indeed the only difficulty in this war. Créquy, entering into Savoy, gained the city of Montmélian about midnight, but not the castle.

The Pope, alarmed by the first sparks of this fire, and fearing lest it should set all Italy alight, set himself immediately to extinguish it. He dispatched a prelate, who bore the title of Patriarch of Constantinople, to point out to Henry the evil consequences of this rupture, and to conjure him in the name of God not to carry it any farther. The King assured him that he had no design to trouble the peace of Italy; that he was a Christian and a just prince; that God had given him a kingdom sufficient to content him, but that he desired to regain what belonged to his crown; and that if he had had other and greater designs, he would have made greater preparations.

In a few days he departed and entered into Savoy. His presence so much astonished the city of Chambéry that he made the garrison depart by a quick capitulation. He then made himself master of Tarentaise and La Morienne, by taking in two or three days the city of Conflans, and that of La Charbonnière, which until then were thought to be impregnable.

Still the Duke of Savoy did not stir. He was so little concerned that he hunted and danced whilst his provinces were being despoiled, and he seemed rather to be a spectator than an adversary. His subjects likewise did not seem much astonished at the King's progress; they said that if he took any places in Savoy, their duke would take others in France. It could not be divined from whence this great security proceeded. Some believed that the duke assured himself by I know not what prognostications of astrologers, who had foretold that in the month of August there should be no King in France—which happened to be very true, for at that time he was victorious in the midst of Savoy. Others believed that the duke yet trusted to the understanding he had with the Marshal de Biron, whose fidelity, much shaken by his artifices while he was in France, was now almost entirely alienated by the fresh reasons of discontent the marshal had suffered during this war. For the King showed that he no longer had any trust in him; he did not treat him with such great freedom as he had done before; and he committed the principal direction of this conquest to Lesdiguières, who, indeed, was better acquainted with the country and the manner of making war in those mountains than Biron. This preference furiously incensed so proud a spirit, for he believed nothing could or ought to be done without him. Afterwards the refusal of the King to give him the government of the city of Bourg put him quite out of his senses. From this time he had none but extravagant and criminal thoughts, and began, as it was said, to treat with the Duke of Savoy for the purpose of kindling a new civil war in France. I cannot relate the particulars of this design, because they were never clearly known.

The Duke of Savoy believed his fortresses of Montmélian in Savoy, and of Bourg in Bresse, impregnable, and felt sure of the safety of his country in regard to them. He was much surprised to learn that the Marquis of Brandis, governor of Montmélian, had agreed to surrender it in a certain time. Upon this news he put himself in the field, and used all his endeavours to get into a position to relieve it. He had recourse to the assistance of the Spaniards; but the Count of Fuentes, who desired to further complicate matters, refused his forces in his need, and in the meantime, the term of the capitulation having expired, he lost Montmélian, to the great astonishment of his subjects and no less shame of Brandis. Want of victuals and ammunition caused him likewise in some weeks to lose the citadel of Bourg, in which the governor held out to the last extremity.

The King, passing by the side of Geneva, subdued the country of Chablais and Faussigni. The inhabitants of Geneva took the fort of St. Catherine, which the Savoyards had built to annoy them, and demolished it. After this the King desired to visit Geneva, famous as being one of the ramparts of the Protestant religion. Theodorus Beza, the chief in age as well as in doctrine of all the Huguenot ministers, spoke a few words to him. The Marshal de Biron, having considered the place, which the inhabitants had taken forty years to fortify with much care and expense, either to cause himself to be esteemed a great captain, or to show the zeal he had for the Catholic religion, boasted he could take it in twenty days. The King was not pleased with this speech, because France had taken Geneva under its protection since the reign of Francis I., and was obliged to defend it against the Duke of Savoy, who claimed that that seignory belonged to him.

In the meantime the Pope, desiring above all things to extinguish the fire of this war, had dispatched to the King and the duke his nephew the Cardinal Aldobrandin, who incessantly laboured to make peace. His greatest difficulty was to find knots strong and sure enough to hold the Duke of Savoy, for those of his promises and his faith were so uncertain and so slippery that one could not trust them.

At the same time the King, whose thoughts upon his marriage the war had not interrupted, embarked on the Rhône and went down to Lyons, where the Queen his new spouse had arrived and was expecting him.

The legate would not discontinue his entreaties for peace. He followed him to Lyons for this purpose, where he made his entrance fifteen days after the Queen. The ambassadors of Savoy followed him; but their power was given in such terms that the duke might find means to disavow them. However, when they saw the citadel of Bourg reduced to extremity, they urgently solicited the legate to renew the overtures of peace. But he would do nothing until they had told him in writing that they desired it for the good of their master's affairs.

When the articles were drawn up and agreed to, they were signed on the one part and the other; and the peace was published at Lyons on the 17th of January, 1601, by which the duke yielded to the King, and to the kings of France, his successors, the country and seignories of Bresse, Bugey, and Valromey, and generally all that appertained to him lying along the river Rhône, from the egress of Geneva, and also the bailiwick and barony of Gex; this to be in exchange of the marquisate of Saluces, which the King absolutely resigned to the duke and his heirs. The treaty agreed likewise that all the places taken by the King from the Duke of Savoy should be restored; but all the King's pretended rights against the said duke should be reserved to him, according to the provisions of the treaties of Cateau in Cambresis, and of Vervins.

By this exchange both the one and the other equally gained. The King, for a marquisate of little extent, distant from all his territories and encompassed by those of Savoy, and which he could only keep by great garrisons, which would consume twice as much as the revenue it yielded, gained a country of more than twenty-five leagues in extent, which bordered upon and enlarged his frontier, in which he had eight hundred gentlemen, and which was very fertile and abundant, principally in grazing land. The duke, in appropriating to himself the marquisate, took a troublesome thorn out of his foot, or rather a sword which pierced through his body, and placed himself in a position of security; for while the French held it he dared not go out of Turin, except with three or four hundred horse for convoy, and he was forced to maintain large garrisons in the middle of his country.

The treaty being signed, the King departed from Lyons by post, to return to Paris, whither the Queen followed him by easy stages. Soon after her arrival he

took her to see his buildings of St. Germain-en-Laye.
This was one of his delights, and certainly a very
innocent one, and which agrees well with a powerful
prince after he has paid his great debts and eased his
people of their heavy load of oppressive impositions;
for by raising these proud edifices he leaves the fair
marks of his greatness and riches to posterity; he em-
bellishes his kingdom, attracts the admiration of his
people, makes strangers know that his coffers swell with
treasure, gives life and bread to a great number of poor
workmen, labours profitably for his own convenience
and for that of his successors; and last, but not least,
makes architecture, sculpture, and painting flourish,
which have ever been highly esteemed by all the most
polite nations of the world.

Our Henry only took this diversion to recreate his
spirit after labours, and not to employ it. For he had
a soul too great and a genius too elevated to dedicate
itself wholly to such mean things, much less to fix it
on vain amusements. It is true that he built, that he
hunted, that he was merry; but this was without
diverting himself too much from his affairs, without
abandoning the helm of state, which he held as firmly
and diligently during the calm as during the tempest.

Moreover, he took care not to grow sleepy whilst
it was fair weather, which is often deceitful; for besides knowing that a good king ought to labour for
his country during peace as well as during war, he
knew that the Spaniard and the Savoyard still grum-
bled and secretly plotted against him. The Count of
Fuentes, having raised a great army to assist the
Savoyards, was annoyed because the peace had de-

prived him of the occasion to employ it. Some places he had taken in Picardy during the war between the two crowns had made him vain, and caused him to believe that he should always gain the advantage over the French. At the same time the King of Spain had put to sea a fleet, commanded by one Doria, which would doubtless have made a descent upon Provence if the peace had not been made. And although it was concluded, this did not prevent Fuentes from making an attempt upon Marseilles, with the object of again causing a rupture. Those whom he informed of his plans offered the King to draw six or seven hundred men into a snare, and keep them prisoners or cut them to pieces. But the King did not deem it worth while to give an opportunity to his enemies to break the peace, and to re-enter upon a war which might have proved very dangerous, they being so powerfully armed. Moreover, he feared lest there were still in France some fire concealed under the embers which, in the confusion of war, might more easily show itself in attempts upon his person. For, to tell the truth, he had more reason to fear their knives and daggers than their swords. He therefore wisely discountenanced this enterprise, and answered the Marseillians that he knew not how to steal a victory; that ambuscades were not honest except in war; and that it was necessary for his honour to take heed that he did not in any manner contribute to that rupture his enemies had a design to make.

After this the Spaniards, finding that this wise Argus had too many eyes and too much vigilance to be surprised on any side, resolved to employ their arms in pious and honourable enterprises. A part of their army was sent to Hungary, which was then being attacked by the Turks. The Duke of Merceur, having gone to seek in that country a juster glory than in the civil wars of France, commanded the Emperor's forces. He made known to the infidels, by many gallant exploits, and more particularly by the memorable retreat of Canise, that French valour was chosen by God to sustain the Christian religion. Nor was there any doubt but that he would have quite chased them out of the kingdom, of which they had invaded more than one half, if he had not died the following year of a fever, which seized him at Nuremburg as he was about to pay his devotions at the shrine of the Lady of Loretto.

Sometime after this an accident happened by which the King took occasion to let the Spaniards know that he would not suffer anything against his honour nor against the dignity of his estate. Rochepot was his ambassador in Spain. Some gentlemen of his train, of whom one was his nephew, while bathing in the river chanced to have a quarrel with some Spaniards, and killing two, took refuge in the ambassador's house. The friends of the Spaniards so much excited the people that they besieged the house, and were ready to set it on fire. The magistrate, to prevent the tragic effects of this fury, was constrained to do an injustice, and to violate the freedom of the ambassador's house; so he repaired thither with assistance, and led them to prison. The King of Spain, being troubled at having violated the right of nations, sent to demand pardon of the ambassador; yet the Frenchmen still remained prisoners.

There were many things said and written concerning the rights and privileges of ambassadors. It is true, said some, that an ambassador alone has right of sovereign justice in his palace; but the people of his train are subject to the justice of the nation in which they are, for those faults they commit outside his palace, and so if they be taken outside of it they may be proceeded against; and though this rigour is not generally observed, and the respect shown to the ambassador's person is usually extended to all those that follow him, yet, however, this is a courtesy, and not a right. But it is not permissible to search for the criminal in the palace of the ambassador, which is a sacred place, and a sanctuary for his people. It should not, however, be abused, or used as a retreat for wicked persons, nor give sanctuary to the subjects of a prince against the laws of his realm; for in such cases, on complaint to his master, he is bound to do justice.

Now the King being justly offended at the injury done to France in the person of his ambassador, and not judging the satisfaction the magistrate had given him sufficient, commanded the ambassador to return immediately; which he did, without taking leave of the King of Spain. He forbade at the same time all commerce with Spaniards; and foreseeing that in these circumstances they might make an attack on the towns of Picardy, he with great diligence departed from Paris to visit that frontier, and came to Calais.

The people, who had begun to taste the sweetness of repose, and to till their lands with patience, trembled for fear lest a new war should expose them once more to the license of the soldiers. But God had pity on

these poor people. The Pope having undertaken to
remedy those mischiefs which threatened Christendom,
happily settled the quarrel without bloodshed. The
Spaniards gave up the prisoners, whom his Holiness
consigned some days after into the hands of the Count
of Béthune, ambassador of France at Rome; and the
King afterwards sent the Count of Barraut as ambassador
to Spain.

Whilst the King was at Calais, whither, as we have
said, he went, the archduke, who was pursuing before
Ostend the most famous siege[1] since that of Troy,
feared with some reason lest the King's approach should
retard the progress of his enterprise, in which he had
already lost so many men, and spent so much time,
shot, money, and ammunition. He sent therefore to
compliment him, promising him on the part of Spain
satisfaction for the violence done to the lodgings of his
ambassador, but entreating him not to permit the
besieged to take advantage of the state of affairs. The
King, who never let himself be overcome with courtesy
any more than by arms, sent the Duke of Aiguillon,
eldest son of the Duke of Mayenne, to assure him that
he desired to maintain peace, that he had only advanced
on the frontiers to dissipate some designs which were
being contrived, and that he trusted the equity of the
King of Spain, which he doubted not, would do him
justice.

Whilst he was in Calais Queen Elizabeth sent Lord
Edmonds, her principal confidant, to visit him. In
answer to which obliging civility, he sent the Marshal

[1] This siege lasted three years, three months, and three days,
from July, 1601, to September, 1604.

de Biron to England, accompanied by the Count of Auvergne, and the choice of the nobility of his court, to represent to her the regret the King felt, while he was so near to her, at not being able to enjoy the pleasure of seeing her.

This Queen endeavoured by all means possible to show the French her greatness and power. One day, holding Biron by the hand, she showed him a large number of heads fixed on the Tower of London, telling him that thus they punished rebels in England, and recounting to him the reasons for which she put to death the Earl of Essex, whom she had once so tenderly loved. Those who heard the discourse remembered it afterwards, when they saw the Marshal de Biron fallen into the same misfortune, and lose his head, after having lost the favour of the King.

We must not forget to relate that before the King made his voyage to Calais he had taken the Queen with him to enjoy the jubilee in the city of Orleans, where the Holy Father had ordained the stations for France to begin. His sincere and unfeigned piety gave a fair example to his people, who saw him go to processions with great devotion, and pray to God with no less attention, his heart agreeing with his lips. He laid the foundation-stone of the church of the Holy Cross at Orleans, which the Huguenots had thrown down forty years before, and gave a considerable sum of money to rebuild it.

All France, during this holy jubilee, had earnestly prayed to Heaven that it would be pleased to give them a Dauphin, to deliver them from those misfortunes in which they would be plunged if the King should die without male children. Their vows were heard, and the Queen was happily brought to bed of a son at Fontainebleau, on the day of St. Cosmo (27th of September). They gave him at his baptism the name of Louis, so sweet and dear to France for the memory of the great St. Louis, and of the good King Louis XII., father of the people. He was afterwards given the surname of the Just; and at the present day we consider it not the least of his titles to have been the father of Louis the wise and virtuous. His birth was preceded by a great earthquake, which happened some days before. The birth was very hard, and the infant laboured until he was all of a purple colour, which possibly ruined the principal organs of health and good constitution. The King, invoking on him the benediction of Heaven, gave him his blessing, and placed his sword in the infant's hand, praying to God that He would give him the grace to use it only for His glory and for the defence of the people. The princes of the blood which were with him in the Queen's chamber saluted the Dauphin one after another. I omit to tell at length how express couriers carried the news into all the provinces, and of the public rejoicings throughout the whole kingdom, particularly in the great city of Paris, where the people as much loved Henry the Great as they had hated his predecessor, of the compliments the King received from all the potentates of Europe, and of the accustomed present from the Holy Father on all occasions, to wit, the blessed swathing-bands, which he sent by Seigneur Barbarino, who became Cardinal and afterwards Pope Urban VIII.

Five days before, the Queen of Spain had been brought

to bed of her first child, a daughter, whom at the font of baptism they called Anne. The Spaniards rejoiced no less than if it had been a son, for in that country females may succeed to the crown. The most far-seeing amongst the French likewise took part in this joy, but for another reason, which was that this princess being of the same age as the Dauphin, it seemed that Heaven had ordained them for one another, and that she ought one day to be his spouse; as, indeed, Louis XIII. had this happiness, and France still possesses it, admiring on all occasions the rare wisdom, the exemplary piety, and heroic constancy of this great princess.[1]

In acknowledgment of the grace which God had done to the King in giving him a Dauphin, which was the sum of his wishes, he redoubled his care and diligence to acquit himself well of his duty to his state, to better, as he said, the succession of his son. We will here recount some establishments and orders he made to that purpose.

Need of money had obliged him during the siege of Amiens to create triennial officers in his revenues. The necessity having now passed away, he knew that there was no need of so many people to rifle his purse, and that it was impossible but something should every day remain in the hands of each one of these. He therefore discharged these new officers, and commanded that the old system should be re-established. From this suppression were excepted the treasurers of the exchequer, and those of casual forfeitures or fines.

[1] Louis XIII. married Anne of Austria, daughter of Philip III. of Spain and Margaret of Austria.

Rosny had so well bridled both the gatherers and the farmers that they could no longer rob the exchequer with impunity. But this was not enough; they had filled their purses so well before he was superintendent, that the King with infinite justice ordained a tribunal, composed of a certain number of judges chosen out of the sovereign courts, and called it the Chamber Royal. This tribunal he instructed to make an exact search of the misdemeanours of those who had managed the King's moneys, and it made a great many disgorge. A large number, however, found means to escape; some out of consideration of their alliances, others by force of money gaining those who were near the King, principally his mistresses, and even corrupting the judges themselves. So much is it true that gold pierces everywhere, and that nothing is proof against this pernicious metal. We need not then wonder that those people filled their coffers as full as they could, since the fuller they heaped them, the easier was their justification.

I have already said it, and I say it again (for it cannot be too often nor too much observed), that there is but one remedy for this disorder, which is the greatest of disorders in the state, and the cause of all others, and that is the vigilance and exactness of the King. He must himself hold the strings of his purse, keep his eye upon his coffers, know exactly what is in them and what comes out of them. He must know how his moneys accrue, to what uses they are employed, and those who manage them; and above all, he must make them give a good account, as our

Henry did, so that if they be honest men they cannot be corrupted, and if they are knaves they will have no opportunity for their knavery.

He was informed that there were two other disorders in his realm, which extremely impoverished it, and took from it all the gold and silver. The one was the transportation of it to strange countries, into Italy, Germany, and Switzerland, where the smaller potentates melted it and made money of a baser alloy. The other was the luxury which consumed likewise a great quantity in embroideries, silver and gold lace on clothes, and no less in the gilding of wainscots and chimney-pieces, and various articles of furniture.

He made two severe edicts, which prohibited these abuses. For the first, he renewed the ancient orders concerning the transport of gold and silver, adding the punishment of death to the transgressors; and he commanded all governors to take great care that these prohibitions were observed, and not to give any passports to the contrary, or else they would be considered as accessories.

By the second he prohibited, under penalty of great fines for the first time, and of imprisonment for the second, the wearing of gold and silver upon clothes, or employing it in gildings. This edict was rigorously observed, because it excepted no person. The King himself submitted to the law he had made, and looked with disfavour on a prince of the blood who did not obey this reformation.

A prodigious amount of money was likewise expended in silks, by the buying of which a large sum of money had got into the hands of strangers. The King seeing this, and considering that the use of these stuffs was very good and desirable, thought it best to introduce the manufacture into France, in order that the French might profit by it instead of strangers. To this purpose he gave instructions for the planting of a large number of white mulberry trees in those parts of the country where they would best thrive, and particularly in Touraine, to rear silkworms. He also ordered that persons who understood the manufacture should be brought to France, for the purpose of teaching the French people.

If care had been taken after his death to maintain this order, and to extend it to other provinces, it might have saved France more than five millions, which it sends out every year to provide silk stuffs. Besides, a million persons, useless for other labours, such as old people, young women, and children, might have gained a living by it, and the employers would have been able more easily to pay the imposts and taxes out of the profit on their industry.

There was yet a much greater mischief, which, as we may say, dried up the very entrails of the kingdom : this was the excessive usury. Those who managed their affairs badly, that is to say, the greater part of the nobility, borrowed money at 10 or 12 per cent. In this there were two great inconveniences. The first was that the interest gradually dug up the foundations of the richest and most ancient houses, which are the props and pillars that uphold the state. The second, that the merchants, taking the opportunity to lay out their money to such great advantage and without any risk, absolutely abandoned all commerce, the streams of which once dried up, there must needs follow a famine of gold and silver in the kingdom, for France hath no other mines than its traffic and the sale of its merchandise.

These considerations compelled the King not only to prohibit all usury, but ordain as penalty the confiscation of the sum lent, and heavy fines besides. Afterwards the parliament appointed councillors in all provinces to make inquiry after usurers, and to reduce all interests or mortgages to $6\frac{1}{2}$ per cent. They were before this 10 or 12 per cent., as we have said. The reason of this high percentage was that when usury was instituted money was much more scarce; but now that since the discovery of the Indies it was greatly multiplied, it was only just to abate its interest.

With the same object of enriching his people and of bringing abundance and plenty into his kingdom, the King always listened to proposals which might serve to enlarge commerce, to bring comfort to his people, and to till and make fruitful the most sterile places. He endeavoured as much as it was possible to make rivers navigable; he caused all bridges and causeways to be repaired, and the great roads to be paved, knowing that whilst they are not well kept, travelling is difficult, and commerce is by that means interrupted. From whence happen the same disorders in a kingdom as in a man's body when the passage of the blood and senses are not free.

When he passed through the country he carefully regarded all things, took notice of the necessities and disorders, and remedied all with promptitude. Under his favour and protection were established in many

parts of the kingdom manufactures of linen and woollen cloths, laces, ironware, and other things.

Following his example, the burgesses repaired their houses which the war had ruined. The gentlemen, having laid by their arms, having only a switch in their hands, devoted themselves to the management of their estates, and to augmenting their revenues. All the people attended their work; and it was a wonder to see this kingdom, which five or six years before had been, we may say, a den of serpents and venomous beasts, being filled with thieves, robbers, vagabonds, and good-for-nothing persons, changed by the diligence of the King into a hive of innocent bees, who emulated each other in giving proofs of their industry and in gathering wax and honey. Idleness was a disgrace and a kind of crime; and indeed it is, as the proverb says, the mother of all vices. The mind which takes no care to employ itself seriously in something is unprofitable to itself and pernicious to the public. And therefore the provosts made diligent search for loiterers, vagabonds, and low persons, and sent them to the galleys to serve the King, to make them work whether they would or no.

There is no happiness so stable and assured that it may not be easily troubled. There happened this year two things which might have overturned all France, had not the King averted them in good time.

The assembly of the notables or chiefs at Rouen, which was held in the year 1596 to raise money for the King to continue the war and pay his debts, had granted him, as we have said, the imposition of one sou per pound on all merchandise carried into walled cities.

"The state," says Tacitus, the greatest politician among historians, "cannot be maintained without forces, nor the forces without payment, nor these paid without impositions; consequently they are necessary, and it is just that everyone should contribute to the expenses of a state of which he makes a part, as well as partake of those conveniences and that protection it enjoys. But these impositions ought to be moderate, proportionate to the power of every one; and every one ought to bear his part. Moreover, care should be taken that the expense of raising them exceed not the principal; that they be not levied so as to appear odious, as on commodities which are the sustenance of the poor; and that they be blood drawn gently from the veins, and not marrow forced from the bones." Now this imposition of a sou per pound was not of this nature. It was very oppressive; for in every city they searched the merchants' goods, opened their bales, and saw all that was brought to them, so that liberty was quite lost in the kingdom. Moreover, it was excessive; for on any merchandise ten or twelve times sold, it was found that it paid as much in taxation as it was worth. There was also great expense in the sale of it; for men were forced to employ as many factors as would have formed an army, who, all desiring to make themselves rich as well as their masters, were so vexatious to the merchants that the latter became desperate. And the strangest thing of all was that there were in the King's council pensioners to these farmers, who supported them in their violences, and rejected all the complaints made of their misdemeanours.

The people are always subject to the criminal error

of considering that when justice is denied them they may do it themselves, and have recourse to force when their prayers are of no avail. This is the cause of almost all seditions, and it made all those beyond the Loire, incensed at this imposition, drive away the factors, and even kill some of them. The farmers on the other hand increased the mischief by their furious threats that they would dismantle the rebellious cities, and that they would build citadels to keep them in awe. And I believe that these gentlemen desired it to be so, not from love to the King's authority, of which they were always talking, but for their own private revenge and advantage.

The King, hearing of these commotions, and fearing lest they were raised by the emissaries of the faction of the Duke de Biron, which he had just then discovered, shortly after Easter departed from Fontainebleau, arrived at Blois, and went from thence to Poitiers. There he favourably hearkened to the complaints of his people, and remonstrated with the deputies of the cities of Guienne, saying that the imposts raised were not to enrich his ministers and favourites, as had been the custom of his predecessor, but to provide the necessary expenses of the state; that if his means had been sufficient for it, he would not have taken anything out of his subjects' purses; but since he had first employed all his own,[1] it was just that they should contribute some of theirs; that he passionately desired the ease of his subjects, and that none of his predecessors had so much wished for their prayers to God to bless the years of his realm as he; that those stories told

[1] He had sold the lands of his patrimony.

them of his design to build castles in their cities were false and seditious, for he desired to have no other forts than the hearts of his subjects.

By these gentle remonstrances he calmed all the seditions without having need of chastising them, excepting that the consuls of Limoges were deposed, and the *pancarte* (for so they called the tax) established. But this was only for the honour of the royal authority, for shortly after this the prince, the best and most just that ever lived, knowing the great vexation it caused, revoked and entirely abolished it.

The second thing, which gave him yet more trouble, and which bid fair to overthrow his kingdom if it were not remedied, was the conspiracy of Marshal de Biron. It should be understood that Laffin had been the principal instrument in the intrigue between the marshal and the Duke of Savoy. He had carried letters to and fro, and had had conferences with the duke and with the Count of Fuentes, so that he understood the whole business. But, seeing that there was no faith to be placed in the words of the Savoyard, and that Biron seemed to waver, he resolved to reveal the whole plot to the King, either because he feared that if he too long delayed it it might be got wind of by other means, or because he hoped by this service to gain a substantial reward and restore himself to the favour of the King, with whom he was on very bad terms.

Having laid his plans, he employed the Vidame[1] of Chartres, his nephew, to obtain from the King his grace and forgiveness for all he had done, on condition that he disclosed to him his accomplices in the

---

[1] *Vidame* is a lord who holds his lordship in fief of a bishop.

conspiracy and furnished him with proofs. He had preserved several letters committed to his keeping; but they were not sufficiently incriminating. He therefore took steps to procure one which would serve his purpose.

Biron had some notes written with his own hand, wherein the conspiracy was fully set out. Laffin pointed out to him that it was imprudent to keep them and to communicate them, because his writing was too well known, and that it would be safer to make a copy and burn the original. Biron approving his counsel, gave them to him to transcribe. He therefore transcribed them whilst Biron was in bed. Then, giving him the copy and crumpling up the original, he made a pretence of casting it into the fire; but by a premeditated cunning he cast in some other papers and kept the original. A thing of this importance was worthy the care of Biron himself, so that he might be sure of the documents being burnt; but he not taking it, because God so willed, that negligence cost him his life, as we shall see.

After this Laffin, continuing his endeavours to gather some more important secrets, went disguised to Milan. He conferred with the Count of Fuentes; but this close and able Spaniard, knowing well that he would betray them, showed himself more reserved. It has been reported that Laffin, having knowledge of this distrust, was fearful lest he should cause him to be got rid of, and therefore returned by unfrequented roads. The Duke of Savoy, being informed of this by Fuentes, kept prisoner the secretary of Laffin, named Renazé, for fear lest he should go and bear witness against Biron.

In their conferences they had proposed to dismember the kingdom of France. The Duke of Savoy was to have Provence and the Dauphinate; to Biron was allotted Burgundy and La Bresse, with the third daughter of the duke in marriage, and fifty thousand crowns for dowry; while some others were to be lords of other provinces, with the quality of peers. All these petty sovereigns should hold their right from the King of Spain. To accomplish this design, the Spaniards had agreed to enter the kingdom with one powerful army, and the Duke of Savoy with another. They intended to arouse the Huguenots, and at the same time revive discontents in various places and animate the people, already much incensed by the *paucarte*.

All these propositions, it is said, were made at the time of the war against Savoy; and the Marshal de Biron, being incensed at the King's refusal to give him the citadel of Bourg, had not only lent his ear, but had involved himself very deeply in these damnable designs. However, he seemed to have repented of them, for he had confessed them to the King while walking with him in the cloister of the Cordeliers[1] at Lyons, and had asked pardon of him; but he had neglected to obtain a written forgiveness, contrary to the advice of the Duke d'Epernon, who was wiser and more prudent than he.

Shortly after, sorry that he abandoned his designs, he again commenced to intrigue against the King. Moreover, he spoke of the King with little respect, belittling the splendour of his worthy actions, glorifying his own, and boasting that he had put the crown on

[1] The Franciscan monks.

the King's head and preserved France. In fact, all his discourses were bravadoes, rhodomontades, and threats.

All this was reported to the King. He was informed that Biron undervalued his great deeds, extolled the power of the King of Spain, praised the wisdom of that prince's council, his liberality in rewarding all good services, and his zeal in defence of the true religion. The King answered cleverly and prudently to those who brought him these reports, that he knew the heart of Biron, and that it was faithful and affectionate; that, in truth, his tongue was intemperate, but that in consideration of those good actions he had done he would pardon his unwise speech.

Now two things consummated his ruin, and obliged the King to search to the very bottom of his wicked designs. The first was the too great number of his friends, and the affection of the soldiery, which he made boast of, as if they had been entirely dependent on his command and ready to do whatever he wished. The second was the great friendship he had with the Count of Auvergne, brother by the mother's side to Mademoiselle d'Entragues, who was called the Marchioness of Verneuil. By the first he made the King jealous, and caused himself to be feared; and by the other he rendered himself odious to the Queen, who imagined, and possibly not without cause, that he would make a party in the kingdom to maintain that rival and her children, to the prejudice of the Queen.

Now the King desiring to sift this affair to the bottom, sent for Laffin, who came to Fontainebleau, more than a month before the King departed for Poitou. He had at first some secret interviews with

him, and afterwards very open ones. Laffin gave the
King a large number of papers, amongst others, those
notes in Biron's own hand of which we have before
spoken. Laffin's information to the King caused great
disquietude in his spirit, so that all the time he was
at Poitiers he was observed to be extremely pensive,
and the court after his example was plunged in a
sad astonishment, though none could divine the cause.

On his return from Poitiers to Fontainebleau he
sent for the Duke de Biron. The duke at first hesitated about coming, and excused himself with many
weak reasons. The King pressed him, and sent some
of his squires to him; afterwards the president Jeannin
brought him word that he should receive no harm,
provided he prepared himself to receive grace, and did
not aggravate his crime by his pride and impenitence.

Biron knew that Laffin had been to the court, but
he was more assured of that man than of himself.
Moreover, the Baron de Lux, his confidant, who was
there at the time, had told him that Laffin had undoubtedly kept his counsel, and had not revealed
anything which might injure him. De Lux believed
this to be true, because the King, after having entertained Laffin, had told him with a merry countenance,
"I am glad I have seen this man; he has eased me
of many distrusts and suspicions."

In the meantime the friends of Biron wrote to him
not to be such a fool as to come to the court; that
it would be safer for him to justify himself by attorney
than in person. But notwithstanding this advice, and
against the warning of his own conscience, after having
deliberated for some time he came to Fontainebleau,

when the King no longer expected him, but was making preparations for his arrest.

The histories of that time recount exactly all the circumstances of the trial, imprisonment, and death of the marshal. I shall content myself with the most important.

The insolence and blindness of this unhappy man cannot be sufficiently wondered at, nor, on the contrary, can the goodness and clemency of the King, who endeavoured to overcome his obstinacy, be enough praised. Confession of a fault is the first sign of repentance. The King, speaking to him privately, conjured him to confess all those communications and treaties he had made with the Duke of Savoy, pledging his faith that he would bury all in eternal oblivion. He told him that he knew well enough all the particulars, but desired to hear them from his mouth, swearing to him that though his fault should be greater than the worst of crimes his confession should be followed by an unconditional pardon. Biron, instead of acknowledging it, or at least excusing himself with modesty, as speaking to his justly offended King, insolently answered him that he was innocent, and that he had not come to justify himself, but to learn the names of his backbiters, and demand justice, which otherwise he would procure for himself. Though this too haughty answer greatly aggravated his offence, the King nevertheless gently told him to think further of it, and that he hoped he would take better counsel.

The same day, after supper, the Count of Soissons exhorted him likewise, on the part of the King, to confess the truth, concluding his advice with that sentence of the wise man, "Sir, know that the anger of the king is as the messenger of death." But Biron answered him more fiercely than he had the King.

The next morning the King, whilst walking in his gardens, again conjured him to confess the conspiracy, but he could draw nothing from him but protestations of innocence and threats against his accusers.

Upon this the King felt himself agitated even to the bottom of his soul with conflicting thoughts, not knowing what he ought to do. The affection he had borne him, as well as his great services, withheld the King's just anger from him; but the gross blackness of his crime, added to his pride and obstinacy, gave rein to his justice, and incited him to punish the criminal. Besides, the danger with which both his state and person were threatened seemed impossible to be averted otherwise than by cutting off the head of a conspiracy the foundation of which was scarce visible.

In this trouble of spirit he retired to his closet, and, falling on his knees, prayed to God with all his heart to inspire him with a good resolution. He was accustomed to act thus in all his great affairs, esteeming God as his surest counsellor and most faithful assistance. After his prayer, as he said afterwards, he found himself delivered from his trouble, and resolved to hand Biron over to justice, if his council found that the proofs they had in writing were so strong that there could be no doubt of his guilt. He chose for this purpose four of his council, to wit, Bellièvre, Villeroy, Rosny, and Sillery, and showed them the proofs. They declared with one voice that they were more than sufficient.

Yet after this he made a third attempt to subdue this proud heart. He employed this time remonstrances, prayers, and assurances of pardon if he would acknowledge his crime; but he answered still in the same manner, adding that if he knew his accusers he would break their heads.

At last the King, wearied with his rhodomontades and obstinacy, left him, saying, "Well, then, we must learn the truth in another place. Farewell, Baron de Biron." These words were as lightning, the forerunner of the thunderbolt which was to overwhelm him. The King, by degrading him from the many dignities with which he had honoured him, showed that he was about to abase him much more than ever he had raised him.

On coming from the Queen's chamber, where he had been playing at *primero*, Vitry, captain of the King's guard, demanded his sword, and arrested him as his prisoner. Praslin, also captain of the guard, secured the Count of Auvergne. The next day they were conducted, under a strong escort, by water to the Bastille.

Biron had a very large number of friends; but on this occasion wherein he was accused of having conspired against the person of the King, they were all mute. His relations at the Court cast themselves on their knees before the King, not to demand justice of him, but to implore his mercy. Lord de la Force, afterwards Marshal of France, spoke for them all. If Biron had at first spoken with as much humility and submission as they did, he would doubtless have obtained the King's grace; but it was now too late.

There was now no room for clemency; it had given place to justice.

The King commanded his parliament to conduct the trial, and sent a special commission to the chief president, to the president Potier de Blancmesnil, and to two councillors, to draw up the instructions at the request of the attorney-general.

The proofs were very strong, and the defence of Biron very weak. He showed plainly at his trial, which was a matter of life and death, that he had less brains than heart; for he acknowledged his writing, which he might have denied, and thus have gained time until it could be proved. The document had been written at the time of the war against the Duke of Savoy. He pretended that the King had pardoned him at Lyons for all his rebellious actions. But the King sent letters under his great seal to the parliament, by which he revoked that grace; but little account was taken of it, because, firstly, the grace he had granted him was but verbal; and, secondly, the parliament held that there were crimes the King could not pardon, such as those of *lèse-majesté*, divine and human, and those which are of great scandal and prejudice to the public. When they came to the re-examination and confronting of witnesses, and presented Laffin to Biron, instead of reproaching him as a man who was incapable of bearing true witness, he acknowledged him as an honest man and a brave gentleman; but afterwards, when he heard his deposition read, he began to upbraid him and to call him traitor, magician, and devilish fellow. But it was too late, and his reproaches no longer availed him.

He believed that Renazé was still a prisoner in Piedmont; but he had escaped some time before, and was now presented to him. He fancied that he saw a phantom or ghost. He remained astonished and dumb; and without reproaching him, heard his deposition, which agreed with that of Laffin. They deposed, besides what we have already stated, that he had plotted with the governor of Fort St. Catherine to kill the King when he went to reconnoitre that place, Biron arranging to march a little before him clad in a certain fashion, in order that he might be recognised. They said likewise that another of his designs was to seize the King when he was hunting, or otherwise ill-accompanied, and carry him off into Spain.

The impeachment being thus made in the Bastille by four commissioners, he was conducted to the palace down the river, escorted by the regiment of guards. He was tried in parliament, seated on the *sellette* or defendant's stool, all the chambers of the assembly except the peers being present, though they also had been called. Afterwards he was taken back to the Bastille.

On the morrow (31st of July, 1602) it was put to the vote. Of one hundred and fifty judges, there was not one who did not concur in the sentence of death. He was declared attainted and convicted of the crime of *lèse-majesté*, for the conspiracies made by him against the person of the King, designs upon his estate, treasons, and treaties with his enemies, he being marshal of the armies of the said King. And for reparation of his crimes he was deprived of all his estates, honours, and dignities, and condemned to have his head cut off in the Place de la Grève; his goods, movable and immovable, taken and confiscated to the King; his lands of Biron for ever deprived of the title of peerage; and those and all his other lands reunited to the demesnes of the crown.

The King, under pretext of doing a favour to his kindred, but really fearing some tumult, because he was much loved by the soldiery and had a great number of friends at court, changed the place of his execution to the Bastille. The chancellor, going with the chief president, caused him to be led to the chapel, where about ten o'clock he pronounced his sentence, which he heard with one knee on the ground, with a great deal of patience; only when they came to the words, "conspiracies against the person of the King," he rose up and cried out, "There is no such thing; that is false; blot out that!" Finally, the chancellor, according to form, redemanded of him the collar of his order, his ducal crown, and his marshal's staff. He had not the two last with him, but the first, which he drew out of his pocket and gave up.

It is unnecessary to recount all his discourses, his reproaches, his passions, his lamentations, his exclamations, and a hundred other extravagances (for so we may call them) to which he was carried away.

About five o'clock that evening he was led to the scaffold, where he had his head cut off. It was observed that it bounded three times, forced by the impetuosity of his spirits, and that there issued more blood from it than from the trunk of his body.[1] He

---

[1] It is stated that the executioner was obliged to strike him unawares.

was carried to the church of St. Paul, where he was buried without any ceremony, but amidst a great concourse of people, who all had tears in their eyes, and lamented that brave spirit, which a detestable ambition and a too violent pride had brought to so unhappy an end.

It is worthy of notice that the marshal was very ignorant, but extremely curious about the predictions of astrologers, diviners, necromancers, and other deceivers. It was held likewise that Laffin had gained his favour by making him believe that he held communication with the devil, who had assured him that Biron would become a sovereign. It was said likewise that when he was young he went disguised one day to see a fortune-teller, who foretold that he should be a very great lord, but that he should have his head cut off, upon which, being annoyed, he outrageously beat him. Another diviner told him that he should be a king, if a blow from a sword behind did not prevent it. It was also foretold that he should die by the hand of a Burgundian; and it was found that the executioner who cut off his head was a native of Burgundy.

Laffin and Renazé obtained full pardon. Hebert, secretary to Marshal Biron, suffered the ordinary and extraordinary[1] questioning without confessing anything, yet he was condemned to perpetual imprisonment. Shortly after the King gave him his liberty; yet the resentment of what he had suffered having more power over him than the favour, he fled to Spain, where he ended his days.

The Baron de Lux, Biron's chief confidant, came

[1] The rack.

to court by the king's command. He told him all that he knew, and possibly more. By this means he obtained his pardon, and was confirmed in his offices, and also in the government of the castle of Dijon and the city of Beaune. The King kept the government of Burgundy for the Dauphin, and gave the lieutenancy to Bellegarde, who afterwards became governor-in-chief.

Montbarot Lord Breston was sent to the Bastille on certain evidence against him, but being found innocent, he was soon released.

The Baron of Fontanelles, a gentleman of good family, was not so fortunate. For having a hand in the conspiracy, and, in addition, treating on his own account with the Spaniards with regard to the surrender of a little island on the coast of Brittany, he was broken on the wheel by sentence of the great council. The King, in consideration of his family, which was illustrious, granted that in the sentence he should not be called by his proper name, but history could not be silent about it.

The Duke of Bouillon, finding himself likewise somewhat involved in the Biron affair, judged it convenient to retire to his viscounty of Turenne, where the King, being informed that he was still plotting against him, sent for him to come and justify himself. Instead of coming, he wrote a very eloquent letter, in which he stated that, knowing that his accusers were both extremely wicked and very cunning, he entreated the King to dispense with his coming to court, and grant that, to satisfy his Majesty, all France, and his own honour, he should be heard at the chamber of Castres, by virtue of the privilege granted to those of the pretended reformed religion, and that he would send thither his accusers and accusations. In pursuance of which he came to Castres, presented himself to the chamber, and recorded his appearance. The King was not at all pleased with this answer. He blamed the judges of Castres for what they had done, and sent to tell him that there was as yet no question of handing him over to justice, and that therefore he desired him to come to court as soon as possible.

Being informed by his friends at court of the resolution of the King, who had sent the president Commartin to make known his will, the duke departed from Castres, went to Orange, passed Geneva, and retired to Heidelberg to the Prince Palatine, saying—sage politician that he was—that he ought neither to come to terms with his King nor go near him whilst his anger lasted. This business stood still some years, and we shall see in its place how it terminated.

It must here be acknowledged that the favour of Rosny served at this time as a pretext to almost all the discontents and conspiracies of the nobles. The King had given him four or five important posts, because he believed he could not sufficiently recompense those services he had rendered him. In this the King merits only praise, for a good master cannot do too much for a good and faithful servant. But though the troublesome and discontented spirits might complain that the King gave him too many posts and employments, yet they could not lament his giving him too much power, or that he gave it to him alone; for we may truthfully say that Rosny had not the liberty to do anything of his own accord. He was forced in all things to address himself directly to the King, who would himself distribute his favours and recompenses to those he thought worthy, so that they might acknowledge the whole obligation as coming from him. This great prince knew well that he who gives all may do all, and that he who gives nothing is nothing but what it may please him who gives all. He had too much courage and too much glory to suffer that another should act in the most noble function of his royal authority. Whatever favour or familiarity any had with him, if they did not conduct themselves with a profound respect, or if they failed to speak or act as they ought with their master and their King, they would doubtless soon fall into disgrace; this was, as we have observed, one of the causes of Biron's fall. Judge, then, if he who would not allow any to act the companion with him would allow them to act the sovereign. Judge also if he would have been content that his ministers should simply take his consent on any matter, or that they should speak to him of things for conscience' sake, after having themselves resolved on them. No; without doubt he wished everything to proceed from his initiative, that the choice should be his, that he alone should have the power to raise up and cast down, and that none but himself should be the arbiter of the fortunes of his subjects. Not but that he considered, as was just, the recommendations of the great men of his realm as well as of his ministers in conferring favours, employments, and posts, but it was always in such a manner that he made the recipients know that they owed them to him alone, which the following example well demonstrates.

The bishopric of Poitiers having become vacant, Rosny instantly besought him to consider on this occasion one Frenouillet, well known as a clever man and a great preacher. Notwithstanding this recommendation the King gave it to the abbot of Rocheposai, who himself possessed many good qualities, and was son of a gentleman who had served him well with his sword in wars, and with his knowledge and talents in embassies. Some time after, the bishopric of Montpellier became vacant. The King himself sent for Frenouillet, and told him that he would give it to him, but on condition that he should acknowledge no obligation to any but him. By this it may be seen that he really considered the recommendation of Rosny; but it may likewise be perceived that the power of that favourite who was the cause of so much jealousy was limited. I call him favourite because he had the most splendid employments, though actually he had no pre-eminence over others of the council, for Villeroy and Jeannin were more considered than he in negotiations and foreign affairs, as were Bellièvre and Sillery for justice and policy and home affairs; and it must not be imagined that either in any way depended on Rosny. There was only one head in the state, and that was the King, who chose all his members, and from whom alone they received spirit and force.

About the end of this year, the Duke of Savoy, thinking to revenge and compensate himself for the loss of his county of Bresse on the city of Geneva, attempted to take it by storm. The enterprise was planned by Lord d'Albigny, and the duke, having passed the mountains, believed it to be infallible. D'Albigny conducted two thousand men to within half a league of the city, yet was not so rash as to expose himself, but left the direction of the attack to others. At first it was completely successful; more than two hundred men mounted the ladders, gained the ramparts, and ran through all the city without being perceived. In the meantime the burgesses were awakened by the cries of some of the guard, who had seen some of the assailants, and who had been attacked by them. A gunner, who was to have broken a gate inside, to enable those without to enter, was slain, after which they were overwhelmed on all sides. The greater part endeavoured to regain their ladders, but these having been broken to pieces by the cannon, there was no means of escaping, and they were nearly all slain, or broke their necks by leaping into the ditch. Thirteen were taken alive, mostly gentlemen, amongst them being Artignac, who had served as second in command to Don Philipin. They yielded on the assurance that they should be treated as prisoners of war, but the furious cries of the common people, who represented the danger in which their city was of massacres, violation, universal destruction, or perpetual slavery, forced the council of this little republic to condemn them, like thieves, to the infamous death of the gibbet. Their heads, with fifty-four others of those who were killed, were stuck on poles, and their bodies cast into the Rhône.

The Duke of Savoy, disheartened by such ill-success, and overwhelmed with the reproaches of all Christendom for having attempted such an enterprise in time of peace, hastily recrossed the mountains, leaving his troops near to Geneva, and endeavoured to excuse himself to the the Swiss, under whose protection, as well as under that of France, the city was, for having attempted to surprise it, saying that he had not done it to trouble the repose of the confederation, but to hinder Lesdiguières from seizing it for the King.

The dukes of Savoy had long pretended that this city appertained to their sovereignty, and that the bishops, who bore the title of earls and were for some time lords of it, held it from them. This, however, the bishops never acknowledged, always maintaining that they depended immediately on the Empire. The Genevese, on their part, maintained that it was a free city, and subject in temporal things neither to their bishops, whom they expelled in 1533 when they unhappily renounced the Roman Catholic religion, nor to the Duke of Savoy, but to the Empire alone, for which reason they always bore the eagle displayed on their gates. Both had very specious titles to show their rights; but at that time the city of Geneva enjoyed full liberty, and had done so for more than sixty years, having become an ally of the cantons of Switzerland. Now the Swiss were comprehended in the treaty of Vervins as allies of France, and in consequence so was the city of Geneva. This the King had declared to the Duke of Savoy; but it did not, however, deter the latter from this undertaking, hoping that if it succeeded the King of Spain and the Pope would uphold him in it, and that the King for so small a thing would not break the peace.

The Genevese, furiously incensed against him, began to make war courageously. They entered his country and took some small towns, hoping that the King and the Swiss would second these expressions of their resentment, and that all the princes of Germany would likewise come to their assistance. But the King desired to keep the peace, and was too wise to kindle a war in which he could not make religion and policy agree or unite the honour and interests of France, who was obliged to protect her allies, with the good graces of the Pope, whose duty inclined him to destroy the Huguenots. He therefore sent De Vic to assure the Genevese of his protection, and gave them to understand that peace was necessary for them and war ruinous, and that they ought to embrace the one and shun the other. Having little power by themselves, and not being able to do anything without the King's assistance, they were obliged to consent and enter into a treaty with the Savoyard, in which it was clearly laid down that they were included in the treaty of Vervins, and that the duke could not build any fortress within four leagues of their city.

It happened about the same time that the city of Metz rose against the governor of the citadel, who was named Sobole. He had been made lieutenant by the Duke d'Epernon, to whom Henry III. had given the government-in-chief, but had deserted this duke and placed himself under the protection of the King. He had a brother who was second to him in command.

During the last war against Spain these two brothers had accused the principal inhabitants of Metz of having conspired to deliver the city to the Spaniards. Many were imprisoned, and some put to the rack; but none were found guilty. Therefore the burgesses, believing with reason that this was a calumny, conceived a hatred against these Soboles, and drew up several petitions against them, accusing them of a great number of exactions and cruelties. The Duke d'Epernon, who without doubt upheld these burgesses at the court, was sent by the King to settle this difference. The Soboles, who had offended him, no longer trusted him. They would not permit him to enter the strongest citadel, nor let the garrison go out to meet him; so that being justly incensed, he made matters worse instead of better, and roused the anger of the inhabitants to such a pitch that they barricaded themselves against the Soboles. The King who knew that the least sparks were capable of kindling a great fire, was not content with sending La Varenne, but went himself, being desirous of visiting that district. Sobole gave the place into the King's hands, and he gave it to Arquien, lieutenant-colonel of the regiment of guards, with the rank of lieutenant of the King, to command in the absence of the Duke d'Epernon, the governor, who had no great power while the King lived.

The King stayed until after Easter at Metz. Whilst he was there, he listened to the request which the Jesuits made for their re-establishment. He reserved his decision until he went back to Paris, and gave leave to Father Ignatius Armand and Father Coton to come and plead their cause. This they did; and Father Coton, being clever and witty, and a very famous preacher, soon gained the favour of all the court, and pleased the King so well that he obtained from his Majesty the reinstating of the society in the kingdom, contrary to the opinion and advice of some of his council.

He then re-established them by an Act which he caused to be confirmed in parliament; and caused the pyramid to be thrown down which had been erected before the palace, and on which were many cutting sarcasms in verse and prose against these fathers. Thus their banishment was gloriously repaired; and, what was more important, the King kept with him Father Coton as his chaplain-in-ordinary and confessor and director of his conscience. This was not, however, till the year 1604.

In the years 1602 and 1603 we have still three or four important things to observe. The first is that the King at his departure from Metz went to Nancy to visit his sister, the Duchess of Bar, who died the year following, childless. The second, that he renewed the alliance with the Swiss, and some months after, with the Grisons, notwithstanding the obstacles which the Count of Fuentes put in the way of it. The third is, that on returning to Paris he received news of the death of Elizabeth, Queen of England, one of the most illustrious and most heroic princesses that ever reigned, and who governed her realm with more prudence and power than any of her predecessors had ever done. There was nothing wanting to the happiness of her kingdom save the Catholic religion, which she banished from England. And we might give her the name of good as well as great, if she had not dealt so cruelly as she did with her cousin-german, Mary Stuart, Queen of Scotland, whom she kept as a prisoner for eighteen years, and then beheaded, on account of some conspiracies which the servants and friends of that poor princess had made against her person.

James VI., King of Scotland, and son of Mary,

being the nearest of the blood-royal of England, succeeded Elizabeth, who had put his mother to death. He caused himself to be called King of Great Britain, so as to unite under the same title the two crowns of England and Scotland.

The alliance of so powerful a king either with France or Spain might make the balance incline to whichever side it were turned. Therefore the kings of both nations immediately sent magnificent ambassadors to salute him, each endeavouring to draw him to his side. Rosny went on the part of Henry the Great. He obtained the confirmation of the ancient treaties between France and England. The ambassador of Spain was not so fortunate in his negotiations. The Spaniards were forced to allow that the place of treaty should be appointed in England, and to grant the English free traffic in all their territories, even in the Indies, and also give them liberty of conscience in Spain, so that they should not be subject to the Inquisition nor obliged to salute the holy sacrament in the streets, but only to turn aside.

France was in a profound peace, externally by the renewal of the alliances with the Swiss and with England, and internally by the discovery of the conspiracies, which were now quite overthrown. The King enjoyed a repose worthy his labours, and his past troubles made his pleasures all the more sweet. However, he was not idle, for he endeavoured with as much diligence to preserve peace as he had used courage and valour in making war.

He was often heard to say that though he could make the empire of France as powerful in Europe as that of the Ottomans was in Asia, and easily conquer all the territories of his neighbours, yet he would not do so great a dishonour to his word, by which he was bound to preserve peace.

His most ordinary diversions during this time were hunting and building. He at the same time maintained workmen at the church of the Holy Cross at Orleans, at St. Germain-en-Laye, at the Louvre, and at the Place Royale.

The nobility of France during this peace could not be entirely still. Some passed their time in hunting, other with ladies; some in pursuit of learning, others in travelling into foreign countries; while others again continued the exercise of war under Prince Maurice in Holland. But the greater part, whose hands, as it were, itched, and who sought to signalise their valour without departing from their country, became punctilious, and for the least word, or even for a wry look, put their hands to their swords. Thus that madness of duels entered into the hearts of the gentlemen; and these combats were so frequent that the nobility shed as much blood in the meadows with their own hands as their enemies had made them lose in battle.

The King therefore issued a second and most severe edict, which prohibited duels, confiscating the goods of those who disobeyed his orders, and rendering their persons liable to arrest. For a while this prohibition chilled the ardour of the most violent; but because the King often pardoned this crime, not being able to refuse it to those who had faithfully served him in his need, in a little time the trouble became almost as bad as before.

His custom of receiving from all persons any information that might enrich his kingdom, caused him to learn that there were in various places in France very good gold, silver, copper, and lead mines; and that if they were worked, there would be no need to buy from strangers. He considered also that though no great profit might accrue from working them, yet many idle persons might be employed; and likewise that those criminals whose offence did not merit death might be condemned for so many years to work in them. He therefore made an Act which renewed the ancient orders concerning the officers, directors, and workers of mines; and they began to work in the Pyrenees, where it is most certain that there formerly was gold, and that there still is. Had they continued this labour, they might, to all appearance, have gained notable advantages; but either through the negligence of the overseers or the impatience of the French, who become discouraged with everything that does not at once fulfil their desires, this work was discontinued.

Another very great convenience for Paris was undertaken, viz., the joining of the rivers Loire and Seine by the Briare canal. Rosny laboured in this undertaking with much outlay, spending upon it nearly three hundred thousand crowns; but the work was interrupted, for what reason I do not know. It was resumed in the reign of Louis XIII., and was then completed.

Another scheme was also proposed, the object of which was to join the Atlantic and the Mediterranean, by uniting the Garonne, which falls into the Atlantic, and the Aube, which falls into the Mediterranean

below Narbonne. This was to be accomplished by
means of canals connecting the two rivers. The
county of Languedoc offered to contribute; but difficulties arose which hindered this enterprise.

Navigation was established by the great care which
the King had taken to keep his coasts in security,
and to punish pirates severely when they were caught.
Ships were no longer content to make voyages to the
ordinary places, but went also to the New World, the
way to which they had almost forgotten since the time
of Admiral Coligni. A gentleman of Saintonge named
Du Gas made, with the King's commission, the
voyage to Canada.

Among all these things we must not forget a large
number of new religious companies which were organised at Paris. Amongst these were the Recollets,[1]
who were a branch of the order of St. Francis, the
Capuchins, and the Feuillantines.[2] There were also
the Carmelites and the Barefooted Friars, both of
which orders came from Spain; and the Brothers of
Charity, vulgarly called the "ignorant brothers," who
came from Italy. All of them built convents out of
the alms and charity of devout persons.

In the midst of this profound calm, which the
King enjoyed, and during all these fair occupations
which were worthy of him, he was not without
troubles and vexations which perplexed his spirit. He
had none greater than those in connection with his
wife and his mistresses.

[1] So called because only those were admitted who were of a
collected, serious mind.
[2] Founded at Feuillant, in Languedoc.

We have already related how Mademoiselle d'Entragues had conquered him. He had given her the land of Verneuil, near Senlis, and had made it a marquisate. After he was married his infatuation for her continued, and he took her with him on all his journeys, and gave her apartments at Fontainebleau.

These things extremely offended the Queen. The pride of the marchioness more furiously incensed her, for she always spoke of the Queen in terms either insulting or disdainful, sometimes saying that if justice were done she should occupy the place of that fat banker.[1]

The Queen, on her side, with reason hated her, and made complaints of her to all her friends. But this was not the way to gain the favour of the King. She would have acted more wisely if she had dissembled her displeasure, and by her kindness made herself paramount in that heart which rightly belonged to her. The King loved to be flattered, and was to be gained by tenderness and affection. The philtre of love is love itself; and it was this that she ought to have employed with him, and not grumblings, scorn, and evil looks, which only serve more and more to disgust a husband, and make him find more pleasure in the allurements of a mistress who takes care to be always agreeable and obliging. But instead of acting in this manner she was always in contention with the King. She exasperated him continually by her complaints and reproaches; and when he sought to find repose from the cares of state he encountered nothing but gall and bitterness.

[1] Alluding, I suppose, to the dukes of Florence, who are all merchants.—TRANSLATOR'S NOTE.

She had among her attendants a Florentine woman, daughter of her nurse, named Leonora Galigay, a creature extremely ugly, but very clever, who had won the affections of her mistress to such a degree that she exercised almost unlimited authority over her. It has been said that this woman, fearing that the Queen her mistress would love her less if she perfectly loved the King her husband, kept her from him as much as she could, in order that she might the better retain her influence over her. Afterwards, so that she might have an accomplice in her designs, she married a Florentine domestic of the Queen, named Conchini, of slightly better extraction than herself, being grandson of Battista Conchini, who had been secretary to Cosmo Duke of Florence.

The common opinion was, that these two persons laboured conjointly, as long as the King lived to keep alive an evil spirit in the Queen, and to make her always troublesome and ill-humoured towards him; so that, in the seven or eight years they were together, if he had one day of peace and quiet with her he had ten of discontent and vexation. In this the King's fault was the greater, because he gave the occasion of these troubles; and the husband being, as St. Paul says, the head of the wife, ought to set her a good example, and keep faithful to her.

We have observed this once for all; but we cannot too often reflect "that sin is the cause of all disorder, and that for a little pleasure it causes a thousand troubles and a thousand mischiefs, even in this world itself." The King being now but just fifty years of age, began this year to have some slight attacks of gout, which possibly were the effects of his excessive voluptuousness, as well as of his labours.

To return to the marchioness. It happened one day that the Queen, being very much offended at her discourse, threatened her, saying that she ought to know how to bridle her evil tongue. The marchioness upon this seemed sad and grieved. She shunned the King, and told him that she desired that he would no longer demand anything of her, because she feared that the continuation of his favours would be prejudicial both to her and her children. Her design was to inflame his passion more by showing herself more difficult. But when she saw that her cunning had not all the effect she hoped, and that the Queen's anger was increased to such a point that indeed there was some danger to her and her children, she decided on another plan. D'Entragues, her father, demanded permission of the King to carry her out of the kingdom to avoid the vengeance of the Queen. The King granted her demand more easily than she thought he would; whereupon, being excessively enraged, her father and the Count d'Auvergne, her brother by the mother's side, began to treat secretly with the ambassador of Spain with regard to taking refuge in the territories of his King, casting themselves absolutely into his arms.

The ambassador thought that this business would be very advantageous to his master, and that, in the proper time and place, he might avail himself of the promise of marriage which the King had given to the marchioness. He therefore readily granted them all that they asked, and added all the fair promises with which weak and feeble spirits are liable to be intoxicated.

The King had granted them permission to retire from France, but without the children, believing that they would go to England, to the Duke of Lennox and the Earl d'Aubigny, of the house of Stuart, who were their near kinsmen. When, however, he understood that they were desirous of retiring to Spain, he resolved to hinder them, but at first to employ fair means to do it. He therefore sent for the Count d'Auvergne, who was then at Clermont, and was so much beloved in the province that he believed he might securely stay there. He refused to come before he had his pardon granted in due form for all that he might have done. This was a sort of crime to dictate terms to his King, who, however, sent him the pardon, but with the proviso that he should make his immediate appearance.

This, however, did not allay his misgivings. He remained in the province, where he kept himself on his guard, with all precautions imaginable. Nevertheless, cunning as he was, the King by a clumsy artifice entrapped him. Being colonel of the French cavalry, D'Auvergne was desired to attend a muster of a company of the Duke of Vendôme. He went well mounted, keeping himself at a good distance, that he might not be surprised. Nevertheless, D'Eurre, lieutenant of that company, and Nerestan, approaching him to salute him, mounted on ponies so as to remove his suspicion, but with three soldiers disguised as attendants, cast him from his horse, and made him prisoner. They led him to the Bastille, where he was seized with a great fear when he found himself lodged in the same chamber where the Marshal de Biron, his great friend, had been.

Immediately afterwards the King caused D'Entragues also to be arrested, who was carried to the Conciergerie;[1] and also the marchioness, who was left in her lodgings under the guard of the Cavalier de Guet. Then, desiring to make known by public proofs the ill-intention of the Spaniards, who seduced his subjects and excited and fomented conspiracies in his realm, he handed over the prisoners to the parliament, who, having convicted them of conspiring with the Spaniards, declared (1st of February) the Count d'Auvergne, D'Entragues, and an Englishman named Morgan, who had been the agent of the negotiations, guilty of treason, and condemned them to be beheaded as such. They also ordered the marchioness to be conducted with a strong guard into the convent at Beaumont, near Tours, where she was to remain until more ample evidence had been produced against her, at the request of the attorney-general.

The Queen spared no solicitations to get this sentence pronounced, believing that its execution would satisfy her resentment, but the goodness of the King was proof against her vindictiveness. The love which he had for the marchioness was not so entirely extinct that he could resolve to sacrifice what he had adored, and he would not permit them to pronounce the sentence. Two months and a half afterwards, to wit, on the 15th of April, he, by letters under his great seal, commuted the penalty of death on the Count d'Auvergne and the Lord

[1] These were prisons in the jurisdiction of "Parlements" before the Revolution.

d'Entragues, into perpetual imprisonment; and that on Morgan to perpetual banishment. Some time after he changed the imprisonment of D'Entragues into confinement to his house at Malesherbes in Beauce. He likewise permitted the marchioness to retire to Verneuil, and seven months having passed without the attorney-general procuring any proof against her, he caused her to be declared absolutely innocent of the crime of which she was accused.

There now remained only the Count d'Auvergne, who, being the most to be feared, was the worst treated; for the King not only kept him prisoner at the Bastille, where he lay for twelve whole years, but likewise deprived him of his property in the county of Auvergne. He had received the title from King Henry III.

Queen Margaret maintained that the gift of the title was not valid, because the marriage contract of Catherine de Medicis, her mother, to whom that county belonged, allowed substitution of her goods, and that substitution, she said, extending to daughters in default of males, the county was to come to her after the death of Henry III., nor could he give it to her prejudice.

The parliament having listened to her reasons and seen her proofs, annulled the donation made by Henry III., and awarded her this county. In recompense of this obligation and many others she had received from the King, she bequeathed all her estates to the Dauphin, only reserving the usufruct of them for herself during her life.

The Count d'Auvergne, thus despoiled, remained

in the Bastille until the year 1616, when Queen Mary de Medicis, having need of him during the troubles, delivered him from thence, and caused him to be justified. She caused likewise the registers of parliament and of the notaries to be taken off the file, with all informations which might preserve the memory of his crime. By this an example may be seen how time causes a mutability in all things, and how it changes the greatest hatreds into the strongest affections, and on the contrary, transmutes the strongest affections into mortal hatreds.

By searching into the plot of the father of the marchioness to deliver her with her children to the Spaniards, the designs of the Duke of Bouillon were likewise discovered, who was from that time the only person able to give the King any trouble in his own kingdom. It is most certain that this prince had conferred on him very great favours, having given him the staff of marshal of France and arranged his marriage with the heiress of Sedan ; and this lord had likewise very well served him in his greatest necessities. But after the King became converted to the Catholic faith, Bouillon diminished much of his affection, and, moved partly by zeal for his false religion and partly by ambition, he conceived vast designs of making himself chief and protector of the Huguenot party, and under that pretext of becoming master of the provinces beyond the Loire. It was believed that with this object he had much helped to exasperate the spirit of the Marshal de Biron ; and also that he had made a treaty with the Spaniards, who were to furnish him with what money he desired, but not with forces, for fear of becoming odious to the Protestants.

It was but too visible that, after the conversion of the King, Bouillon had incessantly laboured to arouse distrust and discontent in the spirits of the Huguenots, and to unite them into a compact body, persuading himself that that body must necessarily have a head, and that they could choose no other but himself; and for these reasons many assemblies were called, and many particular and general synods of those of this religion held, wherein nothing was heard but complaints and murmurs against the King, whom they continually wearied with new requests and demands.

Moreover, it was found that this duke had emissaries and servants in Guienne, and particularly in Limousin and Quercy, who held private councils among the nobility, distributed money, and took oath of those who promised him service, and who had formed designs against ten or twelve Catholic cities.

The King, judging that he ought to dig up the root of this mischief before it extended further, and not knowing indeed how far it might extend, resolved to go and apply the remedy himself. He departed from Fontainebleau in December, having sent before him Jean Jacques de Mesmes, Lord of Roissy, to Limoges, to take proceedings against those who were culpable.

Immediately all this conspiracy vanished in smoke. The best advised came to the King to cast themselves at his feet. The chief agent of the Duke of Bouillon being informed that an order had been given for his arrest, came to the King and told him all he knew before, and a great deal that he did not know. The others either fled out of the kingdom or else hid themselves. Five or six unfortunate persons being taken were beheaded at Limoges, and their heads stuck on the tops of the gates, their bodies burnt, and the ashes thrown into the air. Three or four others suffered the same punishment at Périgord. There were ten or twelve condemned for contumacy and their effigies hanged; amongst others, Chappelle-Biron and Giversac of the house of Cugnac. But in all these proceedings there were found no proofs in writing, nor yet by any formal deposition against the Duke of Bouillon, so cunningly had he managed this business.

Before these executions the King, having made his entrance into Limoges, returned to Paris. He earnestly desired that after this the Duke of Bouillon should acknowledge and humble himself; for if he remained impenitent he would be obliged to prosecute him to the utmost, and if he did prosecute him he offended all that great body of Protestants who were his faithful allies. He therefore secretly employed all means which he could devise to induce him to depend on his clemency rather than on the intercession of strangers, which could not be pleasing to a sovereign, in the case of his officer and subject. The duke desired even more than he to extricate himself from this trouble; but he believed he could not find security at court, because Rosny, who was not his friend, and who was jealous at seeing him of more consequence than himself in the Huguenot party, had such great influence with the King. So that after many treaties and negotiations, the King resolved to go after him at Sedan with an army.

Rosny laboured with great zeal to make preparations

for this expedition. The King confided much to him;
and by honouring him, he desired to testify to the
Huguenots that if he attacked the Duke of Bouillon, it
was not against their religion, but against rebellion,
that he was angry. For this purpose he made the land
of Sully into a duchy and peerage; and, therefore, we
shall henceforward call Rosny Duke of Sully. Sully's
opinion was that the King should pursue the Duke of
Bouillon to the utmost. Villeroy and the rest of the
council were of a contrary judgment; they did not think
it advisable to hazard the siege of Sedan, because the
length of that undertaking might possibly revive divers
factions in other parts of the kingdom, and give time
to the Spaniards to assault the frontiers of Picardy, to
the discontented Duke of Savoy to cast himself with the
forces of the Milanese on disarmed Provence, and to
the Huguenots and Protestants of Germany to come
to the assistance of their friends.

The King clearly foresaw all these inconveniences;
and, therefore, having advanced to Donchery during
the absence of Sully who had gone to provide artillery,
he treated with the Duke of Bouillon and received him
into his favour, on condition that he should humble
himself before his Majesty, receive him into the city
of Sedan, and deliver up the castle to him to keep it
with what garrison he should think fit, for four years.

These were the public conditions; but by secret
articles the King promised the duke to stay but five
days in Sedan, and to put only fifty men in the castle,
who should immediately depart upon humble suppli-
cation made by the duke. All these things were
faithfully executed, and without the least distrust

either on the one side or the other. The duke came to meet the King at Donchery, where he besought his pardon. The King received him as if he had never done any wrong, and five or six days after entered into Sedan, where he stayed only three days, and then returned to Paris. The duke accompanied him as far as Mousson; but some days after, when he understood that the parliament had confirmed his pardon, in which were likewise comprehended his friends who had been condemned by default at Limoges, he came to the court, where he received more honours and kindnesses than ever. This was the custom of that great king. He had a heart like a lion's against the proud and against rebels; but he was pleased to relieve with an unparalleled goodness those he had overcome, when by their submission they rendered themselves worthy to receive his grace. And the Duke of Bouillon, who perfectly knew his nature (for they had long lived and fought together), was careful to comport himself with all that prudence and compliancy which an intelligent man, such as he was, could be capable of.

Notwithstanding this great generosity and goodness of the King, his kingdom was no less troubled with incredible treacheries and conspiracies. Such were the treason of L'Oste, the attempt on the city of Marseilles by Mérargues, and another on Narbonne and Leucate by the Luquisses.

L'Oste was secretary to Villeroy, and his godson. It was his duty to decipher the dispatches. This unfortunate man revealed all the secrets of the King's affairs to some members of the council of Spain, who had bribed him with a pension of twelve hundred crowns, which they promised him whilst he was in that country with the ambassador Rochepot. On his treachery being discovered he fled, and as he was pursued by the provosts and the marshals he drowned himself in the river Marne, near the ferry of Fay. It may easily be judged that Villeroy, whose fidelity by this means remained exposed to the King's reasonable suspicions and to the calumnies of his enemies, was sensibly troubled. He would undoubtedly have had some difficulty in clearing himself of this business, however innocent he might have been, if the King, who saw him in such great affliction, had not had the goodness to visit him himself, and by that honour brought him the comfort of justifying him in the face of all calumnies which the envious might sow against him.

Mérargues was a gentleman from Provence, of a very good family, who, having assurance that he should the following year be sheriff[1] of Marseilles, had promised to deliver that city to the Spaniards during his shrievalty. He was so imprudent and so foolish as to reveal his design to a slave in the galleys at Marseilles, who gave information of it to the court, thinking by this means to gain his liberty.

Upon this information Mérargues, who was then at Paris, was watched so closely that they found him conferring with the secretary of the ambassador of Spain, and almost all they said was heard. They searched him, and found in the fold of his garter a note containing the plan of the conspiracy. He was arrested, and beheaded by sentence of the parliament

[1] *Viguier:* a magistrate under the old monarchy in the south of France, subordinate to the "seneschal."

of Paris on the 19th of December. His body was quartered, and his quarters fixed before the city gates; his head was carried to Marseilles, to be stuck on a pike upon a tower of one of the principal gates. The secretary of the ambassador was arrested as well as he, and would have been in great danger if the King had been as furious as those who counselled him, who desired a rupture with Spain.

This affair gave rise to considerable discussion amongst politicians concerning the rights of ambassadors and their people; but Henry the Great himself decided the question thus: "Ambassadors," said he, "are sacred by the right of nations. They abuse this right when they contrive any treason against the state or against the prince to whom their master has sent them, and consequently this right ought not to secure them from being sought out and punished. Moreover, it is not to be presumed that they are either ambassadors or that they represent the sovereign who sends them when they commit those treacheries which their masters would neither commit nor avow. However, there is more generosity in not behaving on this point with extreme severity, but in reserving the right to chastise them without it." And to this purpose, being well read in history, he alleged that example of the Roman senate, who having discovered that the ambassadors of the Allobroges were concerned in the conspiracy of Catiline, contented themselves with commanding them to depart the city. This was his opinion, and as he always followed the most generous maxims, he forbade that any action should be taken against the secretary, whom the judges were about to question.

In the meantime the ambassador, thinking to cloak this perfidy by his exclamations, came to complain to the King that the rights of nations were being violated, and in them the dignity of ambassadors; and that the King his master would resent it as became a great prince when offended. The King, answering him with a wise coldness, represented unto him what his secretary had conspired with Mérargues. The ambassador, not willing either to own the man or approve his action, turned the business another way, and complained that the King had made the first breach of the peace of Vervins by assisting the Hollanders with men and money. The King replied that, as regarded the men, they did not go by his orders, and that there were Frenchmen in the service of the archduke as well as in that of the Hollanders; but that it was in his power to do what he pleased with his money, and to lend it or give it without anyone having a right to say anything. The ambassador was very angry, and some high words passed on one side and the other. Finally the King returned him his secretary, as he had resolved to do in the first instance.

The Luquisses were two brothers, Genoese by extraction, who had made an agreement with the governor of Perpignan to deliver to him Narbonne and Lucate. It is certain that it was not in their power to execute this design, and that there was more ill-will in them than danger of its success. Nevertheless, they were taken and carried to Toulouse, where the parliament sent both to the gibbet.

It seemed that not only the malice of men, but folly itself now conspired against France; for the same day that Mérargues was executed an unhappy fool made an attempt on the sacred person of the King, throwing himself upon him with a dagger in his hand as he passed on horseback over the Pont-Neuf, returning from hunting. The attendants of the King running up, made him let go his hold, and would have killed him on the spot if it had not been forbidden by the King, who caused him to be taken prisoner to Fort Evêque. He was called John de l'Ile, and was a native of Vineux, near Senlis. He was examined by the president Jeannin, who could get no reasonable answer from him, for he was indeed quite out of his senses. He believed himself king of all the world, and said that, Henry IV. having usurped and taken France from him, he wished to chastise him for his temerity. Upon which the King, judging that he was sufficiently punished by his folly, commanded that he should only be kept in prison, where he died not long after.

Those who desired war did not fail to take advantage of all these conspiracies and undertakings of the Spaniards to incense the King's spirit. They represented to him that he ought not to wait for others from his perpetual enemies; that having used all their endeavours to hinder him from coming to his crown, they continued daily to attempt something against his repose and life; that their ambushes were more to be feared in peace than in war; that it were better to break with them, because they would have less means to hurt him, being no longer within his realm; that he had more to gain in attacking them by open force than in counter-plotting all their treacherous devices, which they concealed under the cloak of peace and friend-

ship. They moreover represented to him the bad state
of the Spanish finances; that having expended all their
treasure in the wars in the Low Countries, they were
obliged to have recourse to extraordinary means to re-
plenish it. But above all, they did not fail to lay
before him the great and advantageous qualities that
he had over Philip III., his adversary, in order that
he might be the easier induced to attack a man whom
they taught him to despise and consider weaker.

I may say, in connection with King Philip III.,
that although his mind was very acute, and his father,
Philip II., had given him all knowledge necessary to
govern, nevertheless from a certain timidity and distrust
of himself, too common in many great men, shunning
trouble and hardships, he had allowed the government
to devolve almost entirely on the Marquis of Denia,
whom he made Duke of Lerma. It would be difficult
to tell how this man rendered himself odious, and how
the other was little esteemed so long as this lasted;
but God finally opened the eyes of this young prince.
He broke his chains; and he who had become, as it
were, his master, thought there was no better way of
diverting all the calamities which might happen than
by becoming a churchman and a cardinal.

We may in passing make some reflections on the
pitiful state to which a sovereign reduces himself, who,
for not maintaining his dignity as he ought, necessarily
becomes an object of disdain and aversion to his subjects. Without doubt the greatest misfortune that can
befall him is to be regarded as inferior and subject to
another; to have his ears continually filled with the
voice of his people, crying on all sides, "Govern us!"

and to permit himself to be guided by five or six wicked
flatterers, who make him believe that he is master,
though he exercises not one function, rather than by
the truth or judgment of his whole kingdom. For if
he desire to know whether he be truly sovereign or
no, he need only regard himself without flattery. If
it be he that gives commands on his own initiative; if
he himself chooses the persons; if the officers about
him are of his own making; if he has ever said, "I
will have it so," in any affair of importance; if he see
himself always followed and accompanied by grandees;
if those who have business, who seek employments,
and who have need of his favour, are in his ante-
chamber; and, finally, if none of his realm have more
respect paid to them, or are sought more assiduously,
then he shall clearly know who it is that reigns. But
it is not enough for him to know who it is. He must,
after the example of Philip III., of whom we were just
now speaking, endeavour to put himself in possession
of his authority. It is in this that the courage of a
prince principally consists; for in what can he better
make known his resolution and valour than in taking
upon himself that degree and power which God has
given him? Is there a truer point of honour for a
king than to maintain in his person the rights of
his royalty? Without dissembling, it shows more
weakness and shame for a sovereign to submit to him
who ought to be dependent on his will than to flee
in the day of battle before his enemies; for the bravest
sometimes run away, and the courage of a king consists
much less in fighting with his hands than in governing with his head. What use is it for him to over-

come his enemies if he see himself beneath his own subject, who under pretext of serving him reduces him and his kingdom into fetters, and who dares invest himself with all the glory and all the advantage of command, making him believe that it is to ease him of the burden?

Our Henry was not of this temper. His goodness was extreme, but it was neither sluggish nor timid; his knowledge and understanding were not useless, but always laborious and active. Nothing was above him but God himself; nothing on any side of him but justice and clemency, his two faithful counsellors. The most hardy of his ministers trembled when he but bent his brow; all familiarities immediately ceased, and none dared to speak when he was pleased to take the tone of master.

Now this great King thus preserving the splendour of his majesty, we cannot wonder if he were esteemed above Philip III., who at that time suffered himself to be absolutely governed. And therefore, because they knew he understood his weakness, they believed that he would be more easily persuaded to make war against him. Indeed he was sufficiently resolved to that; and after so many injuries as he had received from the Spaniard, his resentment had no great need of a spur. However, before he would undertake so arduous a task, he wished to make all his arrangements so exactly, gather together so much money, artillery, and ammunition, fortify so well his frontiers, keep such good order within his kingdom, assure himself of so many friends and allies, raise such powerful armies, and, finally, make his party so strong, that the success should not at all be doubtful, and that when he encountered that ambitious power, he might be assured of overthrowing it; and therefore he judged it not to the purpose too much to hasten.

In the meantime he neglected not other means to acquire reputation, thinking it not less glorious to blazon forth his name by the repute of his wisdom in counsels than by the power of his arms. By the latter he had been victorious over the rebels and the Spaniards; by the former, he rendered himself arbitrator of the great differences of Christendom, and acquired a superiority so much more noble, because given him without constraint.

Pope Clement VIII. having died about the end of the year 1605, Henry wished to employ his influence in causing the choice of the cardinals to fall on one of his friends. The Cardinal of Joyeuse, his ambassador, and his other agents laboured so well that they elected Alexander de Medicis, Cardinal of Florence. He took the name of Leo XI., but he died at the end of seventeen days; so the business had to be gone through again. The King did not wish that they should take pains in the choice of another of his friends; and declared that France took no other interest than that an honest man should be chosen. The conclave in the end chose Cardinal Borghese, who was named Paul V.

In the first years of his papacy a great difference which was begun under his predecessors was rekindled, which would have set on fire all Italy, and possibly all Christendom, if our Henry had not taken care to extinguish it.

The seigniory of Venice had formerly made an ordinance or decree which prohibited the monks from purchasing lands in their dominions above the value of twenty thousand ducats, and enjoining everyone who had purchased above that value to remit it to the seigniory, who would reimburse them the purchase-money and the improvements they had made on the property. Following in the footsteps of this ancient decree, they made another, which forbade the founding or building of new churches, convents, and monasteries without express permission of the seigniory, under penalty of banishment, and confiscation of such foundations and buildings.

It was, indeed, part of the function and charge of bishops to prevent this multiplication of convents; but either through negligence or through being too easily persuaded, they gave permission to all that asked; so much so that the commonwealth, instead of the prelates, found themselves obliged to take notice of it; otherwise it would soon have happened that all their cities would have been nothing else but convents and churches, and all their revenues, which ought to bear the charge of the state and serve for the support of married people, who furnish it with soldiers, merchants, and labourers, would have been expended only in the maintenance of nuns and friars.

The seigniory therefore made another decree, which prohibited ecclesiastics from purchasing any real property, except by permission of that body. At the same time it happened that an abbot and a canon, being accused of horrible crimes committed in the territories of the seigniory, were imprisoned upon secular authority, which was considered very strange on the other side of the mountains, where the ecclesiastics are not at all subject to secular justice.

Now Paul V., on coming to the pontifical chair, was not able to overlook, he said, all these attacks of the secular power on the ecclesiastical, and dispatched at the same time two briefs[1] to his nuncio at Venice, one containing the revocation of the decrees made by the seigniory with regard to the purchasing of temporal estates, and the other commanding the restitution of the abbot and the canon to the chapter of the church. The nuncio announced this to the seigniory, who answered sharply that their authority came from themselves; that no person but they had to do with it; and that they would know how to maintain it against any who attempted to oppose it. Both sides employed the best scholars of the time to defend their rights and confute the arguments of their adversaries. A very large number of manifestoes and treatises were written, full of legal arguments, passages of Holy Scripture, authorities of fathers and councils, and parallels drawn from history.

In the meantime the Pope, extremely offended at this answer, thundered out an excommunication against the Doge and the seigniory, if within twenty-four days they did not revoke their decrees and consign the two prisoners to the hands of the nuncio. The seigniory was not at all moved by this, but boldly declared the sentence of excommunication null and out of rule; nor was there any ecclesiastic in their whole territories who attempted to publish it, or dared to observe the

[1] Pastoral letters.

interdict or stop Divine service. The Capuchins and the Jesuits, however, resolved to depart, and asked permission of the seigniory. They granted it to the Capuchins, with liberty to return when they pleased; but the Jesuits were prohibited from ever re-entering their dominions.

While the quarrel between these two powers was becoming very grave, the Spaniards were looking out with a sharp eye to make their profit out of these divisions, and secretly fomented the strife while pretending to be desirous of healing it. On the one side they encouraged the Venetians, and emboldened them to maintain their rights; and on the other they commanded their governors of Naples and Milan to serve the Holy Father with all their powers. Henry the Great, more sincere and more disinterested, embraced this opportunity to establish his power in Italy in a more fair and just manner. He assured the Pope that, as the eldest son of the Church, he would always sustain its interests, and that in case of rupture he would go in person to its help with an army of forty thousand men; but he entreated him that, before it came to this, he would grant that he might use his best endeavours to settle matters peaceably.

He answered likewise to the ambassador of Venice, who asked for his assistance, that he owed it to the Holy Father before all others; and therefore he exhorted the seigniory to permit him to mediate in the affair, which they might do without wounding their honour or rights.

Both parties having accepted his mediation, he dispatched Cardinal Joyeuse into Italy, who managed this negotiation with so much address, that in the end he effected a reconciliation. The treaty contained four principal articles: 1. That the seigniory should consign the two prisoners in the hands of the ambassador of France, to remit them to his Holiness. 2. That they should revoke the manifesto and declaration they had made against the apostolic censors. 3. That they should restore to all ecclesiastics their property. 4. That the Pope should give them absolution, and that in requital they should send to thank him by a noble embassy, and assure him of their filial obedience.

On the morrow the Cardinal de Joyeuse, coming to the place assigned by the seigniory, the doors being shut, in the presence of the Doge and twenty-five senators, and of the ambassador of France, revoked the excommunication, and gave absolution to the seigniory. All this was effected without the slightest intervention on the part of the Spaniards, though they endeavoured to share in it. Thus both parties had some sort of satisfaction by the good offices of Henry the Great.

The business of the Jesuits, however, for some months retarded the treaty. It came very near breaking it off altogether, because the Pope, considering that they were driven away for his sake, firmly resolved that the seigniory should re-establish them in their property, and the seigniory were equally obstinate, preferring rather to hazard all than to consent to it. At last the Pope, persuaded by the eloquence of Cardinal Perron, who was then at Rome, thought it better to waive this point than hazard the outbreak of a war throughout Christendom; and the Jesuits therefore remained banished from the lands of the seigniory. Alexander VII., by his intercession, afterwards caused them to be re-established.

If the accommodation of the differences between the Pope and the Venetians added much to the renown and reputation of our Henry, reviving the credit of France beyond the mountains, where it seemed dead, and depressing by as much that of the Spaniards, which before seemed paramount, the treaty which he managed between the King of Spain and the States or United Provinces purchased him no less fame among the Protestants and the people of the north. I will briefly relate the circumstances.

The United Provinces, commonly called Holland, from the name of the largest of the seven provinces which composed this body, had some reason to complain that the King had made the treaty at Vervins without their consent, and that he had bound himself not to assist them, either directly or indirectly. He had, however, kept them supplied with money, and also had permitted a large number of volunteers, including many nobles, to enlist themselves in their service to such an extent that there were many regiments composed entirely of Frenchmen. It was not therefore without apparent reason that the Spaniards cried out that he had clearly infringed the treaty of Vervins; but these reproaches were not just, for they had broken it beforehand by a hundred attempts, of which we have mentioned some.

In the meantime the King, who was very careful of his money, was weary of furnishing the United Provinces with so much, and earnestly desired to see them in a position in which they would not put him to so much expense. There was only one way to effect this, and that was by securing them peace with the Spaniards. He therefore resolved to work for this end, and chose the president Jeannin, a man of great good sense, to manage this negotiation.

The two parties at first consented to a truce of eight months, during which the estates of the United Provinces, in order that they might treat with more reputation and security, prayed the King to grant them an offensive and defensive alliance. This, of which the following are the principal articles, he willingly granted them.

He promised faithfully to assist and aid them by all means in his power to obtain from the King of Spain a good and assured peace. If it pleased God that they should obtain it he would cause it to be faithfully observed, and would defend them against all who should dare to infringe it; and to this end he would maintain in their service ten thousand foot at his own expense, so long as they should have need of them. Reciprocally the states agreed that if he were assaulted in his kingdom they would assist him with five thousand foot at their own expense; and they would leave it to the King's choice to take this assistance in soldiers, or in ships fitted and furnished at all points to fight at sea.

The Spaniards were extremely alarmed at this alliance. Don Pedro de Toledo, one of the greatest lords of Spain, passing through France to go to the Low Countries, made great complaints to the King; but many imagined that all the noise he made tended only to oblige him to treat of peace with the Hollanders, for Spain was exhausted with a war so long, so tiresome, and so bloody, with such great expense and so little progress.

Don Pedro, as is characteristic of the true Spanish nobility, was of an austere and grave countenance, high and magnificent in his words when it was a question of the honour and glory of his nation and the power of his king, but otherwise courteous and civil, submissive and respectful where he should be so, gallant, witty, and clever. We must not omit to mention several interesting incidents which took place during his visit to the King.

The King, believing that he had brought him threats of war, and knowing that the Spaniards had spread abroad a report that he was quite lame with the gout and unable to mount on horseback, wished to show him that his health and activity were not at all diminished. He received him in the great gallery at Fontainebleau, and made him take twenty or thirty turns at so great a pace that he put him out of breath, then saying to him, "You see now, sir, how well I am!"

At this first audience Don Pedro brought his beads in his hand. He represented to the King the general interest that all Catholic princes had in the ruin or conversion of heretics, and the great wars which his master had waged for this purpose. Afterwards changing his discourse, he told him that the Catholic King earnestly desired to ally himself more closely with him, and to make marriages between their children, provided that the King would renounce the alliance and protection of the Low Countries. The King frankly answered that his children were of as noble blood as could be found; that he desired no constrained friendships nor conditions; that he could not abandon his friends; but that those, who would not be such, would repent of being his enemies.

Don Pedro upon this exalted the greatness and power of Spain. The King, without being moved, let him know that it was like the statue of Nebuchadnezzar, composed of several sorts of materials, and which had feet of clay. Don Pedro then came to reproaches and threats. The King, however, was more than a match for him, and told him that if the King of Spain continued his attempts, he would carry flames even into the Escurial, and that if he once mounted on horseback he would soon be at Madrid. The Spaniard arrogantly answered him, "King Francis was there, indeed." "Therefore," replied the King, "I would go there to revenge his injuries, those of France, and my own."

After some high words, the King with a calmer voice said to him, "My lord ambassador, you are a Spaniard and I a Gascon, let us not grow angry." They returned then to the language of sweetness and civility.

Another time the King, showing him his buildings at Fontainebleau, asked him what he thought of them. He replied that in his opinion God was lodged very narrowly. There were then but two chapels, which were in the court, and were certainly very small. The King could not bear to have his piety accused, and therefore answered him very sharply: "You Spaniards know not how to give God other than material temples; we Frenchmen lodge God not only in stones, we lodge

Him in our hearts; but though He should be lodged in yours, I fear it would be in stone still."

From Fontainebleau they came to Paris, where the King one day showed him his gallery of the Louvre, and asked his opinion of it. "The Escurial is just such another thing," said Don Pedro. "I believe it," replied the King; "but has it a Paris about it like my gallery?"

One day Don Pedro, seeing at the Louvre the King's sword in the hands of one of his cloak-bearers, advanced to it, and putting one knee on the ground, kissed it, "rendering this honour," he said, "to the most glorious sword in Christendom!"

During the eight months' truce of which we have spoken, the president Jeannin incessantly laboured for a treaty. There were two great difficulties; one, that the King of Spain would not treat with the United Provinces but as with subjects, and they on their part wished to be acknowledged as free and independent; the other, that the Prince of Orange, whose power and authority would be extremely weakened by the peace, opposed it by a thousand artifices, being upheld in it by the province of Zealand, which was always anxious for war, and by some cities of its faction.

These two obstacles were in the end surmounted. The Spaniard yielded on the first, and acknowledged the states as free states, provinces, and countries; and for the second, the King spoke so sharply to the Prince of Orange that he dared not stop the course of the treaty. It did not end, however, in a peace, as was to be desired, but only in a truce of twelve years, during which time the commerce of both countries was to be free and assured.

The renown of this negotiation carried the King's glory throughout all Europe. The Doge of Venice told the French ambassador in the senate that the seigniory had fresh cause to admire the prudent conduct of the King, who never deceived himself in his undertaking, nor ever gave blow in vain ; that he was the true upholder of the repose and felicity of Christendom ; and that nothing more could be desired for the happiness of his kingdom but that he might reign for ever. A eulogy so much the more worthy and glorious because we may say with truth that Venice has always been the seat of political wisdom, and that the praises which come from that senate are as so many oracles.

The friendship and protection of this great king was sought on all sides. All was referred to his arbitration, and all implored his assistance. And as he was equally powerful and wise, feared and loved, there was none who dared contradict his judgment, or attack those whom he protected. But he was so just that he would not encroach upon the rights of another, nor maintain the rebellions of subjects against their sovereign, a notable proof of which he gave in the affair of the Moors.

It is well known that the Moors or Saracens invaded Spain towards the year 725. The Christians, with the aid of the French, had regained it from them little by little, so that there remained to them no more than the kingdom of Granada, which was small in extent, but very rich, and extremely populous, because all the remnants of that infidel nation had retired into that little space. Ferdinand King of Arragon, and Isabella Queen of Castile, completed the conquest of that kingdom in the year 1492, and so put an end to the government of the Moors and to the Mohammedan religion in Spain, forcing the infidels to accept baptism, or to retire into Africa.

Now as those who had thus professed the Christian religion only did so because they were obliged to, they for the most part remained Mohammedans in their hearts, or Jews (for there were many Jews amongst them), and secretly brought up their children in their unbelief. To this, however, the Spaniards themselves largely contributed, by putting great distinction between the new Christians and the old; for they would not receive the new ones either to charges or holy orders, they would not intermarry with them, and, what is worse, levied blackmail upon them, and oppressed them with excessive imposts. So that these unfortunate people, seeing themselves thus trampled on, and being too weak to free themselves from their yoke, resolved to address themselves to some foreign power, but which should be Christian, because that of the King of Morocco, or the other princes of Africa, would have appeared too odious. With this object they secretly had recourse by deputies to our Henry, when he was still only King of Navarre. Afterwards, in the year 1595, when they saw that he had overcome the League, and had got the upper hand in his affairs, they again implored his protection. He listened favourably to their propositions, sent disguised agents into Spain to see the state of their affairs, and gave them hope that he would assist them. And he might easily have done it, since he was at war with the King of Spain, and it is lawful to make use of all sorts of arms to defend ourselves against our enemies. In the year 1608 they again returned and earnestly solicited him to accept their propositions and offers, and to give them an answer from his own mouth. He told them plainly that the quality of most Christian King which he bore prevented him from undertaking their defence so long as the peace of Vervins lasted; but that if the Spaniards should first openly infringe it, he would have just cause to receive them under his protection.

Their deputies having lost all hopes in this quarter, addressed themselves to the King of England, whom they found still less disposed than he to lend them assistance. In the meantime, their plots, having taken wind in the court of Spain, caused both fear and astonishment, for there were nearly a million of them, and they owned almost all the commerce, particularly in oils, which is very great in that country.

King Philip III. could see no safer way to hinder the dangerous effects of their conspiracies than banishing them from his territories. This he did by an edict of the 10th of January, 1610, which was executed with much cruelty, inhumanity, and treachery; for in transporting these unfortunate people into Africa, as they had begged, part were drowned in the sea, others despoiled of all they had, so that those who had not yet departed, perceiving the ill-treatment of their companions, fled towards France, one part by land to St. Jean de Lus, to the number of one hundred and fifty thousand, others in French vessels, which brought them into various ports of the kingdom. But those who came by land were not much better treated by the French than the others had been by the Spaniards, for in crossing the Landes[1] they were almost all robbed and stripped, and their wives and daughters ravished; so that finding so little safety in a country wherein they had believed they would find refuge, they embarked by the King's permission at the ports of Languedoc, and crossed over into Africa, where they have become implacable and most cruel enemies to all Christians. Some few families remained in the maritime cities of the kingdom, as in Bordeaux and Rouen.

The King, instead of protecting these infidels, was planning a gigantic undertaking towards the Levant, for the glory and extension of the Christian religion. But he would not declare himself till he had so ordered the affairs of Christendom that there should be no fear of any trouble or division, and that it might make use of all its forces against so powerful an enemy as the Grand Turk. In pursuance of this idea he had sent three or four gentlemen into the Levant, who, under the pretext of travelling and visiting the holy places, reconnoitred the country, the disposition of the people, the state of their forces, and the garrisons and government of the Turks; which having well considered, he estimated that after having settled the interests and procured the union of the Christian princes, he might in three or four years at most ruin this terrible power, and that with an army of thirty-five thousand foot and twelve thousand horse only. Alexander the Great had no more forces to destroy the empire of

[1] Dry, sandy ground.

the Persians, which without doubt was greater and more powerful than that of the Turks.

I shall recount what his great design for the reunion of Christendom was when I have briefly observed some important things which happened in the three or four last years of his life.

As he laboured diligently to heap up money, the sinews of war, so he listened to all propositions made for gaining it, so much the more willingly because his design was to abolish all taxes and impositions.[1] This could not be done without greatly diminishing his revenue, so it was necessary to find some other way of getting funds in its place. Now this he hoped to find in the demesnes of the crown, which he desired entirely to release and increase by a number of new rights, and particularly by that of the *greffes*,[2] which had been quite withdrawn for five or six years, but had brought him in fifteen million francs a year. After his death, however, Queen Mary de Medicis re-established it on a much larger scale than before.

As for the impost, our Henry had a desire to buy from the owners all the salt-marshes of Poitou and Brittany, and then when he had them in his own hands, to sell the salt upon the spot at what price he pleased to the merchant, who would again retail it through the whole kingdom without constraint or imposition. This would have done away with the necessity for so many overseers, controllers, factors, officers, and a hundred others, who, without exaggera-

---

[1] *La gabelle:* excise duties, principally in salt.

[2] The *greffes* was a due to the King of £3 3s. 9d. upon the sale of wood in several places.

tion, amounted to nearly twenty thousand, all fed and paid at the expense of the King and public, and against whom he had often very great complaints. Thus the poor country people would not be burdened by them with the imposition on salt, forcing them willy-nilly to take yearly a certain quantity; and it is certain the people would have had it a great deal cheaper, and the King have raised much more money, without expense, trouble, or vexation of his subjects.

Now it must be acknowledged that the King, in seeking means to fill his coffers, and to find some other way than taxes, made some imposts and also created officers; but it must also be admitted that he removed many things which gave cause of complaint. And moreover, to pay his old debts and find means for the rewards and pensions due to those who had served him in his wars against the League, he was obliged to enact for their benefit several things which they proposed, so that he loaded himself with envy and reproaches which ought more justly to have fallen upon those people than upon himself. But those who knew his intentions did not blame him, for they called that prudence and wise economy which some termed avarice and insatiable covetousness.

Moreover, though this prince was desirous for the comfort of his people and the grandeur of his state, nevertheless it cannot be denied that he was sometimes deceived in the choice of the means, which were not always so innocent as his intentions. Two in particular are worth relating, of which the one made some noise but never succeeded, and the other has had very dangerous consequences.

The first was an inquisition of the rents at the Hôtel de Ville, by which those who had not come by them honestly were to be compelled to give them up. This in itself was very just; but the greater part of the rents having changed owners, or been parted, he must perforce trouble an infinite number of families, so that all Paris was roused, and the tenants had recourse to their provost of the merchants. This was Miron, who was likewise civil lieutenant, a man very zealous in the service of the King, as he had shown on several occasions, but withal a very honest man, and one whom no interest in the world could bribe against the people, whose magistrate he was. He boldly championed the cause of the people, and spoke in the assemblies of the Hôtel de Ville, acted with the superintendent vigourously, and made remonstrances to the King. But in these remonstrances his warmth caused him to make some odious comparisons, not of the King's person, but of some of his council.

The Louvre stormed; the people of the court cried out that he had blasphemed; those whom he had mentioned in his speeches, and those who were interested in this inquisition after rents used all their endeavours to incense the King and to persuade him rigorously to punish this boldness. On the other hand, the people, hearing that their magistrate was threatened, unanimously rose up to protect him. The burgesses came in troops about his house to defend it; but Miron entreated them to retire, and not to make him a criminal. He told them that there was nothing to fear; that they had to do with a king as sweet and just as he was great and wise, and who would not let himself be carried away by the persuasions of evil counsellors.

Upon this, those who wished him ill employed all their endeavours to persuade the King to take him by force, and to assert his supreme authority. But he wisely answered these people that authority does not always consist in pushing matters to the utmost extremity; that the time, the persons, and the cause ought to be regarded; that having been ten years extinguishing the fire of civil war, he feared even the least sparks; that Paris had cost him too much to hazard the least danger of losing it, which seemed to him certain if he followed their counsel, because he should be obliged to make terrible examples, which would in a few days deprive him of the glory of his clemency and the love of his people, which he prized as much as, nay above, his crown; that he had on a hundred other occasions proved the fidelity and honesty of Miron, who had no ill-intention, but without doubt believed himself obliged by the duty of his office to do what he did; that if some inconsiderate words had escaped him, he might well pardon them for his past services; that after all, if this man affected to be the martyr of the people, he would not give him that glory nor bring upon himself the name of persecutor or tyrant; and, finally, that it was not on such valuable occasions that he ought to prosecute a man, when people desired his destruction.

Thus this wise King knew how to prudently dissemble a little fault; he did not even want to know what had passed, for fear of being obliged to strike some blow of authority which might possibly have had dangerous consequences. He received, therefore, very favourably the excuses and humble submission of Miron, and afterwards prohibited the inquisitions of rents, which had caused so much trouble.

The second means of which he availed himself to raise money, and which was of very dangerous consequence, was the *paulette*, or annual right. To understand this properly we must go back a little in history.

The offices of judicature, of police, and of the revenues had formerly been exercised in France, under the first and second race of our kings, by gentlemen; for the nobility were obliged to study and understand the laws of the kingdom. They were chosen for the maturity of their age and judgment; they were changed from time to time, from one seat to another; and they took no fees from suitors, except a very moderate salary which the public paid them rather for honour than recompense. Afterwards, towards the end of the second race and at the beginning of the third, the nobility became ignorant and weak, and the plebeians and burgesses, having gained a knowledge of the laws, raised themselves little by little to these charges, both judicial and financial, and began to make them of higher value, because they drew all their honour and dignity thence, not having any other by birth, as the gentlemen had. Yet they had not very much to do, for the churchmen possessed almost all the jurisdiction, and had their officers who administered justice.

In the meantime the parliament, which before was as the council of state of the kingdom, and an epitome of the States-general, took upon themselves the decision of differences between particular persons, whereas before they only treated of great affairs of policy; therefore Philip the Fair, or, according to some others, his son, Louis X., made it stationary at Paris. Now this company of judges became most illustrious, because the King often took his seat amongst them, the dukes, peers, and prelates of the realm formed a part of them, and the most able people in legal matters were chosen to fill places there. They made the power of other judges-royal depend upon them, to wit, the bailiffs and seneschals, who, though before this they had been sovereign judges, became now subordinate to them.

At various times after, other kings created many other parliaments, but with the sole intention of causing justice to be administered without any pecuniary interest, and by it they filled their coffers with wages to pay these officers.

At this time the number of the officers of justice was very small, and the order which was observed to fill the vacancies in parliament perfectly good. The custom was to keep a register of all the able advocates and lawyers, and when any office was vacant they chose three, whose names they carried to the King, who chose one of them. But the favourites and the courtiers soon corrupted this order. They persuaded the kings not to confine themselves to those presented, but to name one of their own choosing, the object, of course, being that these favourites might extract some present from him who should be made on their recommendation. And the abuse was so great that often the offices were filled with ignorant and low people; and so people of merit held the position of an advocate much more honourable than that of a counsellor.

The mischief daily increased, and the rich people becoming extremely desirous of these posts for lucre, and their wives out of vanity, those who governed began to make a regular traffic in them. Thus under Louis XII., his coffers being exhausted by the long Italian wars, the offices of the revenue commenced to be openly sold. However, that good king having soon foreseen the dangerous consequence, resolved to reimburse those who had bought them ; but dying without fulfilling his good intention, Francis I., of whom he had well predicted that he would spoil all,[1] sold likewise those of judicature. At various times afterwards new ones were created, with the sole purpose of raising money.

Afterwards Henry II., his son, created the presidents, and Charles IX. and Henry III., heaping ill upon ill and ruin upon ruin, made a great number of other creations of all sorts, in order to have these wares to sell; and, moreover, they sold offices when they were vacant, either by death or forfeiture.

Hitherto the evil had been great, but not incurable. When these offices became vacant, a part only need have been suppressed, and the rest filled with persons of capacity and merit. Thus in twenty years this ants' nest of officers might have been reduced to a very small number, and those honest people.

But the business was not in this way made known to Henry the Great; they represented it to him in another sense. They gave him to understand that

[1] He had often said, "That fat boy will spoil all."

since he drew no profit from vacant offices, being almost always obliged to give them, he would do well to find the means to discharge in this way a part of the wages he paid his officers, which he might do by granting them their offices for their heirs, reserving a moderate sum of money which they should yearly pay, yet without forcing anyone, so that it should be a favour and not an oppression. This was named the annual right, otherwise the *paulette*, from the name of the proposer Paulet, who gave the counsel and was the first farmer. All the officers were only too pleased to pay this right, so as to assure their offices to their heirs. We need not here tell the mischief and inconvenience which this wicked invention caused.

I will not weary the reader with all the ceremonies and rejoicings made at the birth and baptism of all the children of Henry the Great, nor at the various marriages of the princes and grandees of the court, amongst others, of the Prince of Condé and the Duke of Vendôme, which were celebrated in July, 1609.

The Prince of Condé espoused Charlotta Margarita of Montmorency, daughter of the Constable, who was wonderfully fair and had a splendid presence, which the King having noticed, was more struck with her than he had ever been with any other, which shortly after caused the retreat of the Prince of Condé, who carried her into Flanders, and thence retired to Milan. The King was extremely displeased at seeing the first prince of his blood cast himself into his enemies' hands.

The Duke of Vendôme espoused Mademoiselle de Merceur, to whom he had been affianced since the year 1597, as we have said before. The mother of the lady, however, being very proud and haughty, threw so many obstacles in the way of this marriage that it would never have taken place if the King had not concerned himself in it. This was not the least difficult thing in his life, for he had a high and obstinate spirit to bend; however, he employed only ways of gentleness and persuasion, acting in this business only as a father who loved his son, and not as a King who would be obeyed.

I do not think it necessary to dwell at any very great length on the King's ordinary diversions, these being hunting, building, feasts, play, and walking. I will add only that in feasts and merriments he would appear as good a companion and as jovial as another; that he was of a merry humour when he had the glass in his hand, though very sober; that his mirth and witticisms were the best part of the good cheer; that he showed no less agility and strength in combats at the barrier, courses at the ring, and all sorts of gallantries than the youngest lords; that he took delight in balls and sometimes danced. Some thought it wrong that so great a prince should descend to such follies, and that a greybeard should take pleasure in acting the young man. It may be said in his excuse that the great cares of his mind had need of these diversions. But I know not what to answer to those who reproach him with too great a love for playing at cards and dice, little befitting a great king; and that withal he was no great gamester, but greedy of coin, fearful at great stakes, and petulant upon a loss. To this I must acknowledge that it was a fault in this great king, who was no more exempt from blots than the sun.

It might be wished for the honour of his memory that he had been only guilty of this; but that continual weakness he had for fair ladies was much more blamable in a Christian prince, in a man of his age, who was married, to whom God had shown so many graces, and who had conceived such great designs in his spirit. Sometimes he had desires which were passing, and only fixed for a night; but when he met with beauties which struck him to the heart, he loved even to folly, and in such transports of passion he resembled anyone rather than Henry the Great.

The fable says that Hercules took the spindle and spun for the love of the fair Omphale. Henry did meaner things for his mistresses. He once disguised himself like a countryman, with a wallet of straw on his back, to gain access to the fair Gabrielle; and it has been reported that the Marchioness of Verneuil had more than once seen him at her feet bewailing her disdain and insults.

Twenty romances might be made of the intrigues of his loves with the Countess of Guiche, when he was but King of Navarre; with Jacqueline of Bueil, whom he made Countess of Moret; and with Charlotta d'Essards, without counting many other ladies, who held it a glory to have some charm for so great a king.

The high esteem and affection which the French had for him hindered them from being offended at such scandals; but the Queen his wife was extremely annoyed at it, and it hourly caused controversies between them. The King, who was in fault, endured it very patiently, and employed his greatest confidants, and sometimes his confessor, to appease his spirit, so that he continually had a reconciliation to make. These contentions were so common that the court, which at first was astonished at them, in the end took no notice.

Conjugal duty without doubt obliged the King not to violate his faith to his legitimate spouse, or at least not to keep his mistresses in her sight. But if in this point he ought to have been a good husband, so ought he to have been likewise in that of authority, and in accustoming his wife to obey him with more submission, and not trouble him as she did with hourly complaints, reproaches, and even threats.

The trouble and displeasure of these domestic vexations certainly retarded the execution of the great design which he had formed for the good and perpetual repose of Christendom, and for the destruction of the Ottoman power.

It has been variously spoken of, but I have extracted the following from the memoirs of the Duke of Sully, who certainly must know something about it, being as he was so great a confidant of this king.

The King desiring to put in execution those projects he had conceived after the peace of Vervins, believed that he ought first to establish in his kingdom an unshaken peace, by reconciling all spirits both to him and among themselves, and taking away all causes of bitterness; and that, moreover, it was necessary for him to choose people capable and faithful, who might see in what way his revenues or estates might be bettered, and to make himself so well acquainted with all his affairs that he might discern the good from the ill, feasible from impossible enterprises, and such as were proportionate to his revenues; for an expense made beyond them draws the people's curses, and those are generally followed by God's.

He granted an edict to the Huguenots, in order that the two religions might live in peace. Afterwards he made a certain and fixed order to pay his debts and those of the kingdom contracted by the disorders of the times, the profuseness of his ancestors, and by the payments and purchases of men and places which he was forced to make during the war with the League. (Sully showed him an account in the year 1607, by which it appeared that he had paid eighty-seven million francs.) This re-established the reputation and credit of France among strangers, by whom it was before held in very low estimation.

That done, he continually laboured to join in his great design all Christian princes, offering to give them all the fruit of his undertakings against the infidels, without reserving anything for himself; for he did not wish, he said, for any other kingdom than France.

He likewise endeavoured on all occasions to extinguish disorders and to pacify differences among the Christian princes as soon as they arose, and that with no other interest than that of the reputation of a generous, disinterested, wise, and just prince.

He became very friendly with all nations and their princes that seemed best disposed towards France, such as the United Provinces, the Venetians, the Swiss, and the Grisons. After having bound them to him by very strong ties, he endeavoured to negotiate with the three great kingdoms of the north, England, Denmark, and

Sweden, to discuss and decide their differences, and likewise to endeavour to reconcile them to the Pope, or at least to minimise their hatred and enmity, so that they might live together. This would have been advantageous to the Pope, for they would thereby have acknowledged him as the first prince of Christendom as to temporal affairs, and in that case rendered him all respect. He endeavoured to do the same thing among the electors, the states and cities of the Empire, being obliged particularly, he said, to take care of an empire which had been founded by his predecessors. Afterwards he sounded the lords of Bohemia, Hungary, Transylvania, and Poland to know if they would concur with him in the design of taking away and rooting up for ever all causes of trouble and division in Christendom. He treated after that with the Pope, who approved and praised his plan, and desired to contribute on his part all that was possible.

He desired perfectly to unite all Christendom, so that it should be one body, which would have been, and rightly so, called the Christian commonwealth. To effect this, he had determined to divide it into fifteen dominions or states, so as to make them of equal power and strength, and whose limits should be so well specified by the universal consent of the whole fifteen that none could pass beyond them. These were to be the Pontificate or Papacy, the Empire of Germany, France, Spain, Great Britain, Hungary, Bohemia, Poland, Denmark, Sweden, Savoy or the kingdom of Lombardy, the seigniory of Venice, the Italian commonwealth, Belgium or the Low Countries, and the Swiss.

Of these states there were to have been five successive: France, Spain, Great Britain, Sweden, and Lombardy; six elective: the Papacy, the Empire, Hungary, Bohemia, Poland, and Denmark; four republics; two of which were to be democratic, to wit, the Belgians and the Swiss, and two aristocratic or seigniories, that of Venice and that of the small Italian princes and towns.

The Pope was to have, besides those lands he possessed, the whole kingdom of Naples, and was also to receive the homage of the Italian commonwealth and of the island of Sicily.

The seigniory of Venice were to do homage to the Pope for Sicily, by kissing his toe and giving a golden crucifix every twenty years.

The Italian commonwealth would have been composed of the states of Florence, Genoa, Lucca, Mantua, Parma, Modena, Monaco, and other small places which were likewise to be held of the holy see, by payment of a crucifix of gold worth ten thousand francs.

The Duke of Savoy, besides those lands he possessed, was likewise to have Milan, and all was to be created a kingdom by the Pope, under the title of the kingdom of Lombardy, and which would have taken Montferrat in exchange for Cremona.

Franche-Comté, Alsatia, Tyrol, and the country of Trent with their dependencies were to have been incorporated with the Helvetian or Swiss republic, and simple homage was to be done by them to the Emperor of Germany every twenty-five years.

All the seventeen provinces of the Low Countries, Protestant as well as Catholic, were to have been established as a free and sovereign republic, except for a like homage to the Empire; and this dominion was to have been increased by the duchy of Clèves, of Juliers, of Berghe, of La Mark, Ravenstein, and other small neighbouring seigniories.

To the kingdom of Hungary were to have been joined the states of Transylvania, Moldavia, and Wallachia.

The Emperor was to renounce aggrandising himself by any confiscation, disinheritance, or reversion of male fiefs, but was to be able to dispose vacant fiefs in favour of persons not of his kindred, by the consent of the electors and princes of the Empire. It was likewise to have been agreed that the Empire should never upon any occasion whatsoever be held successively by two princes of one house, for fear of its becoming hereditary, as it has been for a long time in Austria.

The kingdoms of Hungary and Bohemia were to have been likewise elective by the voice of seven electors; to wit (1) that of the nobles, clergy, and cities of that country; (2) of the Pope; (3) of the Emperor; (4) of the King of France; (5) of the King of Spain; (6) of the King of England; (7) of the Kings of Sweden, Denmark, and Poland, who were to count as one.

Besides, to regulate the differences which might arise between the confederacy, and to decide them without violence, there was to have been established an order and form of procedure by a general council, composed of sixty persons, four on the part of each dominion, which was to have been situated in some city in the midst of Europe, such as Metz, Nancy, Cologne, or some other equally convenient. There were likewise to have been established three other councils, each of twenty men, which were to report to the grand council.

Moreover, by the consent of the general council, which was to be called the senate of the Christian commonwealth, there was to be established an order and regulation between sovereign and subjects, to hinder on one side the oppression and tyranny of princes, and on the other side the complaints and rebellions of subjects. There was likewise to have been raised and assured a reserve of money and men, to which every dominion was to contribute according to the assessment of the grand council, for the assistance of the dominions liable to the attacks of infidels, to wit, Hungary against those of the Turks, and Sweden and Poland against those of the Muscovites and Tartars.

When all these fifteen dominions had been well established with their rights, their governors and limits, which he hoped might be done in less than three years, they were together to have chosen three general captains, two military and one naval, who were at once to have assaulted the Ottoman empire. To this each dominion was to have contributed a certain quantity of men, ships, artillery, and money, according to the tax imposed. The total sum which they were to furnish was to amount to 265,000 foot, 50,000 horse, a train of 217 pieces of artillery, with waggons, officers, and ammunition proportionate, and 117 great ships and galleys, besides vessels of less power, fireships, and ships of burden.

This establishment would have been advantageous to all Christian princes and states. There was only the house of Austria which would suffer any loss, and which was to be despoiled for the benefit of others. But the plan was to make them consent either willingly or force them to it in this manner. First, we must suppose that, on the part of Italy, the Pope, the Venetians, and the Duke of Savoy were to be informed of the King's designs, and would then assist with all their forces, especially the Duke of Savoy, who was then greatly pleased, because the King gave his daughter in marriage to Victor Amadeo, son of the duke. In Germany four electors, to wit, those of Palatine, Brandenburg, Cologne, and Mentz were likewise to know it and favour it. The Duke of Bavaria had their word, and that of the King, to raise him to the Empire; and many imperial cities had already addressed themselves to the King, to beseech him to honour them with his protection, and to maintain them in their privileges, which had been abolished by the house of Austria. In Bohemia and Hungary communication was held with the lords and nobility, and the people, desperate with the weight of that yoke, were ready to shake it off, and to throw themselves into the arms of him who should first extend them.

All these dispositions being so favourable to him, the business of Clèves happened, which furnished him with a fair occasion to begin the execution of his projects, which was to be carried out in this manner.

Having raised an army of forty thousand men, as he did, he was in his march to send to all the princes of Christendom, to give them the knowledge of his just and holy intentions. After this, under the pretext of going to Clèves, he was to seize all the passages of the Meuse, and at once assault Charlemont, Maestricht, and Namur, which were badly fortified. At the same time the cities of the Low Countries would cry out for liberty, and the lords put themselves in the field for the same purpose, and blazon the Belgian lion with the *fleur-de-lis*. The Hollanders would infest the coasts with their ships to hinder the commerce of the Flemings by sea, as it was shut up by the French by land, which was to have been done to hasten the people to shake off the Spanish rule, and to address themselves to the King and to his allies, asking them to pray the King of Spain to give them liberty, and out of his goodness to restore peace to them, which they could never hope for so long as they were under his dominion.

In all probability, at the approach of so great an army, the understanding between the principal lords, the insurrection of the great cities, and the love which these people had always had for liberty, would have caused all Flanders to rise, especially when they had seen the wonderful order and exact discipline of the King's soldiers, who would live like good guests, paying for all, and not doing the least outrage upon pain of death; and when it became known that he laboured only for the safety of the people, not reserving for himself anything of all his conquests except the glory and the satisfaction of having restored those provinces to their liberty, without keeping so much as a castle or village to himself.

At the same time that he had put Flanders into a free state, and settled the difference of the succession of Clèves, all the princes interested in this business, the electors we have named, and the deputies of many great cities, were to come to thank him, and entreat him that he would join his prayers and his authority to the supplications they had to make to the Emperor, to dispose him to restore the states and cities of the Empire to their ancient rights and immunities; above all, in the free election of a King of the Romans, without using any constraint, promises, or threats. To this effect it was to be from that moment resolved that they should elect one of another house than that of Austria. They had agreed among themselves that it should be the Duke of Bavaria. The Pope would join with them in this request, which would have been made so urgently that it would have been difficult for the Emperor, unarmed as he was, to refuse it.

The like request was to have been made to the King and his associates by the people of Bohemia, Hungary, Austria, Styria, and Carinthia; above all, for the right they had to choose their own prince themselves, and to put themselves under that form of government they should think best, by the advice of their friends and allies. To which the King condescending, would use all sorts of fair means, prayers and supplications, even below his dignity, that it might be seen he intended not so much to avail himself of force as of equity and reason.

After this the Duke of Savoy would demand of the King of Spain, with all sorts of civility and in the name of his children, that he would be pleased to give them a dowry for their mother as good and advantageous as he had to their aunt Isabella; and in case of refusal, the King was to permit Lesdiguières to assist him with fifteen thousand foot, and two thousand horse, for the conquest of Milan or the country of Lombardy, in which he would have been favoured by the greater part of the princes of Italy.

This done, he with his associates were to beseech the Pope and the Venetians to become arbitrators between him and the King of Spain, to terminate peaceably those differences which were ready to break forth between them, by reason of Naples, Sicily, Navarre, and Roussillon. And then, to show that he had no thought of his own aggrandisement, nor other ambition than to secure the peace of Christendom, he would be ready to yield to the Spaniards Navarre and Roussillon, provided that they restored Naples and Sicily; not for himself, for he desired no other kingdom than France, but for the Pope and the Venetians, to whom he would have yielded his right over those countries.

Finally, by an apostolic legate and by the remonstrances of all his associates, he would have let the King of Spain understand his design, together with the princes of his house, and would conjure them by the blood of Jesus Christ to consent to it, as being holy, pious, charitable, glorious, and profitable to all Christendom. They would lay before him the advantages which would come to himself, and endeavour to make him comprehend that he would be richer, less disturbed, and more peaceable; and that in twenty years Spain, which was almost deserted, would be repeopled, and become the most flourishing state of Europe. I believe it would have been difficult to persuade him to it; for irregular and ill-advised ambition embraces chimeras rather than solid things, and chooses rather to possess vast and desert countries than a reasonable extent well

cultivated and well peopled; but possibly arms might have convinced him, had reason failed.

For the rest, the King had resolved to renounce all pretension; not to keep anything of what he conquered; not to attempt anything which should not be approved by his allies, and which he saw them not disposed to contribute to; not to begin in many distant places at a time, but to pursue his expeditions by degrees, waiting for the success of the first before he engaged in others; to show himself to be without ambition, without covetousness or pride in the distribution of quarters, victuals, spoils and conquests; to favour the weak and necessitous states; to always send some honourable and profitable acknowledgment to all the captains or soldiers who had performed some worthy exploit; never to enter into those difficulties which so often arise between friends and allies, but to always appear an equal, just, and common friend; to treat honourably the men of war with praises or reproofs when they deserved them, and to maintain strict discipline, prohibiting disorder, violations, and burnings, so that he might be received as the restorer of nations and one who brought peace and liberty, not ruin and desolation.

He had prepared his designs, made his preparations, and arranged all his means to this end, with all the diligence imaginable, for the space of eight or nine years. He had made friends and allies on all sides, and kept up communications everywhere. He had won over the college of cardinals by great pensions, had drawn to his service all the good captains in Germany and Switzerland, and had likewise enlisted all the good writers in Christendom on his side; for indeed he would have chosen rather to persuade than force people, and instruct them so well in his intentions that they should regard his arms as forces held in reserve, to be used only as a last resort.

This was the groundwork of his design, which, without dissembling, was so great that it may be said it was conceived by an intelligence more than human. But great as it was, it was not above his power; for if princes do not limit their undertakings by their power it happens that they ruin their states, just as a man who undertakes a suit at law, or makes greater bargains than his purse is able to sustain, is obliged in the end to sell his stock and is swamped in a sea of debts and troubles.

Besides his forces, which were great in number, but ten times greater in valour, being all chosen men, and having amongst them four thousand gentlemen, daring all things in the sight of their King, the Prince of Orange was to put himself in the field with fifteen thousand foot and two thousand horse, and the Prince of Anhalt in Germany with ten thousand. The Electors and the Duke of Bavaria had in readiness twice as many, who would have met at places agreed upon at the first sound of the trumpet. The Venetians and the Duke of Savoy would each have been ready with a considerable army at the first signal given. As for the Swiss, besides a levy of six thousand chosen men who came to the King, he might have had as many more as he desired. As regards money, all his troops were paid for three months, his garrisons well furnished, all his storehouses on the frontiers full, and his captains honoured with great presents which he had made them. He had fourteen million livres in the Bastille, seven millions in the hands of the treasurer of the exchequer, which formed the profits of the preceding year, and two millions in other hands. Moreover, there was the current revenue, which was more than twenty-seven millions; and besides all this, Sully, his chief treasurer, assured him of forty millions extraordinary for three years; so that he might maintain a four years' war without burdening his subjects with new charges. But he proposed to carry it on so vigorously that it could last but a short time; for he held that a wise prince when he is obliged to declare war ought to make it powerful and short, and at once astonish the world with formidable preparations, because by this means the greatness of the expense becomes economy, and the conquests made through fear of his arms reach further than those made by his arms themselves.

I have told you what was his design; none but God knows what would have been its success. We may say, however, judging according to appearances, that it could not but be happy, for there appeared no prince nor state in Christendom who would not have favoured it, or who would have taken the part of the house of Austria, except the Duke of Saxony in Germany, and the Duke of Florence in Italy. But the King might have satisfied them both—the first, by assisting against him the heirs of that Duke William, who had formerly been despoiled of the electorate by the Emperor Charles V.; the second, by stirring up Pisa, Sienna, and Florence to cry for liberty and shake off their yoke under the Medicis.

But it is time that I told you what the business

of Cleves and Juliers was, which had furnished him with an occasion to take arms, and opened ways to him to begin his great design. John William, Duke of Juliers, Clèves, and Berghe, Earl de la Mark and Ravensburg, was the son of Duke William and Mary of Austria, sister to the Emperor Charles V., and grandchild to Duke John. Having died without children, on the 25th of March, 1609, the question of his succession was the cause of trouble in the neighbouring states. He had four sisters, the first married to the Marquis of Brandenburg, the second to the Count Palatine of Neuburg, the third to the Duke of Deux-Ponts, and the fourth to the Marquis of Burgaw. The children of these marriages claimed succession, the nearest excluding the furthest off, and the sons the daughters. The Duke of Saxony, descended from an elder daughter of Duke John, grandfather of Duke William, said likewise that it belonged to him in preference to all the others, because it was concluded, in the marriage contract of that lady, that in the event of there being no male heir to the house of Juliers, the succession should return to him and his descendants; and as this had actually happened, it necessarily followed that the succession was open to him. The Duke of Nevers also pretended to the duchy of Clèves, as he alone carried the name and arms of Clèves; and the Count of Maulévrier for the same reason demanded the county of La Mark, for he was the eldest De la Mark, and in this quality he claimed likewise the duchy of Bouillon and the seigniory of Sedan, which were held by the Viscount of Turenne, Marshal de Bouillon. The Emperor said that all these pretensions were ill founded, for those lands, being male fiefs, could not descend to daughters, but in default of males devolved to the Empire, and therefore he should have the disposal of them. He secretly gave the investiture to Leopold of Austria, Bishop of Strasburg, and sent his forces to seize those lands under pretext of right, and in the meantime commanded the parties to appear before his imperial majesty to prefer their claims.

The Duke of Nevers and the Count of Maulévrier were not very energetic in their claims, because they were given to understand that the fiefs they demanded were united, and could not be dismembered. The claims of the Marquis of Brandenburg and the Marquis of Neuburg appearing to be the best, there was bitter conflict between them. The Landgrave of Hesse, their common friend, became mediator for them, and induced them to agree to decide their difference in a friendly manner, without employing their forces, except against usurpers, the administration of the succession remaining equal and common amongst them, saving the rights of the Emperor. But in the meantime Leopold of Austria arrived with his forces and seized Juliers.

The two princes resolved to drive him out, and sought assistance on all sides, particularly imploring that of the King, to whom they sent the Prince of Anhalt with the letters of the Electors Palatine and of the Duke of Würtemburg, who assured him that his arms would be just, powerful, and by the grace of God victorious. The Prince of Anhalt no doubt conversed with him of many other things touching the "great design." The King gave him a most gracious reception, and received his propositions with an unparalleled joy.

He answered him, in terms as obliging as he could, that he would march in person to the assistance of his good allies; and that until such time as he could set out with an equipage befitting a king of France, he would send some troops on in advance, which he did about the end of the year 1609. But moreover he prayed him to let the confederate princes understand that they would do him great wrong if they thought that he intended any prejudice to the Catholic religion in that country; for he desired above all things that the exercise of it should be preserved as it was before the death of Duke William, who was a Catholic, but Brandenburg and Neuburg were Protestants.

The Emperor likewise sent one of his confidential ambassadors, entreating him not to favour the rebellion and injustice of these princes, and to consider that he could not assist them without doing wrong to the Catholic religion. Henry the Great answered him that, being the most-Christian King, he knew well how to maintain and enlarge his title, but that it was only a question of succouring his friends, to whom he should never be wanting so long as he had life.

During the whole winter he gave orders for all preparations for this expedition, which was only the cover to a greater one. Being resolved to undertake it personally, he endeavoured, before his departure from the kingdom, to establish such good order in the government of it that no trouble could happen during his absence. He believed that the best way to secure this was to leave the regency to the Queen; but because he knew that she was governed by Conchini, whom he did not care for, he appointed a council composed of fifteen persons to assist her, these being the Cardinals de Joyeuse and du Perron; the Dukes of Mayenne, Montmorency, and Montbazon; the Marshals de Brissac and de Fervaques; Château-Neuf, who was to have been keeper of the seals of the regency, for the King wished to take his chancellor with him; Achille de Harlay, first president of parliament; Nicholas, first president of the chamber of accounts; the Count of Château-Vieux and the Lord of Liancourt, two wise gentlemen; Pontcarré, councillor of parliament; Gêvres, secretary of state; and Maupeou, controller of the revenues.

Moreover, he established a council of five persons in every one of the twelve provinces of France; to wit, one person for the clergy, one for the nobility, one for justice, one for the revenues, and one for the body of the cities; and these twelve minor councils were to have correspondence with and dependence on the great one, which was to take its resolutions by voting, the Queen having only her vote. Its power was defined by the general instructions formed by the King, and nothing might be done without informing his Majesty of it, if it were a thing which his instructions did not clearly enough explain. Thus, though absent, he kept the reins of government and tied the hands of the Queen, in case she should be inclined to take too much authority, or be induced to abuse her command.

Whilst he applied his mind to these things, some persons, amongst others Conchini and his wife, put it into the mind of the Queen that she should, to acquire more dignity and splendour in the eyes of the people, and more advantageously to authorise her regency, be consecrated and crowned before the departure of the King. For the same reasons that she desired it, the King found it not agreeable to him; besides which this ceremony could not be performed without a great deal of expense and great loss of time, which would keep him at Paris and retard his designs. He was extremely impatient to depart from that city. I do not know what secret instinct pressed him to be gone as soon as possible, but the consecration troubled him; yet he could not refuse this mark of his affection to the Queen, who passionately desired it.

Sully recounts that he heard him say more than once: "My friend, this consecration presages me some misfortune. They will kill me; I shall never depart from this city. My enemies have no other remedy but my death; they have told me that I shall be killed at the first great magnificence that I make, and that I shall die in a coach. This makes me often, when I am in one, be seized with tremblings, and be fearful in spite of myself."

They counselled him to shun these ill prophecies, to depart on the morrow, and leave the consecration to take place without him. But the Queen was extremely offended; and he obligingly remained to satisfy her. The consecration took place at St. Denis on the 13th of May; and the Queen on the 16th of the same month was to make her entry into Paris, where magnificent preparations had been made in her honour.

Already had the forces of the King met at their rendezvous on the frontiers of Champagne. Already had the nobility, who had come from all parts, sent their equipages. The Duke of Rohan had gone to

organise the six thousand Swiss; and fifty pieces of
artillery had been sent from the arsenal. The King
sent to demand of the Archduke and the Infanta in
what manner they desired that he should cross their
country, either as a friend or an enemy. Every hour
of delay seemed to him a year, as if he had had
presage of some misfortune to himself; and certainly
both heaven and earth had given but too many prognostications of what happened. A very great eclipse
of the whole body of the sun, which happened in the
year 1608; a terrible comet, which appeared the year
preceding; earthquakes in several places; monsters
born in various parts of France; rains of blood, which
fell in several places; a great plague, which afflicted
Paris in the year 1606; apparitions of phantoms, and
many other prodigies kept men in fear of some
horrible event.

His enemies were at present perfectly quiet, which
possibly was not caused only by their consternation
and by the fear of the success of his arms, but also
by the expectation they had of the success of some
great blow, in which lay all their hopes. There undoubtedly were many conspiracies against the life of
this good king, since from twenty places warning was
given of it. Both in Spain and Milan a report was
spread in print of his death. Eight days before he was
assassinated a courier passed through the city of Liège,
who said that he carried news to the princes of Germany that the King was killed. At Montargis a paper
was found upon the altar, containing the prediction of
his approaching death by a premeditated blow. The
report that he would not outlive that year, and that

he would die a tragic death in the fifty-seventh year of his age, ran through France. He himself, who was not over-credulous, placed some faith in these warnings, and seemed as one condemned to death, so sad and downcast was he, though naturally he was neither melancholy nor fearful.

There had been in Paris for about two years a certain wicked rogue named Francis Ravaillac, a native of the country of Angoumois; red-haired, a visionary, with a melancholy look, who had been a monk, but after having quitted the frock turned notary, and came to Paris. It was not known whether he came for the purpose of striking this blow or whether he had been induced to do this execrable deed by those people who, knowing that he had yet in his heart some leaven of the League and that false persuasion that the King was about to overturn the Catholic religion in Germany, judged himself a proper person to deliver the blow.

If it be asked who were the devils who inspired him with so damnable a thought, and who spurred him forward to put it into execution, this history answers that it knows nothing, and that in a thing so important it is not permissible to give currency to suspicions and conjectures as assured truths. The judges themselves who examined him dared not open their mouths, but spoke very reservedly.

On the day after the consecration, being the 14th of May, the King came from the Louvre about four o'clock in the afternoon, to go to the arsenal to visit Sully, who was indisposed, and to see the preparations made at the bridge of Notre Dame and the Hôtel de Ville for the reception of the Queen. He was in the body of the coach, having the Duke d'Epernon by his side; the Duke de Montbazon, the Marshal de Lavardin, Roquelaure, La Force, Mirabeau, and Liancourt, chief equerry, were in front and in the boots. His coach on entering from the street of St. Honoré into that of the Ferronnerie, found on the right hand a cart laden with wine, and on the left another laden with hay. As the street is very narrow because of the shops built against the wall of the churchyard of the Holy Innocents, the coach was obliged to stop. King Henry II. had formerly commanded the shops to be pulled down, to render the passage more free, but it was never carried out. Alas, that one half of Paris had not rather been beaten down than have seen this great misfortune, which has been the cause of so many other miseries! The footmen having passed through the churchyard of the Holy Innocents to avoid the block, and no person being near the coach, Ravaillac, who for a long time had obstinately followed the King to give his blow, observing the side on which he sat, thrust himself between the shops and the coach, and, setting one foot on one of the spokes of the wheel and the other against a post, gave him a stab with a knife between the second and third ribs, a little beneath the heart. At this blow the King cried out, "I am wounded!" But the villain, not in the least terrified, redoubled the blow, and struck him in the heart. The King died immediately, without so much as heaving a sigh. The murderer was so resolute that he gave yet a third blow, which fell on the sleeve of the Duke of Montbazon. Afterwards, he neither attempted to flee nor to conceal his knife, but stood still, as if to show himself and to glory in so fair an exploit.

He was arrested on the spot, examined by the commissioners of parliament, judged by the chamber of assemblies, and sentenced to be dragged to pieces by four horses in the Grève, which he underwent, after having had the flesh of his breasts, arms, and thighs torn off with burning pincers, without testifying the least fear or grief at such terrible tortures. This strongly confirmed the suspicion that certain emissaries, under the mask of piety and religion, had instigated him to do the deed by the false assurance that he would die a martyr if he killed him whom they pretended was the sworn enemy of the Church.

The Duke d'Epernon, seeing that the King was dead, caused the coach to turn back, and carried his body to the Louvre, where it was opened in the presence of twenty-six physicians and surgeons, who found that in the course of nature he might have lived another thirty years.

His entrails were the same hour sent to St. Denis and interred without any ceremony. The Jesuit fathers demanded the heart, and carried it to the church of La Flèche, where this great King had given them his house to build a beautiful college. The body, embalmed, wrapped in lead, placed in a coffin of wood, with a cloth of gold over it, was laid in the King's chamber under a canopy, with two altars on each side, on which mass was said for eighteen days continuously. Afterwards it was taken to St. Denis, where it was buried with the ordinary ceremonies, eight days after that of Henry III., his predecessor. For the body of Henry III. had remained until then in the church of St. Corneille in Compiègne, whence the Dukes d'Epernon and

de Bellegarde, formerly his favourites, brought it to
St. Denis, and caused the funeral rites to be celebrated, courtesy making it necessary that he should
be buried before his successor.

The King's death was concealed from the city all
the rest of the day of the murder and a good part
of the next; whilst the Queen disposed the grandees
and the parliament to give her the regency. She
obtained it without much difficulty, having led the
young king her son to the parliament, the Prince of
Condé and the Count of Soissons, who alone could
have opposed it, being absent. The former was at
Milan, as we have said before; and the latter at his
house at Blandy, whither he had retired discontented
some days before the consecration of the Queen.

When the report of this tragical event was
spread through Paris, and they knew that the King,
whom they believed only wounded, was dead, that
mixture of hope and fear which kept this great city
in suspense, suddenly broke forth into extravagant
cries and furious groans. Some through grief became
immovable as statues; others ran through the streets
like madmen; others again embraced their friends
without saying anything but, "Oh, what misfortune!"
Women were seen with dishevelled hair, running about
howling and lamenting; fathers said to their children,
"What will become of you, my children? you have
lost your Father." Those who had most apprehension
of the time to come, and who remembered the horrible
calamities of the past wars, lamented the misfortune of
France, and said that that accursed blow which had
pierced the heart of the King cut the throat of all

true Frenchmen. It is reported that many were so severely stricken with grief that they died, some upon the spot, and others a few days after. In fact, this seemed not to be mourning for the death of one man alone, but for one-half of all men. It might have been said that everyone had lost his whole family, all his goods, and all his hopes by the death of this great king.

He died at the age of fifty-seven years and five months, in the thirty-eighth year of his reign over Navarre, and the twenty-first of that over France.

He was married twice, as we have said before; first with Margaret of France, by whom he had no children, and the second time with Mary de Medicis. Margaret was daughter to King Henry II., and sister to the Kings Francis II., Charles IX., and Henry III. He was divorced from her by sentence of the prelates deputed for that purpose from the Pope. Mary de Medicis was daughter to Francis, and niece to Ferdinand, dukes of Florence. She bore him three sons and three daughters.

The sons were all born at Fontainebleau. The first, Louis, was born on the 27th of September, 1601. He was king after Henry, and had the surname of the Just. The second was born on the 16th of April, 1607. He had the title of Duke of Orleans, but no name, because he died in the year 1611, before the ceremony of his baptism was celebrated. The third was born on the 25th of April, 1608, and was named John Battista Gaston, and had the title of Duke of Anjou, but on the death of the second son, that of Duke of Orleans was given him, which he bore till his death.

The eldest of the daughters was born at Fontainebleau on the 22nd of November, 1602. She was the second child, and was named Elizabeth, or Isabella. She was married to Philip IV., king of Spain. She was a princess of brave heart, and had a spirit and brain above her sex; the Spaniards therefore said that she was truly daughter to Henry the Great. The second daughter was born at the Louvre on the 10th of February, 1606. She was given the name of Christina; and she espoused Victor Amadeo, Prince of Piedmont, afterwards Duke of Savoy, a prince of the greatest virtue and capacity. The third was born in the same place, on the 25th of November, being the feast of St. Catherine, in the year 1609, and was named Henrietta Maria. She became the wife of the unfortunate King of England, Charles Stuart, whom his subjects cruelly despoiled of his royalty and life.

Besides these six legitimate children, he had eight natural ones, of four different mistresses, without counting those whom he did not own.

By Gabrielle d'Estrées, Marchioness of Monceaux and Duchess of Beaufort, he had Cæsar, Duke of Vendôme, who was born in June, 1594; Alexander, grand prior of France, who died a prisoner of state; and Henrietta, married to Charles of Lorraine, Duke of Elbeuf.

By Henrietta de Balsac d'Entragues, whom he made Marchioness of Verneuil, he had Henry, bishop of Metz, and Gabrielle, who espoused Bernard of Nogaret, Duke of Valette, afterwards Duke d'Epernon.

To Jacqueline de Bueil, to whom he gave the county of Moret, was born Anthony, Count of Moret, who was killed in the service of the Duke of Orleans in the battle of Castelnaudary, where the Duke of Montmorency was taken. This was a young prince whose spirit and courage promised much. Jacqueline de Bueil was afterwards married to the Marquis of Vardes.

By Charlotta d'Essards, to whom he gave the estate of Romorantin, he had two daughters—Jane, who became abbess of Fontevrault, and Mary Henrietta. He loved all his children, legitimate and natural, with a like affection, but with different consideration. He would not permit them to call him Monsieur, a name which seemed to render children strangers to their fathers, and which denoted servitude and subjection, but he desired that they should call him Papa, a name of tenderness and love. And certainly in the Old Testament God took the names of Lord, the Mighty God, the God of Hosts, and others, to set forth His greatness and power; but in the Christian law, which is a law of grace and charity, He commands us to make our prayers as His children, by those sweet words, " Our Father, which art in heaven."

Henry was of middle stature, nimble, active, and hardened to labour and travel. His body was well formed, his temperament able and strong, and his health perfect; but about the age of fifty years he had some slight attacks of the gout, but they soon passed away, and left behind them no weakness. His forehead was broad, his eyes full of vivacity and assurance, his nose aquiline, his complexion ruddy, his countenance sweet and noble, and yet withal his presence warlike and martial; his hair was brown and very thin. He wore his

beard long and his hair very short. He began to grow
grey at the age of thirty-five years, of which he was
accustomed to say to those who wondered at it, "It
is the wind of my adversities which has blown me
this."

Indeed, to consider well all his life from his very
birth, few princes will be found who have suffered as
much as he; and it would be difficult to tell if he had
more crosses or more prosperities. He was born the
son of a king, but of a king despoiled of his states.
He had a mother who was generous and courageous,
but a Huguenot and an enemy of the court. He
gained the battle of Coutras; but he lost shortly after
the Prince of Condé, his cousin and his right hand.
The League stirred up his virtue, and made it known,
but it nearly overthrew him. Henry III. having called
him to his assistance, he found himself at the gates of
Paris, as if God had led him by the hand; but Paris
armed itself against him, and all his hopes were almost
dissipated by the scattering of the army which besieged that city. It was without doubt a great piece
of good fortune that the crown of France fell to him,
there having never been a succession more distant in
any hereditary state; for there were ten or eleven
degrees between Henry III. and him, and when he was
born there were nine princes of the blood before him,
to wit, King Henry II. and his five sons, King Anthony
of Navarre, his father, and two sons of that Anthony,
elder brothers of our Henry. All these princes died
to make room for his succession. But he found it in
such a state of confusion that we may say he suffered
an infinity of labours, pains, and hazards before he

could gather the fair flowers of this crown. While very young he espoused the sister of King Charles, which seemed a match very advantageous for him; but this marriage was a snare to entrap both him and his friends. Afterwards that lady, instead of being his comfort, became his trouble, and instead of being his honour, became his shame. His second wife brought him forth fair children, to his no little joy; but her grumblings and contempt were the cause of a thousand discontents. He triumphed over all his enemies, and became arbitrator of Christendom; but the more powerful he made himself the greater became their hatred and the more means they sought to destroy him; so that after having plotted an infinite number of conspiracies against his life, they found in the end a Ravaillac, who executed what so many others had failed in.

Now, it must be acknowledged that all these adversities which he suffered whetted his spirit and his courage, and that at last he became the greatest of kings, because he came to the crown through so many difficulties and at a very mature age.

And certainly it is difficult and very rare for those who are born to a crown, and bred up in the hope of mounting a throne after the death of their father, or who find themselves too soon raised to it, ever to learn well the art of reigning if they be not so happy as to be educated under the care of a mother so virtuous and so well-intentioned as that great Queen who has so diligently caused King Louis XIV., her son, to be instructed in all good sentiments and in all maxims of Christian policy, or so happy as to be blessed with a minister so wise and so devoted to their good as that young monarch has found in the person of Cardinal Mazarin.

The reasons for this are, that commonly those persons into whose hands they fall during the infancy of the sovereign, desiring to keep to themselves the authority and the government, instead of causing them to apply their minds to things solid and necessary, act so cunningly that they employ them only in trifles unworthy of them. Instead of laying incessantly before their eyes the true grandeur of kings, which consists in the exercise of their authority, they feed them only with appearances and images of that greatness— exterior pomps and magnificences, wherein there is only pride and vanity. In fact, instead of instructing them diligently in what they ought to know and in what they ought to do (for all the knowledge of kings ought to be reduced to practice), they keep them in profound ignorance of their affairs, that they may always be masters, and that they may never be able to do without them. From whence it happens that a prince, though he be great, knowing his own weakness, judges himself incapable to govern; and from the moment that he holds this opinion, he will renounce the conduct of his state, if he have not indeed extraordinary natural qualities and a heart truly royal. Moreover, these persons hinder honest men from approaching those tender ears; or if they cannot hinder their approach, they render them suspected, and deprive them of all credence in the minds of these young princes. Moreover, they have some emissaries who infatuate them with flatteries, with excessive praises and adorations; who never let them know anything but what shall serve their own ends; who accentuate their defects by continual adulation; who make them believe they have a perfect intelligence of all things when they know nothing; who make them conceive that royalty is only a sovereign bauble, that work befits not a king, and that the functions of government being laborious, are in consequence base and servile. In this manner they soon disgust them with their own command; they accustom them to have masters because they have yet neither enough knowledge nor courage to be masters. And thus these poor princes, never being contradicted, but always adored; not having any experience of themselves, nor ever having suffered pain or necessity, become often presumptuous and absolute in their fancies, and believing in their right to be considered as gods, they begin to think of nothing but their passion, pleasure, and caprice, as if mankind were created for them, whilst they were created to order and govern mankind wisely. They let profusion and waste be made of the life and goods of their subjects; and, with an unparalleled insensibility, take no more notice of their laments and groans than of the lowings of an ox whose throat is being cut.

On the contrary, those who come to the crown at a greater distance in relationship and at a riper age, are nearly always better instructed in their affairs. They apply themselves more strongly to govern their states; they will always hold the rudder; they are more just, more tender, and more merciful; they know better how to manage their revenues; they preserve with more care the blood and the goods of their subjects; they more willingly hear their complaints, and do better justice; they do not so rigorously use their absolute power, which often makes the people despair, and causes revolutions.

If the reason why they are so be searched for, it will be found that it is because they have been in a place where they have often heard truth; where they have understood what ignominy it is for a prince not to enjoy his own personal power, but to leave it to another; where, though they have had some flatterers, they have likewise had open enemies, who by censuring their faults have induced a reformation; where they have heard blamed the faults of that government under which they were, and have blamed them themselves, so that they are obliged to do better, and not to follow what they have condemned; where they have studied to govern themselves wisely, because they were dependants, and fearful of punishment; where they have often heard the complaints of individuals and seen the miseries of the people; and where they have understood by suffering what evil is, and to have pity on those who suffer injustice, because they themselves have proved the rigour of a too severe government. We have two fair examples in Louis XII., surnamed the "Father of the People," and in our Henry, two of the best kings who have borne the sceptre of the *fleur-de-lis*.

Now whoever would gather together and worthily arrange all the heroic virtues, noble actions, and eminent qualities of Henry the Great, would make him a crown much more precious and resplendent than that wherewith his head was adorned on the day of his corona-

tion. That fund of freedom and sincerity, free and
exempt from malice, from gall and bitterness, should
be more precious than gold. His renown and his
glory, which will never end, should be the circle.
His victories of Coutras, of Arques, of Ivry, of
Fontaine-Française; his negotiations of the peace of
Vervins; his mediation between the Venetians and the
Pope; and between Spain and the Low Countries;
and that great League with all the princes of
Christendom, for execution of the design of which we
have spoken, should be the branches. Then his warlike
valour, his generosity, his constancy, his good faith,
his wisdom, his prudence, his activity, his vigilance, his
economy, his justice, and a hundred other virtues,
should be the precious stones. Amongst these, that
paternal and cordial love he had for his people would
cast a fire more lively and bright than the carbuncle;
the firmness of his courage, always invincible in danger,
would bear the price and beauty of a diamond; and his
unparalleled clemency, which raised up those whom his
valour had overthrown, would appear like an emerald
which spreads joy before the eyes of all that behold it.
To continue the metaphor, the many wise laws which
he made for justice, for police, and for his revenues;
the many good and useful establishments of all sorts of
manufactures which produced to France many millions
yearly; the many proud buildings, as the galleries of
the Louvre, the Pont-Neuf, the Place Royale, the Collége
Royal, the quays for merchants on the river Seine,
Fontainebleau, Monceaux, St. Germain; the many
public works, bridges, causeways, highways repaired;
the many churches rebuilt in various places of the

realm, should be as the engraving and embellishments.

Let us crown, then, with a thousand praises the immortal memory of that great King, the darling of the French and the terror of the Spaniards, the glory of his age and the admiration of posterity. Let us make him live in our hearts and in our affections, in spite of the rage of those wicked persons who deprived him of life. Let us shout forth as many acclamations to his glory as he has done benefits to France. He was a Hercules, who cut off the head of the Hydra by overturning the League. He was greater than Alexander and greater than Pompey, because he was as valiant, but he was more just; he gained as many victories, but he gained more hearts. He conquered the Gauls as well as Julius Cæsar; but he conquered them to give them liberty, while Cæsar subjugated them to enslave them.

BIOGRAPHICAL SKETCHES

ADMIRAL COLIGNY.

Gaspard de Coligny, the second of that name, admiral of France, and known as the admiral of Châtillon, was born February 16th, 1517. He distinguished himself in the wars of Francis I., and was appointed colonel-general of the French infantry. He afterwards became admiral of France and governor of Picardy and Artois. Towards 1560 he commenced to make open profession of the reformed religion, and became then, with the Prince of Condé, leader of the Calvinist party. He displayed great capacity in the organisation of the forces of his party, and knew how to repair his faults and disasters with a rare ability. On the night of the massacre of St. Bartholomew he was strangled. His assassin, Besme, threw his corpse into the court at the feet of the Duke of Guise, who was waiting for it.

ANNE, DUKE OF MONTMORENCY.

Anne, first Duke of Montmorency, the most illustrious personage of his house, was born March 15th, 1492, died at Paris November 12th, 1567. Son of William of Montmorency and of Anne Pot, he fought at Marignan (1515), and on returning from a mission to England (1520) was appointed first gentleman of the bedchamber to Francis I., with whom he had been brought up. He assisted at the defence of Mézières, and went through the Italian campaign, terminated by the disaster of Italy, being for his services nominated marshal of France. With La Palisse he pursued the Constable of Bourbon, who had invaded Provence, and he was taken prisoner at Pavia. He contributed to the conclusion of the treaty of Madrid, and in the same year became grand master of the King's household and governor of Languedoc.

Created Constable in 1538, he had for several years almost complete control of the home and foreign affairs of France. In consequence, however, of a breach of faith towards Francis I. on the part of Charles V., the Constable was disgraced, and he lived in retirement until the accession of Henry II. Being then recalled to the Court, he regained all his former influence. In 1548 he punished with the greatest rigour the rebels of Bordeaux. He was created duke and peer, and commanded the army which took possession of Lorraine. He showed his military incapacity in the campaign of Flanders, and also afterwards in the battle of St. Quentin, where he was taken prisoner. Released upon parole, he was the chief agent in the negotiation of the treaty of Câteau-Cambrésis, which excited against him general indignation. Again disgraced at the death of Francis II., he was obliged to resign to the Duke of Guise his post of grand master.

On the accession of Charles IX. he reconciled himself with the Duke, and formed with him and the marshal of Saint-André a *triumvirat* directed against the Protestants, whom he hated, and by whom he was made prisoner at the battle of Dreux. The civil war recommenced in 1567, and on the Huguenots menacing Paris he offered them battle on the plain of St. Denis. Here he was mortally wounded, and died two days afterwards.

His wife was Madeleine, daughter of René, bastard of Savoy, by whom he had five sons and seven daughters.

ANNE, DUKE OF JOYEUSE.

Anne, Duke of Joyeuse, admiral of France, was born in 1561. He was first known by the name of d'Arques. He became one of the favourites of Henry III., who loaded him with riches and honours, created him duke, and arranged his marriage with Margaret of Lorraine. The King also bought for him the position of admiral, and appointed him governor of Normandy. Sent at the head of a brilliant army against the King of Navarre, he gave him battle at Coutras on October 20th, 1587, but was defeated and killed.

ANTHONY DE BOURBON.

Anthony de Bourbon, King of Navarre, was born in 1518. Son of Charles de Bourbon (Duke of Vendôme) and Françoise d'Alençon, he married, in 1548, Jeanne d'Albret, daughter of Henry II., King of Navarre, who brought him as dowry the principality of Bearn, together with the title of King of Navarre. He withdrew from public affairs during the reign of Henry II., but after the death of Francis II. was appointed lieutenant-general of the kingdom, and about this time became a Catholic. He commanded the army which besieged Rouen, where he received a wound which his imprudences rendered mortal. He died November 17th, 1562.

BIRON.

Armand de Gontaut, Baron de Biron, a celebrated captain, was born about 1524, and killed by a cannon-ball at the siege of Epernay, July 26th, 1592. He distinguished himself in the wars of Piedmont and in the religious wars, being appointed grand master of artillery in 1569. He negotiated with Mesme the peace of St. Germain. After the death of Henry III. he rallied to Henry IV., and gave evidence of his great military talents at Arques and Ivry.

His son Charles de Gontaut, Duke de Biron, born in 1562, was decapitated at the Bastille, 1602.

COLONEL ALFONSO D'ORNANO.

Alfonso d'Ornano was born in 1548, and died in 1610. Colonel-general of the Corsicans in the service of France, Governor of Valence, then of Pont St. Esprit, he took an active part in the wars of religion, and was one of the first to recognise Henry IV., who created him lieutenant-general of Guyenne and marshal of France.

COUNT OF SOISSONS.

Charles de Bourbon, Count of Soissons, son of Louis, Prince of Condé, and of Françoise d'Orléans-Longueville, born November 3rd, 1566, died November 1st, 1612.

Although a catholic, he fought at Coutras with Henry of Navarre, the sister of whom he sought in vain to marry. In 1589 he went to Tours to join Henry III. who had been chased from Paris, was taken prisoner by the Duke of Mercœur, and confined at Nantes, from which place he succeeded in escaping, then rejoined Henry IV. at the siege of Dieppe, and was appointed grand master of France. He remained some years away from the court, and returned there only in 1600, went through the Savoy campaign, and obtained the government of Dauphiny. He took an active part in the intrigues of Marie Medicis, and contributed to the banishment of Sully.

DE BRISSON.

Barnabé Brisson, president of the parliament of Paris, was born in 1531. After the Day of the Barricades he refused to obey the King, who had transferred the parliament to Tours. He remained at Paris, and replaced Achille de Harlay, who had been imprisoned in the Bastille, as first president. His irresolute conduct caused him to be suspected by the Sixteen, who (November 15th, 1591) arrested him, and he was hanged to a beam in the council chamber at the palace.

D'OSSAT.

Arnaud d'Ossat, cardinal and celebrated diplomatist, was born July 20th, 1537, died at Rome, 1604. Originally valet-de-chambre, he became preceptor to John of Marca. He received the tonsure, and obtained the professorships of rhetoric and philosophy at the University, some time afterwards becoming secretary to Paul de Foix, ambassador at Rome. On the death of the latter he retained his appointments under Cardinals Louis d'Este and de Joyeuse. Scarcely had Henry IV. mounted the throne when d'Ossat commenced the work of reconciling the former with the Pope, and after long negotiations was successful. He remained some time at Rome, and settled some affairs of great importance, amongst others the divorce of Henry IV.

DUKE OF ANJOU.

Hercules-Francis, Duke of Alençon, afterwards Duke of Anjou, fifth son of Henry II. and Catherine de Medicis, was born March 18th, 1554, died at Château-Thierry in 1584. He put himself at the head of the disaffected party in 1574, for which he was arrested, together with Henry of Navarre; he was, however, set at liberty on the accession of Henry III. shortly after.

His whole life was a succession of perfidies; and a wit of the time, in making allusion to the traces left upon his face by the small-pox, said that one ought not to be astonished at his deformity, because it was necessary to have "two noses with a double face."

It was he who, to disembarrass himself of his favourite, Bussy d'Amboise, the lover of Madame de Montsoreau, revealed to the husband of the latter the secret of this adulterous liaison.

DUKE OF AUMALE.

Charles de Lorraine, Duke of Aumale, one of the chiefs of the League, was born in 1554, died at Brussels 1631. Appointed governor of Paris after the murder of the Duke of Guise, he was beaten by the Royalists near Senlis. After the conversion of Henry IV. he surrendered several places to the Spaniards, and being condemned to death *par contumace*, was obliged to quit France.

DUKE OF EPERON.

Jean-Louis de Nogaret, Duke of Eperon, was born in May, 1554, died January 13th, 1642. He attached himself to the Duke of Anjou, and then for a time to the King of Navarre. At the Court of Henry III. he became one of the favourites of the King, who loaded him with honours and riches. He received charge of several governments, and was also appointed admiral, which post he resigned in favour of his brother Bernard. After the death of the King, he refused to serve Henry IV., who left to him, however, the government of Provence, where the duke tried to make an independent principality, but his pride and cruelty rendered him odious. He ultimately became reconciled to the King, and was by his side when the latter was struck by Ravaillac.

FRANCIS, DUKE OF GUISE.

Francis of Lorraine, Duke of Aumale and of Guise, eldest son of Claude, first Duke of Guise, was the most distinguished man of that house. He was born at the castle of Bar, February 17th, 1519, and died before Orleans, February, 1563. Prince of Joinville, Marquis of Mayenne, and peer, he became successively Duke of Aumale, grand master, grand chamberlain, and first huntsman of France, and lord lieutenant of the kingdom. He distinguished himself at the taking of Montmédy (1542), at the defence of St. Dezier (1544), and at the siege of Boulogne. He made himself illustrious by his glorious defence of Metz, which was besieged by Charles V., who was obliged to retire, after having lost 30,000 men. Recalled from Italy, where he had conducted a campaign with varied success, he was created lieutenant-general, and was able in less than a month to become possessor of Calais and Thionville, exploits which caused universal joy in France and placed him at the summit of popularity. His influence became all-powerful when the accession of Francis II. also brought to the throne his niece Mary Stuart. After the death of the King he was exiled. In 1561 he formed with the Constable of Montmorency and the Marshal de Saint-André an alliance under the name of the *Triumvirat*, and retired to his estates, but was soon recalled. It was whilst on his way to the Court that, passing by Vassy, his people had with the Calvinists that bloody quarrel known as the "massacre of Vassy," and which was the signal for civil war. Guise, at the head of the Catholic army, retook Rouen from the Reformers, whom he defeated at Dreux, and then besieged Orleans. It was at the last mentioned place that he was assassinated by Poltrot. A serious wound in the face, received at the siege of St. Dizier, had given to him the surname of *Balafré* (slashed).

DUKE OF GUISE.

Henry of Lorraine, called the *Balafré* (as his father), Prince of Joinville, peer and grand master of France, governor of Champagne and of Brie, was born December 31st, 1550, and was assassinated at Blois, December 23rd, 1588.

At the age of sixteen years he went to serve in Hungary against the Turks, signalized himself at the battles of Jarnac and of Montcontour, compelled Coligny to raise the siege of Poitiers, quitted the Court after the peace of St. Germain, and returned there to prepare the massacre of St. Bartholomew, when he brought about the assassination of Coligny. In 1575 he beat the Protestants at Dormans, and organised the League which the year following the King was compelled to sign. He made an unsuccessful attack on Strasburg, beat the German auxiliaries who had come to the assistance of the King of Navarre, and arrived the following year in Paris, in spite of the prohibition of the King, who had been forced to quit the town in consequence of the *day of barricades*. Appointed lieutenant-general of the kingdom, he attended the meeting of the States-General assembled at Blois, where Henry III., excited to a state of exasperation, caused him to be assassinated.

He married, in 1570, Catherine of Cleves, Countess d'Eu, by whom he had fourteen children.

DUKE OF GUISE.

Charles of Lorraine, Duke of Guise, Prince of Joinville, Duke de Joyeuse, Count d'Eu, peer and grand master of France, admiral of the seas of the Levant, governor of Champagne and of Provence, was born August 20th, 1571, and died at Cuna, September 30th, 1640. He was the eldest son of the Duke Henry assassinated at Blois, and on the day of his father's death he was arrested and committed to the

Château of Tours, from which he at last succeeded in escaping. Having failed in his endeavour to become king by marrying the daughter of Philip II., he submitted, in 1594, to Henry IV., poignarded the Marshal of St. Pol, who reproached him with his defection, and in 1596 he brought Marseilles under royal authority.

DUKE OF JOYEUSE.

Henry, Count du Bouchage, Duke of Joyeuse, marshal of France, brother of the preceding, was born in 1567, died at Rivoli (Piedmont) September 27th, 1608. After having followed for some time a military career, he became a Capuchin upon the death of his wife in 1587. He returned to his former profession when his brother, Antoine-Scipio, was drowned in the Tarn after the combat at Villemur (October 20th, 1592), but it was not until 1596 that he came to an arrangement with Henry IV., who gave him the marshal's bâton.

DUKE OF MAYENNE.

Charles of Lorraine, Marquis then Duke of Mayenne, was born March 26th, 1554, died at Soissons the 3rd or 4th of October, 1611. He was the second son of Francis of Lorraine, Duke of Guise, assassinated by Poltrot, and of Anne d'Este. After having served in the ranks of the Catholic army in the campaign of Jarnac and Montcontour, he went to assist Venice against the Turks, was present at the siege of La Rochelle, was created duke and peer, and accompanied Henry III. in Poland, took an active part in the formation of the League. He was at Lyons at the time that his brothers were murdered at Blois, and, warned in time, was able to avoid the order issued to arrest him.

He raised Burgundy, of which he was governor, went to

Paris in the February following, organized there a government, and marched against Henry III. who had united his forces with those of Henry IV. As is known the assassination of Henry III. took place. Soon declaring war against Henry IV. he was beaten at the battles of Arques and of Ivry. After this last defeat he went to Flanders to seek assistance to permit him to re-victual Paris, which was strictly besieged by the royal army, but which the Duke of Parma succeeded in relieving. It was only at the last that he came to terms with Henry IV., by whom he was treated with every respect. He married, in 1576, Henrietta of Savoy, Marchioness of Villars.

DUKE OF NEVERS.

Louis de Gonzagne, Duke of Nevers, was born the 18th of September, 1539; died at Nesle, October 22, 1595. Son of Frederick II., Duke of Mantua, he became a naturalized Frenchman, was made prisoner at the battle of Saint-Quentin, married Henrietta of Cleves, sister and heiress of the last two dukes of Cleves, became Governor of Piedmont, and protested energetically when Henry III. ceded to the Duke of Savoy the towns which France still possessed on the other side of the Alps. He took an active part in the wars of religion, was one of the organizers of the massacre of St. Bartholomew, when he saved the life of Condé, his brother-in-law. He accompanied the Duke of Anjou to Poland. After having served the League, he attached himself to Henry IV., and was with him at the battles of Ivry and of Aumale, and was sent by him as ambassador to Rome, and created superintendent of the finances.

DU PLESSIS MORNAY.

Philip de Mornay, one of the most illustrious of the protestant party, and surnamed the Pope of the Huguenots, was born at Buhy (Seine and Oise) November 5, 1549; died at the Forêt-sur-Sèvre (Deux-Sèvres) November 11, 1623. He embraced Calvinism early in life, travelled in Italy and Germany, managed to escape St. Bartholomew, passed over to England, and, on his return, attached himself to the King of Navarre, who frequently charged him with most important missions to England and elsewhere. Mornay contributed to the reconciliation of Henry III. and Henry IV., and was successful when sent as ambassador to Queen Elizabeth. After the death of Henry IV., he did his best to prevail upon his co-religionists to obey the regent, but was unsuccessful.

JAMES CLEMENT.

James Clement, the assassin of Henry III., was born at Sorbon (Ardennes) in 1567, killed at St. Cloud, August 1st, 1589. The Leaguers honoured him as a martyr.

LESDIGUIÈRES.

Francis de Bonne, Duke of Lesdiguières, Marshal and Constable of France, one of the greatest captains of his time, was born at Saint-Bonnet de Champsaur (High Alps) April 1st, 1543, died at Valencia, September 28th, 1626. He early embraced Calvinism, and from the first of the religious wars took arms and distinguished himself in Dauphiny. He had followed the King of Navarre to Paris, but an illness of his wife (Claudina de Béranger) recalled him to Dauphiny, and he thus escaped the massacre of St. Bartholomew. The following year he again took arms, compelled the Marshal de Bellegarde to raise the siege of Livron, surprised Gap and obtained favourable conditions of peace for his co-religionists. In 1585 he made himself Master of Montélimart, and of D'Embrun, then entered Provence, where he gained numerous victories over the

Leaguers. He was most successful in all his undertakings, and in 1597 he was made lieutenant-general of the kingdom by Henry IV. In 1608 he received the bâton of Marshal of France, and the title of Counsellor of Honour to the parliament of Paris.

Under the regency of Marie de Médicis, who created him duke and peer, he did all that he could to prevent the protestants taking arms, and refused to join them when the Assembly at Rochelle decided to declare war. After that he had abjured, he was named successively marshal-general and constable.

MARSHAL DE BOUILLON.

Henry de la Tour d'Auvergne, Viscount de Turenne, was a Calvinist much favoured by Henry IV., who created him marshal of France. From this time he was known as the Marshal de Bouillon, he having married Charlotte, sister of the late Duke of Bouillon.

MARSHAL DE COSSÉ.

Arthur de Cossé, marshal of France, called the Marshal de Cossé, was born about 1512, died January 15th, 1582. He distinguished himself at the defence of Metz, of Marienbourg, and at the battle of Montcontour. Beaten by the Calvinists at Arnay-le-Duc, then accused of being in communication with them, he was arrested, and was released only the year following.

MARIE DE MEDICIS.

Marie de Medicis was born at Florence April 26, 1573; died at Cologne July 3, 1643. Daughter of Francis I., Grand Duke of Tuscany, and of Jane, Archduchess of Austria, she married Henry IV., by proxy, at Florence, October 5, 1600.

She set out on the 17th for France, and was met at Lyons
by the King, who was occupied with the Savoy war. The
couple did not agree long, the Queen's sour temper, her
allowing herself to be governed by Italians, and the King's
gallantries, soon caused dissensions between them. Their
misunderstanding was so extreme that, at the time, it was
even rumoured that the Queen had arranged the assassination
of her husband. This has been disproved.

Marie de Medicis was declared regent immediately upon
the death of her husband, thanks to d'Epernon. Sully was
dismissed, and she soon dissipated the savings of her husband.

Her incapacity, and the intrigues of her favourites, raised
against her the princes and nobility, with whom she signed
the treaty of Saint-Menehould (1614), but who continued
hostilities against her until she marched against them at the
head of some troops. The majority of her son was declared
in the month of October of the same year, but she, nevertheless, continued to rule, and caused to be celebrated, at
Bordeaux, in spite of the opposition of the nobility, the
marriage of Louis with the Infanta Anne, and that of her
daughter Elizabeth with the Infante don Philip, and concluded, at Loudon, the peace with Condé. Soon after this
being put on one side, she obtained permission to retire to
Blois, where she was guarded as a prisoner; she escaped
from there and commenced a war against her son, which
terminated with the treaty of Angoulême. Next year she
joined the rebel princes, who, beaten at Ponts-de-Cé, were
compelled to sign the peace at Angers. After the death of
Luynes, Marie was taken into favour again, and showed a
wisdom of conduct, which was owing to the influence of
Richelieu, who, thanks to her, was appointed Cardinal and
Minister of State. Soon jealous of Richelieu's ascendancy
over the King, Marie headed a powerful conspiracy. Vanquished and abandoned by the King, she quitted France and

retired to the low countries, then to Holland, and afterwards to her son-in-law, Charles I. of England, who attempted to arrange for her return to France. Compelled to leave London, she retired to Cologne.

GABRIELLE D'ESTRÉES.

Gabrielle d'Estrées was born about 1571, died 1599. After having been the mistress of Henry III. and several others, she transferred her affections to Henry IV., who became deeply attached to her. He created her Marchioness of Monceaux, then Duchess of Beaufort, and even had thoughts of marrying her; but her death, from apoplexy, prevented this union. She was enceinte at the time, and was believed to have been poisoned.

FRANCIS D'O.

Francis, Marquis d'O, statesman, was born at Paris 1535, where he died 1594. His marriage with Charlotte-Catherine de Villequier (1573) introduced him to the Court, where he became a favourite of Henry III., who made him superintendent of finances, first gentleman of the chamber, &c. After the assassination of Henry III. he rallied to Henry IV.

FRANCIS II.

Francis II., King of Navarre, was born in January, 1544, at the Château of Fontainebleau, died at Ambois, December 5th, 1560. Eldest son of Henry II. and Catherine de Medicis, he married in 1558 Mary Stuart, Queen of Scotland. On July 10, 1559, he succeeded his father, and during his short reign was completely under the influence of the Guises, uncles of his wife.

PRINCE OF CONDÉ.
(Henry I. of Bourbon.)

Prince Henry of Condé was born December 29th, 1552, died at St. Jean-d'Angely, March 5th, 1588. He served from his youth in the Protestant army, and nearly perished at the massacre of St. Bartholomew, but finally consented, with his cousin of Navarre, to abjure. It was suspected that his death was due to poison.

PRINCE OF CONDÉ.
(Henry II. of Bourbon.)

Henry II. of Bourbon, Prince of Condé, posthumous son of the preceding, was born in 1588, died 1646. Brought up in the Catholic religion, he married Charlotte de Montmorency, who inspired such a lively passion in Henry IV. that her husband was obliged to lead her out of France. He returned only after the death of the King.

SULLY.

Maximilian de Béthune, Baron, then Marquis of Rosny, Duke of Sully, one of the greatest ministers that France has ever had, was born in 1560 and died 1641.

He belonged to a younger branch of the house of Béthune, and was the second of the seven children of Francis, Baron of Rosny, and of Charlotte Dauvet. Being a Calvinist he escaped with difficulty the massacre of St. Bartholomew, attached himself to Henry of Navarre, took part in his most perilous expeditions and was named his chamberlain ordinary and counsellor of Navarre. He followed the Duke of Anjou in the expedition to Flanders, then returned to assist at the battle of Coutras, and fought at the side of Henry at Arques and Ivry, where he was covered with wounds.

In 1596 he entered the Council and was charged with other counsellors to make a tour through the provinces in order to verify the accounts of the treasurers and receivers, and was able to bring to the king the sum of 500,000 crowns. Nominated superintendent of the finances (1599) he displayed the rarest ability in the exercise of his function.

He showed an extraordinary perseverance and an inflexible rigour in diminishing the expenses, augmenting the receipts, and reforming abuses. All the friendship of the king was necessary to sustain him against the numerous enemies who rose against him in consequence of his action.

In 1609 he was able to pay a state debt of 100 million francs, to raise the revenue from 9 to 16 millions, and had yet a reserve of 22 millions. The artillery was on a formidable footing, and the arsenals full of arms and provisions. Soon after Henry IV.'s death he resigned.

INDEX.

ABBEVILLE, 152
Aiguillon, Duke of, 226
Albert, Archduke, commander of the Spanish army, 162; married to the Infanta, 193
Aldobrandin, Cardinal, 220
Alençon, Duke of, 19
Amboise conspiracy hatched by Huguenots, 16
Amiens, city of, renounces the League, 153; taken by Spaniards, 165; besieged by Henry IV., 166; is captured, 168
Andely, death of King Anthony of Navarre at, 16
Angers, 170
Anjou, Duke of, 18; elected King of Poland, 24
Armand, Father Ignatius, 256
Arnay-le-Duc, peace concluded at, 20
Arragon, Ferdinand, King of, 7
Auneau, defeat of Germans at, 61
Aussonne, 155
Autun, 155
Auvergne, Count of, 240; arrested, 244
Auxerre, 155

BALAGNY, 152, 159
Baptism of Henry the Great, 13
Bar, Duke of, 193, 209
Bar, Duchess of, 257
Barraut, Count of, 226
Barricades, raising of, 65
Barrière, Peter, 154
Bassompierre, 153
Bastille, the, 134
Battle of the Flour, 127
Beaumont, convent at, 266
Beaune, 155
Beauvais, 152

Bellegarde, Termes, 82
Belleisle, Marchioness of, 194, 195
Bellièvre, 181, 182, 201, 243, 252
Béthune, Count of, 226
Biron, Marshal de, 81, 90; remark to the king, 101; his great authority, 114; remark to his son, Baron de Biron, 137; is killed, 139
Biron, Baron de, succeeds his father, 139; becomes Marshal of France, 152; is praised by the king, 169; created duke and peer, 175; corrupted by Laffin, 211; his vanity, 212; loses his affection for the king, 213; his conspiracy, 238 et seq.; arrested, 244; executed, 247
Birth of Henry the Great, 11
Blancmesnil, Potier de, 245
Blavet, 172, 175
Boisdaufin, Lord of, 161
Borghese, Cardinal, 280
Bouillon, Duke of, 37
Bouillon, Marshal de, 158, 249, 268, 269, 271, 272
Bourbon, Anthony de, Duke of Vendôme, father of Henry the Great, genealogy of, 6; succeeds to the kingdom of Navarre, 15; his death, 16
Bourbon, Cardinal de, 8, 43, 86; death of, 106
Bourbon, John of, 7
Bresse, La, 214, 252
Brie, 138
Brigard, 133
Brissac, Marshal de, 320
Brisson, de, 133, 134
Bruges, retaken from reformers, 16; submits to the king, 149
Burgundy, 156
Bussy le Clerc, 69, 134

CALAIS taken by the Spaniards, 162
Calvinism publicly embraced by mother of Henry IV., 16
Cambray, 152, 158, 159
Capuchins, 261
Carces, Count of, 148
Carmelites, 261
Casaux, Charles de, 161
Castel, John, 154
Castile, Constable of, 155
Castres, 250
Catherine, Madame, sister of Henry IV., marries the Duke of Bar, 193; her death, 194
Cattelet, 158
Caudebec, 136
Caux, 151
Chalons-sur-Saône, 157
Chambéry, 217
Charenton, 137
Charles V., Emperor, demands Jane d'Albret, 9
Charles IX., succession of, 16; married, 20; offers to marry his sister Margaret to the Prince of Navarre, 20; draws principal chiefs of Huguenot party to Paris, 20; mortally sick, 24; sends for Henry of Navarre, 25; death of, 26
Chartres, Henry III. retires to, 65; besieged, 127; Chiverni restored to governorship of, 128; Laffin interceded for by his nephew, the Vidame of, 237
Chastillon, 51
Château-Neuf, 320
Château-Vieux, Count of, 320
Château-Reynard, 58
Châtelet, 133
Chiverny, 181
Christian, Florentius, appointed tutor to Henry IV., 17
Clement VIII., Pope, death of, 280
Clement, James, kills Henry III., 76
Clermont, Count of, 6
Coligny, Admiral, 18
Commartin, President, 250
Conchini, 263, 319, 320
Conciergerie, the, 266
Condé, Henry, Prince of, raises levies for Huguenots, 26; death of, 62
Condé, Louis, Prince of, 8; opposes the Guises, 15; arrested at Orleans with his brother Anthony, 16; killed, 18
Condé, young Prince of, 192
Conflans, 217
Conti, Prince of, 82
Corbeil, besieged by Parma, 116; retaken by Givry, 116
Cossé, Marshal de, 20
Coton, Father, 256, 257
Courtnay, 6
Coutras, battle of, 56 et seq.

D'Aix, Louis, 161
D'Albigny, Lord, 252, 253
D'Albret, Jane, 6; death of, 20
D'Amboise, George de Clermont, 51
Damville-Montmorency, Marshal of, 50
D'Arques, Château, 91; battle of, 91
D'Aumale, Duke, chosen governor of the "Sixteen," 69
D'Aumont, Marshal, 89, 181
D'Auvergne, Count, 264, 265, 266, 267
D'Egmont, Count, 97
Denia, Marquis of, 277
D'Entragues, Count, 264; arrested, 266
D'Entragues, Henriette, mistress of Henry IV., 202-3; the Queen incensed against her, 262
D'Epernon, Duke, favourite of Henry III., 41; incites the King to punish the "Sixteen," 65; retirement of, 67; returns to Court, 72; declines to stay with Henry IV., 85; deprived of his government, 153; sent to Metz to restore order, 256; present at the death of the King, 324
D'Espinac, Pierre, Archbishop of Lyons, 64
D'Est, Alphonso, 191; Cæsar, 191; Anne, 191
D'Estrées, Count, 131
D'Estrées, Gabrielle, mistress of Henry IV., 130; death of, 196, 198
D'Eurre, 265
D'Humières, James, Lord, 35; swears allegiance to Henry IV., 80; killed in battle, 158
Dieppe, 135
Dijon, 155

D'O, Francis, vainly attempts to induce the King to become Catholic, 83; dies, 150; referred to, 184
Dombes, Prince of, 82
Donchery, 271
Doria, 223
D'Ornano, Colonel Alfonso, 148
D'Ossat, 159, 197, 200, 201, 209
Dourlens, 158
Dreux, 97, 145
D'Ussac, Huguenot governor of La Reole, his deformity, 37; enamoured of a lady, 37; jeered at by the young bloods of Henry's party, 37; gives up the city to the enemy, 37-8

EDMONDS, LORD, 226
Elbeuf, Marquis of, 152
Elizabeth, Queen of England, 51; is solicited by the Huguenots, 126; sends Lord Edmonds to Henry IV., 226; her remark to Biron, 227; death of, 257
Emer de Chattes, 89
Epernay, Marshal de Biron killed at, 139
Estampes, 95
Estates, assembly of, at Blois, 35

FERDINAND, King of Arragon, 7
Feria, Duke of, 143
Ferrara, duchy of, 192
Fervaques, Marshal de, 320
Feuillantines, convent of, 195
Feuillantines, the, 261
Florence, contract of marriage signed at, 201; solemnities at, 202
Foix, Catherine du, 8
Fontaine-Française, 156
Fontanelles, Baron of, 249
Fontainebleau, 183; birth of a dauphin at, 228; 241, 262, 269, 288, 289
Fortet, public assembly at College of, 45
Forty, Council of, 133
Francis I, 7
Francis II., succession of, 15; death of, 16
Francis, Duke of Guise, assassinated, 17

Frenouillet, 252
Friars, barefooted, 261
Fuentes, Count of, 158, 222, 223, 237

GALIGAY, Leonora, 263
Gas, du, goes to Canada, 261
Germany, Protestant princes of, 55
Gèvres, secretary of state, 320
Givry swears allegiance to Henry IV., 80; takes Corbeil, 116
Godfathers of Henry IV., 13
Gonde, Cardinal de, 132
Gray, 156
Gregory XIV., Pope, 128
Grenoble, city of, 130, 216
Guet, Cavalier de, 266
Guienne, government of, given to the young Prince of Condé, 192; the King remonstrates with the deputies of the city of, 236
Guise, Duke of, 43-6, 65, 66; assassination of, 67
Guise, Duke of (son), escape of, 131
Guises seize government, 15
Guitry, 181

HAM, held by the League, 153; given up to the Spaniards by the governor, 158; retaken, 158; death of D'Humières at, 158
Harlay, first president of parliament, his eloquence, 210; appointed a member of the regency council, 320
Hebert, Marshal Biron's secretary, tortured on the rack, 248
Heidelberg, 250
Henry d'Albret, sends for daughter, 11; his death, 14
Henry II., death of, 15
Henry III., accession of, 26; conspiracy against, 27; confidence in Henry of Navarre, 28; espoused to Louise of Lorraine, 28; falls sick, 29; is perplexed at the war, 52; excommunicated by the Pope, 70; goes to Tours, 71; dies, 77; his faults, 119
Henry the Great, birth of, 12; treatment by his grandfather, 12-14; brought to Court of France, 15; with Coligny takes Nîmes, towns of St. Julian and St. Just, 19;

becomes King of Navarre, 21; marriage, 21; brought before Charles IX. after massacre of St. Bartholomew, 22; passion for women, 22; goes with Duke of Anjou to besiege Rochelle, 24; is sent for by Charles IX., 25; is closely watched at Court, 27; is enamoured of Madame de Sauves, 27; friendship with Henry III., 28; is commanded by him to kill Duke of Alençon, 29; leaves the Court, 32; returns again to Protestant religion, 32; is admitted into Rochelle, 32; takes possession of his government of Guienne, 33; action with regard to Pope's bulls, 49; interview with Queen-mother, 52; address to Princes Condé and Soissons, 57; assists Henry III., 71; retires to Meudon, 80; raises siege of Paris, 88; goes to Rouen, 89; retires to Dieppe, 90; receives suggestion from Tours parliament, 90; assaults the suburbs of Paris, 95; attacks Normandy, 96; his clemency at Ivry, 102; his acknowledgment to Colonel Thische, 103; storms Paris between St. James and St. Marceau, 116; retires to Senlis and to Creil, 116; flatters Mayenne, 118; different factions in party of, 124; siege of Chartres by, 127; army increased, 136; is wounded, 139; receives communication from Queen Elizabeth, 139; besieges city of Epernay, 139; gives his consent to be instructed in the Catholic religion, 140; conspiracy to seize him at Mantes, 142; notifies his resolution to deputies at Surènes, 144; goes to St. Denis, 146; abjures the Protestant religion, 146; receives absolution, 147; is anointed, 149; enters Paris, 149; besieges Laon, 152; Rheims, Vitry and Mezières return to, 153; his life is attempted, 154, 156; receives notice of the Pope's absolution, 159; has an interview with the Duke of Mayenne, 160; gives recompense to those who submit, 161; Marseilles is delivered to him, 161; takes La Fère, 162; convenes the estates, 163; determines to invest Amiens, 166; captures that city, 168; visits Arras, 168; goes to Brittany, 170; swears to the peace, 175; gives his reasons for wishing for peace, 176; illness at Monceaux, 180; offers his sword and forces to the Pope, 191; is requested to take a wife, 199; is divorced, 199; is engaged, 201; several attempts against his life, 207; receives a visit from the Duke of Savoy, 208-214; his advice to Marshal de Biron, 211; annoyed with him because of his vanity, 213; declares war against Savoy, 216; goes to Lyons to meet Marie de Medicis, 220; goes to Calais, 225; goes to Poitiers, 236; sees Baron de Biron, 242; goes to Metz, 256; sends Rosny to England, 258; prohibits duels, 259; makes Rosny Duke of Sully, 271; decides the rights of ambassadors, 274; his life is attempted, 276; his interview with Don Pedro, 288, and the Prince of Orange, 289; desires to purchase the salt-marshes, 294; causes an inquisition of the rents at the Hôtel de Ville, 296; account of his mistresses, 303; money paid to former opponents, 305; his "Great Design" to unite all Christendom, 306, 307 *et seq.*; decides to leave the regency to the Queen, 319; expresses his fears to Sully, 321; is assassinated, 324

Huguenots, hatch conspiracy, 16
Hulst, siege of, 162

INCHI, BARON OF, 152
Intermittent nature of war, 127
Isabella Clara Eugenia, Infanta of Spain, marriage of, 193
Ivry, battle of, 98—101

JAMES OF SCOTLAND, 257
Jarnac, battle of, 18

INDEX

Jeannin or Janin, President, 86, 128, 181—183, 241, 252, 276, 289
Jesuits, 155
Joyeuse, Cardinal de, 161, 280, 283, 284, 320
Joyeuse, Duke of, 40; army of, 56; death of, 59
Joyeuse, Duke of, 194
Juillet, edict of, 46
Juliers, John William, Duke of, 317

La Boulaye, 51
La Bourdaisière, 127
La Charbonnière, 217
La Chastre, Marshal de, 181
La Châtre, 149
La Fère, 153, 158; siege of, 162
Laffin, 211, 213, 237, 247, 248
La Force, Lord de, 244
La Gaucherie, tutor to Henry the Great, 16; death of, 17
La Mark, Charlotte de, Duchess of Bouillon, 130
La Morienne, 217
Landriano, Marcelin, 129
La Noue, 151
Laon, 133
Larcher, de, 133
La Reole, 37
La Tour, Henry de, 51
La Trémoille, Claudius de, 51
League, the, birth of, 33; Sixtus V. approves of, 47; 158, 161
Le Mans, 95
Leopold of Austria, 318
Lesdiguières, governor of Dauphiné, 51, 181, 218
Liancourt, Lord of, 320
L'Ile, John de, attempts to kill Henry IV., 276
Limoges, 237, 240, 241, 269
Loire, river, joined with Seine, 260
Longueville, Duke of, 89, 195
Lorraine, Duke of, 87, 153
L'Oste, treason of, 272
Loudun, skirmish at, 18
Louvre, the, 134
Low Countries, flight of Leaguers to, 158
Luquisses, the, conspiracy of, 272, 275
Lux, Baron de, 241, 248
Lyons, 148; peace signed at, 220

Mâcon, 155
Manou, 82
Mansfield, Count of, 142
Mantes, King Henry IV. stays at, 105
Margaret, Queen, returns to her husband, 38; comes to Paris, 200
Marseilles, 272
Martel, Charles, 188
Maulévrier, Count of, 317
Maupeou, 320
Mayenne, Duke of, 54, 70; takes title of Lieutenant-General, 71; attacks Tours, 74; his indecision, 85; goes to relief of Rouen, 89; distrusts Spaniards, 92; physical state of, 93; his vacillating policy before Ivry, 95—97; his conduct during the battle, 101; jealous of Duke of Nemours and Duke of Lorraine, 124; receives Spaniards into Paris, 127; his jealousy of the young Duke of Guise, 131; 133—136; calls together the States-general for nomination of a king, 140; surprise at the King's resolution, 144, 145; dismisses deputies, 147; 153, 156, 157; sues for peace, 159; goes to Monceaux to salute the King, 160; 181, 183, 320
Meaux, 112, 148
Medicis, Alexander de, elected Pope under the name of Leo XI., 280; his death, 280
Medicis, Catherine de, causes herself to be declared regent, 16; seizes regency on death of Charles IX., 26; her plots and intrigues, 36 et seq.; death of, 67
Medicis, Marie de, 197, 201, 262, 268, 320, 321
Mérargues, treason of, 272, 273; execution of, 276
Merceur, Duke of, 161, 169, 176, 224
Metz, city of, 255
Miron, champions the cause of the people, 296—298
Modena, 192
Monceaux, 160; illness of Henry IV. at, 180
Monsieur, death of, 42
Montargis, 322
Montcontour, Prince of Navarre and Prince of Condé at battle of, 18

Montmorency, Constable of, mortally wounded at battle of St. Denis, 17
Montmorency, Duke of, 320
Montpensier, Duchess of, 94, 151
Montpensier, Duke of, 82, 89
Montreuil, 152
Morgan, 266
Mornay, Philip du Plessis, 48, 114, 201
Mousson, 272

NANTES, 170; Edict of, 190
Narbonne, 272
Nemours, treaty of, 46
Nemours, Duke of, 76, 87, 95; puts Paris in a state of defence, 107; 148, 191
Nerestan, 265
Neufbourg, 137
Nevers, duke of, 53; sent to Rome, 147; 158, 317, 318
Nimes taken, 19
Nonancourt, 97
Noyon, 131, 142
Nurses of Henry IV., 13

ORLEANS, Francis Duke of Guise assassinated at siege of, 17; the city submits to the King, 149
Ostend, siege of, 226

PARIS, siege of, 76; relieved by Duke of Parma, 114; general assembly of clergy held at, 189
Parma, Duke of, 90; at Condé, 105; delivers Paris, 114; is discontented with French troops, 116; hears of the loss of Corbeil, 116; advises the Council of Spain against Mayenne, 117; goes to help the besieged city of Rouen, 135; wounded, 136; extricates himself from his difficulties, 137; to the King's amazement, 138; expresses his admiration of King Henry's action, 139
Pau, Henry IV. taken from Court of France and led to, by his mother, 17
Pedro de Toledo, Don, 286-288
Pelleve, Cardinal de, 150
Perron, David du, 159, 201, 284, 320
Peronne, city of, renounces the League, 152
Philip II., 151
Phillipin killed in a duel, 195

Picardy, 149, 158, 172, 225
Pierre-Encise, castle of, 148, 160
Piney, Duke of, 83, 84
Pisani, Marquis of, 128, 192
Placenza, Cardinal de, 150
Poitiers, bishopric of, 252
Poltrot, Francis Duke of Guise assassinated by, 17
Pompone de Bellièvre, 171
Pont-à-Mousson, Marquis du, 91
Pontcarré, 320
Pont de l'Arche, 136
Pontoise, 147
Praslin, 244

QUERCY, 269

RAILLERY of Spaniards at birth of Henry IV., 13
Ravaillac, Francis, 323, 324; assassinates Henry IV., 325
Recollets, the, 261
Reggia, 192
Renaud de Beaune, 147
Renazé, 246, 248
René, 51
Rennes, 170
Retz, Marshal de, 195
Rheims, general assembly at, 128; submits to Henry IV., 153
Rochefoucauld, Francis, Count of, 51
Rochelle, siege of, 24
Rochepot, Count of, 177, 224, 273
Rohan, Duke of, 321
Rolet, 89
Roquelaire, 38
Rosny, Captain, 158; counsels Spanish commander, 162; assists in taking of Guinez and Ardres, 162; is killed, 162
Rosny, Marquis of, 164, 181; character of, 184-186; 204, 230, 243, 250, 252; goes to England, 258; created Duke of Sully, 271
Rouen, King of Navarre killed at siege of, 16; siege of, 135; estates convened at, 153; assembly of notables at, 234

ST. BARTHOLOMEW, massacre of, 21
St. Brix, conference at, 54
St. Denis, attacked by Parisians, 127
St. Germain-en-Laye, plot to seize the person of the King at, 166
St. Jean d'Angely, 192

St. Ouen, estates convened in abbey of, 163
Saint-Saviour killed at the battle of Coutras, 59
St. Sorlin, Marquis of, 160
Saluces, question of marquisate referred to the Pope, 204
Sancy, 74, 76, 81, 181, 182, 185
Sanson, 156
Saône, the, 156
Saxony, Duke of, 317
Savoy, Duke of, 51, 130, 172
Savoy, Duke of, his visit to France, 208; plots with Biron, 213; quits France, 214; 217, 238, 239, 242, 252, 253, 254, 271
Sedan, 271, 272
Seine, river, joined with Loire, 260
Selles, 142
Senlis, 262
Sfondrato, Count Hercules, 129
Sillery, Nicholas Brûlard de, 171, 181, 182, 197, 243, 252
Sixteen, the, 65, 105, 118, 129, 132, 133, 134, 149
Sixtus V., Pope, death of, 126
Sobole, 255, 256
Soissons, 153
Soissons, Count of, 82, 154; receives proposition to poison the King, 207; exhorts Biron to seek the King's pardon, 242
Somme, the, 135
Sommerive, 157
Sourdis, Madame de, 198
Stenay, 130
Stuart, Mary, 257
Succession of Anthony, Duke of Vendôme, 15
Sully, Duke of, see Rosny, Marquis of
Surènes, meeting of deputies at, 141

Tardiff, 133
Tarentaise, 217

Teillo, Hernand, surprises Amiens, 165; is killed, 168
Thirdlings, the, 125
Thische, Colonel, 103
Touchet, Mary, 202
Toulouse, 161
Tours, 134, 266
Troyes, 152
Tuileries, 183
Turenne, Viscount de, 129

Urban VII., Pope, 127

Valenciennes, 112
Valladolid, 177
Valois, Margaret de, 8
Vendôme, 95
Vendôme, Cardinal de, 82
Vendôme, Catherine of, 7
Vendôme, Duke of, 199, 265
Venice, Doge of, his opinion of Henry the Great's diplomacy, 290
Verneuil, 262, 267
Vervins, peace of, 6; plenipotentiaries meet at, 171; 204, 254
Vic, Seigneur de, appointed governor of Amiens, 168
Vienne, 161
Villars-Oudan, 156
Villemur, 161
Villeroy, 64, 145, 181 et seq., 201, 243, 252, 271
Vitry, 112, 148, 153, 244
Vitry, Louis d'Hôpital, 84

War of the Lovers, 40
Will of Henry d'Albret, 14

Yvetot, army of enemies shut up there by Henry IV., 136

Zamet, 198

www.ingramcontent.com/pod-product-compliance
Lightning Source LLC
Chambersburg PA
CBHW031418230426
43668CB00007B/353